ROLAND KRIEWALDT

BIO-PSYCHOLOGY

& THE GLOBAL WAR FOR STATUS

How men's competitive urge to win
is causing all of us to lose

Aurora Sky Publishing
www.AuroraSkyPublishing.com

*I dedicate my efforts to those
who value truth above winning.*

*And to the courageous whistleblowers
who reveal to us those who don't.*

First Printing:
Paperback Edition
Copyright © 2024 by Roland Kriewaldt

Published globally by
Aurora Sky Publishing

Ordering Info: www.AuroraSkyPublishing.com
Author's website: www.RolandK.ca

All rights reserved. No part of this book may be copied without the expressed written permission of the author. However, short excerpts may be quoted in print or electronic media for the sole purpose of review or promotion.

ISBN *978-1-7389167-1-9*

Cover / Interior Design / Typesetting: Roland Kriewaldt.
(This book uses a hybrid UK/US English spelling to confuse the enemy.)

CONTENTS

Preface		iv
Introduction		vi

PART 1 — Boys Will Be Boys 11
    Chapter 1   A Simple Question 13
    Chapter 2   What is Bio-Psychology? 25
    Chapter 3   The Very Best of Our Worst 39
    Chapter 4   A Special Kind of Stupid 49

PART 2 — Keeping Other Men Out of Power 63
    Chapter 5   Leading with Fear 65
    Chapter 6   Dominating the Human Mind 77
    Chapter 7   Yachts, Hookers & Blow 91
    Chapter 8   Always Just Out of Reach 103

PART 3 — Keeping Women Out of Power 115
    Chapter 9   Follow the Loser 117
    Chapter 10   Tearing Down the Gender Wall 129
    Chapter 11   Choking Her Out 143
    Chapter 12   Asking for Directions 157

PART 4 — The Aftermath & Fallout 169
    Chapter 13   Man on a Mission 171
    Chapter 14   Faking It 185
    Chapter 15   Fighting for Attention 199
    Chapter 16   This Means War 213

PART 5 — Working Towards Solutions 231
    Chapter 17   Woman Rise 233
    Chapter 18   Speaking Truth to Power 249
    Chapter 19   In Defense of Men 261
    Chapter 20   Citizen Based Social Planning 275

Epilogue	289
Index	292

Preface

The truth is a powerful ally to have on our side, which is why so many people try to lay claim to it. Yet no matter who makes that claim, their truth will always be slightly different than that of anyone else's. In fact, many of our truths contradict one another, which has made life even more confusing for us now that the truth is seemingly lost altogether, whatever it might have been.

More troubling still is that the truth is not always what people seek. Instead, they may only be looking for something to hold over others, like a secret that only they know so they can pretend to be better than those who don't know it, but now wish they did.

Our claiming of such truths is one of many competitive behaviors addressed in this book as part of a game people play to appear special or more important than others. And as we will discover, there are many such games being played in this crowded world wherein we struggle to stand out, even if that requires the telling of lies.

...

I want to bring your attention to this truth-telling dilemma because what I have written here also makes its own claim of being true.

However, my motive is not to appear special or more important, as can often be the case for those hoping to draw attention to themselves for having unique insights. Instead, I am motivated by a desire to have you put all of your attention on yourself based on what I claim is true herein. And by paying more attention to yourself, perhaps you will be inspired to also pay greater attention to the affect you may be having on others in claiming your own truths, whatever they might be. And this might then create a starting point for a greater journey inward.

Obviously, I must be convincing in that regard. As such, I have made sure that my own proclaimed truths are provable by offering only real world examples that you can easily confirm for yourself. Also, nothing herein depends upon faith or fraud — all of it is true insofar as it can be supported by easily accessible evidence.

Unfortunately, one potential downside of conveying provable truths is that they may contradict the "truths" of others that are based on faith or fraud. As such, they may feel offended by what I claim herein, not because it is a lie, but because it challenges them to prove themselves.

To them I say: let the truth prevail, regardless of who speaks it, for the truth takes no sides but its own. What is important is that we not allow our fears of one another's truths to hinder our collective progress, whether it be social, spiritual, intellectual or otherwise.

Ultimately, the truth exists to free our minds to travel and explore, whereas lies exist only to obstruct our way forward.

Today, more than ever, we need the truth to prevail because far too often people choose to lie in serving their own selfish ends. And then, like moths drawn to a flame, we risk following them like some light in the distance that may only turn out to be a dingy lightbulb flickering on someone's sagging front porch. And there we may remain, circling aimlessly around some false source of enlightenment; some counterfeit path to hope and wisdom, as we squander our lives away.

And with that, I invite you to see for yourself if these ideas that I have woven together will also have you nodding in silent approval and saying to yourself: "Now ain't that the truth."

At the very least, I promise you an eye-opening journey.

Introduction

Selfishness is an attitude that helps us to stay alive. In fact, it may be our most important survival instinct in that it prioritizes our needs over those of others in times of crisis.

A basic example of selfishness can be seen among newborn kittens as they fight for access to a vacant nipple within minutes of being born. Such behavior also carries with it great risks, as when hungry brown bears in Alaska steal salmon directly from the mouths of other bears. And while constantly acting on this impulse will not make us popular with others, at least it can help us to avoid dying from starvation.

Human beings can be equally selfish in their behavior towards one another and for reasons that exceed those of animals in the wild. Here as well, by habitually prioritizing our needs over those of others, we strain our relationships and make others want to avoid us for draining them of time or resources like an energy vampire. Yet even generous people may resort to selfish behavior when a selfish person's generosity is not forthcoming. As such, being selfish is also a conscious choice.

Accusing others of being selfish is an exclusion strategy that we may use to manipulate others into doing as we desire — which is a selfish behavior in its own right. As you can see, things can get complicated if we dig deeper into the causes and affects of those human behaviors that we may otherwise take for granted.

Consider, for instance, some behaviors that selfishness can cause:

- ☑ An unwillingness to share; treating others as having lesser value.
- ☑ Hoarding of material goods and assets — even if broken or unusable.
- ☑ Procrastinating, especially if having to make an effort for others.
- ☑ Manipulating others to gain advantages or avoid responsibilities.
- ☑ Showing up late for events; failing to consider the needs of others.
- ☑ Talking excessively about one's self while showing little interest in others.

- ☑ Constantly interrupting others to steal the social spotlight.
- ☑ Dismissing the concerns of others; refusing to listen or take the blame.
- ☑ Wasting people's time by being unprepared or disorganized.
- ☑ Neglecting one's own children — leaving a child to sit in a hot car.
- ☑ Denying or diminishing one's selfish behavior when accused of it.

As evident from this list, our lives can be fraught with conflicts if we allow this basic survival instinct to rage out of control in our personal relationships. It may also surprise you to learn that all of the behaviors cited above were exhibited by one person; a pathologically self-serving man who will never know of his generous contribution to this book. However, where there is one, others can be found, and surely you have met a few of them along your own personal journey through life.

Raising the stakes, let us then consider the worst affects of human selfishness, wherein the largest and most intimidating among us feel a sense of entitlement to take as they want from others. While this kind of behavior is natural among animals in the wild, it remains limited to the taking of another's food, territory and mate, whereas a selfish sense of entitlement among humans has no such limits. For instance:

- ☑ In 1889, the number of wild and captive American bison was estimated at 1091, down from an estimated population of 50,000,000 only 100 years before. Human selfishness was to blame.
- ☑ In 2023, the number of wild western black and northern white rhinos in Africa was estimated to be zero due to their recent extinction. Human selfishness was to blame.
- ☑ The Florida Gulf Coast fishery near the 2010 Deep Water Horizon oil spill is estimated to require centuries to regain its former health — though some species may never recover due to genetic mutations. Human selfishness was to blame.
- ☑ By 1909, Eastern wild turkeys in Canada were wiped out by European settlers hunting them and taking over their habitat. Here again, human selfishness was to blame. Reintroduced in 1984, their hunting resumed.

Based on such negative outcomes in the past, let us now consider a question regarding our future behavior that no longer seems unlikely: What if commercial fishermen wanted to catch all the Alaska salmon and leave none for the bears — because it was more profitable? And what if they had equally selfish allies in government who would allow for such an unnatural harvest of natural resources? Luckily, oversights do exist to prevent such careless profiteering. And so the brown bears do have enough fish for now, despite the fishing industry having taken more than 215 million Alaska salmon in 2023 alone.

Yet human selfishness cannot always be tempered by legislation. For those who want to overfish, they simply go where the over-harvesting of wildlife is more negotiable to those who write the local laws.

And then there are men like Russian president, Vladimir Putin, who seems to have it all, yet still yearns to add the Ukraine to his real estate portfolio. And since the owners won't sell, he has decided to hire men to take by force the land and livelihoods of ordinary citizens because their elected leader won't bow to his selfish demands for more.

But Putin is unremarkable in that regard. His name is among many that fill our history books with tales of self-serving excess wherein one man has decided that satiating his selfish urges outweighs the value of other people's lives — sometimes millions of them. And when that one man has access to armored tanks and nuclear weapons, who can deny him a little extra something to take along to his grave?

This brings to light a further concern when our desire for weapons and over-harvesting technology far exceeds that for peace or ecological sustainability. Yet this is understandable given that selfishness is only the facilitator of our destructive behavior and not its root cause. But rather than look for that underlying motive, we may prefer to simply curb our bad behavior. As such, we often wind up policing ourselves as a stopgap measure rather than working toward a lasting solution based on our deeper understanding of the issue. And that is why we often find ourselves walking in circles as a society and species rather than moving decisively toward our continued conscious evolution.

...

Bio-Psychology and the Global War for Status is meant to keep our minds from trudging in aimless circles by identifying the cause of our worst social behaviors as a problem inherent to male biology. As such, it is also not within the scope of politics, religion or a booming job market to solve. Specifically, it is a problem related to men's inborn urge to win. And from this lone ambition all others arise, leading to an almost endless array of human behaviors that all share a common goal, which is to elevate our individual status by rising above all others. And among those behaviors, most are anti-social and destructive in their nature.

Once we understand the underlying cause of our urge to win and its many manifestations, we will not only understand what is happening to our societies, but also why and how best to deal with the problem.

Furthermore, by gaining such insight, it is hoped that some will feel inspired to begin solving all of the many problems we have created on behalf of those affected — including the people of war-torn nations who were simply trying to make a living before armed strangers began turning their homes into rubble and raping their daughters — further selfish behaviors so typical of men in their ongoing wars for status.

Ideally, the information in this book can be added to the academic toolbox of our collective self-awareness so that educators in the future can assist parents in raising young adults who are not only fluent in technical matters but also in regard to the inner workings of their own minds under the powerful influence of their selfish biology. In this way, we might all become more self-aware and consequential in how we behave towards one another once our true motives lay revealed before us like an open book rather than remaining hidden like a mystery that is largely being protected by our denial.

The ultimate goal here is not to find a miracle cure for everything that ails humankind, but to ensure that we continue to work toward a higher future expression of ourselves in context of a far more peaceful and environmentally healthy setting. And for that to happen, we must first learn how to survive our selfish attitude.

PART ONE
Boys Will Be Boys

CHAPTER 1
A Simple Question

Let us begin with a simple question: based on your own knowledge of human history, *how many wars have been fought by armed hordes of women intent on conquering the people and resources of foreign lands?*

The first thing that should strike you is the absurdity of the question itself. In fact, it seems more like a joke and we're just waiting for the punchline so we can break out in laughter. But this is no joke. After all, women can also be highly competitive, so why wouldn't they have a history of engaging in violent warfare against their own kind?

Moreover, if there is anything comical about all of this, it's that every man and woman knows the answer to the question because we all have certain expectations of women's behavior and going to war is not one of them. As such, you would be correct to say that no wars have been fought by women joining forces to conquer the people of other lands.

But why is that? The answer is *Bio-Psychology*. And for now, we'll just leave it at that.

And naturally, we must then ask the same question of men: based on your knowledge of human history, *how many wars have been fought by armed hordes of men intent upon conquering the people and resources of foreign lands?*

And all at once your mind has reoriented itself to a familiar world and its narrative; no more trying to imagine your mother out planting landmines to disembowel other women; no more trying to imagine your sister sticking a bayonet into someone's chest in a foreign land. Finally the question no longer seems so absurd once men are involved.

Yet this sudden change in mental attitude should be of great concern to us because it is based on what we actually expect of men's behavior. In fact, we encourage men to fight, even giving our young boys video games that feature themes of military warfare and gun violence. All of a sudden, that question no longer seems a joke when directed at men. And naturally, we all know the right answer because human history is mostly the story of armed hordes of male invaders on a bloody quest to defeat anyone standing in their way.

But even though men's violent behavior may seem perfectly natural to us, it does not answer the basic question as to why they have always been the gender to engage in such acts of organized mass murder.

Here as well, Bio-Psychology is the answer. And for now, we'll also just leave it at that.

...

Clearly, there is a significant distinction between men's and women's behavior that is causing the male gender to threaten the destruction of our entire world in their quest to compete against and conquer other men. Are they just natural born killers — and if so, how does this bode for our future? What does this mean to any nation hoping to plant the seeds of a working democracy if there are violent, armed men waiting at the sidelines for a chance to tear it all back down again?

As you can see, this is no joke. This is the world in which we now live and wherein there continues to be as much male violence and volatility as ever, whether in the United States or the Middle East. And this is because all men suffer from the same problem, which is their body's inborn Bio-Psychology and how it causes them to behave.

For that reason, the origin of this term and all that it means to the collective future well-being of humankind is what we will be exploring in the coming chapters. There can be no greater global cause than to ensure that we don't kill ourselves and take everyone else with us.

Men's Work

While this book deals with the problems caused by men's competitive urges, it should in no way be interpreted as being biased against men. And so, in fairness to men, let us not ignore that women's competitive behavior can be an equally dangerous threat. In fact, some women are as dangerous to a peaceful society as any murderous male psychopath.

However, women tend to be more practical in their killing affairs. If she needs more money or personal freedom and has a tendency toward homicidal behavior, then she may simply kill her husband, children or relatives to achieve her desired goal. For this reason, her two primary motives in committing murder are personal gain or to escape the rigors and responsibilities of family life.

In stark contrast, when we hear about a heavily armed sniper who is shooting strangers at random, we can be almost certain that a man is responsible. Aside from killing for personal gain or freedom, men also tend to be "proxy" killers, meaning that their victims *symbolize* those they hate or seek revenge against. And so, if a man cannot kill his government leaders or their value system, he may resort to destroying those who represent them or their values. As such, the infamous 9/11 attacks and bombing of an FBI building in Oklahoma were examples of proxy killings wherein the intended victims were but symbols.

In fact, anything from global warfare to school shootings tend to be male-initiated proxy killings. After all, the soldiers who are shooting at one another on a battlefield do not know one another; they are just symbolic representatives of the "enemy" to be defeated.

Often making matters worse is the response of male leaders to such tragic events. For instance, in the United States where mass shootings occur almost weekly, the solution offered by various male politicians and gun lobbyists is to make more guns available. And in doing so, we see yet another competitive behavior so common to men, which is to offer war and destruction as the means to creating a peaceful society. And sometimes we must give them the benefit of the doubt that they just don't know any better.

But then again, who wouldn't be reluctant to part with the massive profits from gun sales, which offers yet another competitive field upon which men can seek to dominate one another — the weapons industry.

...

No matter where we look in our world, we will find men engaged in some form of competition. This is not just some habitual impulse but one driven by biology. And this makes the urge to compete not only instinctual but a constant aspect of men's daily lives and thinking.

Things take a turn for the worse when that urge to compete is no longer aimed at mere sport or throwing darts at a local pub. And this is yet another of the benefits of unraveling the greater mystery of men's Bio-Psychology because it can help us to understand how and why our nations and societies, our governments and businesses, our honorable learning institutions and even our religions have come to be tainted by the competitive urges of men fighting for dominance.

After all, the original purpose of the spiritual journey was surely not to go to war against other religions for ownership of heaven or which truth should govern our minds. And yet, in the heat of their battles for alpha male status, even the leaders of our world religions seem to lose their way.

And where are all the female leaders of those world religions? Here too, it seems an almost absurd question to ask because we already know the answer. As with the waging of war; the running of industries; the overseeing of our economic systems, and the governing of our nations, so has the ruling of religion and its claimed engagements with God been historically considered "men's work."

But what does this mean for our collective future if the gender in charge of determining that future is also the one habitually engaged in destroying all we have built up each time their genocidal killing mood strikes? Moreover, even in times of peace, men's instinctual wars for dominance continue to rage within societies turned into economic battlefields that are fast becoming hostile to life itself.

All of this represents a serious problem for the future of humankind and our natural world that is currently not being addressed because the gender causing the problem is also the one in charge. It is men who largely control everything from our governments and industries to our social destinies. As such, they have little incentive to stop engaging in their various global wars for status, even if that means killing the rest of us in their efforts to win.

And so, we see a constant escalation in physical threats to our safety, from industrial polluters to nations with nuclear arms, while no one seems able to clearly articulate why they must keep grasping for more and more, including those multi-billionaires who surely have amassed sufficient money to prove whether it can buy them happiness or not.

For that reason, we must take it upon ourselves to uncover the truth behind these unconscious urges that are driving men to behave in so many self-destructive and socially destabilizing ways. And in doing so, we must also challenge many of the existing male-sponsored political and religious dogmas, along with various gender and class stereotypes that currently limit the growth potential of most human societies.

Our collective challenge as both men and women is to work toward the betterment of our species by defying not only the call of nature to engage in dangerous biological games of chance, but also to realize that, based on men's failed past efforts to govern peacefully, it is time for the ruling of our societies to be designated as "women's work."

Born To Be Wild

As we progress toward a better understanding of male competitive behavior and the kind of world it has created, we will be met by many surprises along the way, both pleasant and disturbing. Some take the form of connections we can make between aspects of our everyday life as they relate to men's perpetual quest for dominance. As such, what may once have seemed trivial may now take on a greater significance as we explore ever deeper the mystery of men's competitive struggles seemingly against peace itself.

Among the non-trivial details we may uncover are the lyrics of many popular songs, especially in the rock genre. No one can argue that rock music is one of humankind's greatest creations in having brought so much unconditional joy to people around the world in a language that we can all understand. Yet if we actually do understand the language of a song's lyrics, then we may hear messages being directed at the competitive mindset of youthful male listeners — something to get them excited and feeling good about themselves at a time when feeling good is not always easy.

While some song lyrics seem written only to rhyme, genuine artists tend to speak their minds to their audiences. In such cases, their lyrics may address the rigors of male adolescence and its accompanying drive to compete for power, sexual pleasure or group status. Moreover, their songs are often written from direct experience in having faced some of the same struggles as their audiences, thus fostering a deeper feeling of loyalty among their fans.

Beyond providing a soundtrack for flipping over cars or running drunk through bonfires, rock music can also offer some thoughtful insights about the disparities of life under the influence of greedy men battling for control of our world. This speaks to many of the young as they begin falling victim to the political and economic machinations of a ruling minority, whether in losing their incomes or having to work as modern day slaves for insatiable hoarders of material wealth.

For their part, artists try to counter these negative feelings to ensure a proper winning attitude among their listeners. This is why many song lyrics tend to be anthemic in condemning various social injustices or in celebrating one's personal victory over the trials and tribulations of living in a competitive world that seems determined to defeat us.

A perfect example of an adolescent male anthem is *TNT* as sung by Bon Scott, late singer for Australian rock band, AC/DC. Bon had a knack for speaking to young working class men as they struggled for significance in a world that sought to dismiss them. As such, his songs tended to be compensatory — making up for a lack of status or wealth by boasting instead of one's physical might — as nature had intended. Among his anthemic words of conquest, he wrote:

> "*TNT* — *I'm dynamite*
> *TNT* — *I'm gonna win that fight*
> *TNT* — *I'm a power load*
> *TNT* — *watch me explode*"

Music is obviously written to be enjoyed, not analyzed. Yet here the song's message is clearly directed at the awakening competitive urges of young men in their quest for dominant status. This is a successful theme for the band, as are those of drinking, tribal bonding, fighting in the streets and a young man's troublesome encounters with women. In that regard, they speak to the experiences or expectations of many a young, working class male, which is also why AC/DC became one of the most popular rock bands in the world.

On the more thoughtful, poetic side of lyric writing, we find songs such as *Hotel California* by the Eagles that are a condemnation of the tragic, lonely existence of those competing for status through displays of material excess and beauty. Adding tension is the protagonist's own attempt to escape this shallow world of pretense and posturing.

> "*Last thing I remember, I was*
> *Running for the door*
> *I had to find the passage back*
> *To the place I was before*"

The song's lyrics act as a reminder of the inescapable nature of our biological drive to compete; an urge that many aging billionaires and patriarchs seem unable to surrender even in approaching death.

In addition to songs about fighting or fleeing, we have classic rock anthems such as *Born To Be Wild* by Steppenwolf which speak to the raw urges of the male psyche as it yearns for the freedom to seek out new adventures. The song gained great popularity for its declaration of independence from the restraints of an oppressive, paternalistic social order that seemed to advocate that we were instead born to be caged like human animals by politics, religion, our duties as tax payers and the patriotic call to war. Then along came the 1960's.

> *"Get your motor runnin'*
> *Head out on the highway*
> *Looking for adventure*
> *In whatever comes our way...*
> *Like a true nature's child*
> *We were born, born to be wild"*

And finally, in a blatant act of self-promotion, I offer to you the lyrics from one of my own songs, *Too Big To Fail,* addressing the primary obstacles to success we collectively face while providing a convenient introduction to the main theme of this book:

> *"But it was dirty business as usual*
> *As the rich consumed the poor*
> *While the have-nots kept pretending*
> *That someday they'd have more*
> *Mirror, mirror, tell me who can I trust?*
> *Show me a world not ruled by lust"*

Granted, analyzing the lyrics of rock songs may not save our world from its current downward decline, but it does prove how the theme of competing for dominance and its negative fallout are embedded in the expressions of modern culture. We are either complaining about it or surrendering to its selfish demands by boasting about our elevated status and special privileges, not unlike the *gangsta rappers* of old who bragged of their guns, gold and body counts. Ultimately, wherever we look, we are sure to find the destructive taint of male competition.

Delving into the theme of music lyrics also serves a further purpose in preparing us for more surprises to come — hidden gems of insight to make our reading journey more memorable and worth sharing.

As we begin our formal investigation into the destructive influence of men's competitive urge upon our world, we will become aware of its infiltration and impact not only upon our quest for success but also on our future survival as a species. What we will discover is that our lives have been socially-engineered with little else but competition in mind, from being tempted to buy consumer products meant to symbolically elevate our status in the eyes of others, to the processes of marketing to ensure the victory of our dominant retail franchises over all others. As such, almost anything we buy or sell will have been tainted along the way by someone else's competitive lust to win.

But rest assured, as we set out upon this path of discovery, we will also find the intellectual tools to solve many of the problems that have been plaguing human societies for thousands of years.

Between Misery and Death

In the coming chapters, many questions will be answered. For that reason, it would serve us best to continue highlighting the negative consequences of men's various global and social wars for status to make these future insights more relevant and meaningful.

What we can suggest at this point is that men have a proven bias to engage in warfare and social domination. And this is based on a desire to compete that also dooms many men to a state of mind not designed for peaceful cooperation with other men. This can be observed in men who are second-in-command yet feel an urge to take the lead — which is the basis for many a political coup and rivalry among siblings having to share ownership of a family business or inheritance.

What this also reveals is that men are not biologically equipped to let other men get ahead of them. At least not for long. Subsequently, whether in politics, business or religion, we see an endless clashing as men at every level of society and in every facet of life feel driven to take a leadership role — even when unqualified for that position. After all, this unconscious urge to compete does not care about such details as intellect or competence, which is another reason why our world is in such disarray in having elected leaders who prove better at dominating and destroying their rivals than leading us to greater prosperity. In short, they're just too selfish to take on such a selfless role.

And this also does not bode well for democracy when there is no desire among our male political dominators to share their power with the rest of us. In this book's final chapter, a solution is offered.

...

Ironically, the cause of most of our human social problems has always been right in front of our eyes in the competitive behavior of other animal species. Here we also find males engaging in various battles for dominance, thus proving that there is also something in *their* minds that makes them unwilling to let other males get ahead of them. This also dooms many to a solitary life of growling at others for appearing to be a threat to their selfish ambitions, just as it does with many men.

Conversely, we find that the females of other species tend to be far more social, peaceful and cooperative as an expression of their needing to give birth and protect their young. This also inclines them to be far more cautious in their confrontations with others. After all, it does not serve her offspring if a mother is constantly engaging in fights that will leave them unattended or have her returning with life-threatening injuries. The same is true of human females whose children would not be well-served by having their mothers return from war in a body bag or a wheelchair. They need a responsible parent in their lives.

In addition, the offspring of most animal species thrive without a father in attendance because their mothers are outfitted by nature with a portable food supply and a lesser inclination to engage in activities that could endanger their lives, whether it be physical combat, or street racing in cars at speeds that could render them useless in seconds.

Conversely, the ability of solitary human males to take greater risks also explains why they have taken over our world, having both the time and competitive inclination to turn our societies into a battleground to prove their dominance through various kinds of warfare.

...

Fortunately, there are exceptions to every rule and among human males there can be so many exceptions that we may want to reconsider our book of rules altogether.

For instance, one man might be brought to tears by watching a deer cross his backyard, whereas another may be filled with the urge to kill that animal, not for food, but to prove his dominance over it, much like the impulse that inspires serial killers to victimize innocent people.

Peaceful departures from typical male domination behavior cannot be explained within the confines of any debate about nature versus nurture. Instead, we will find that our behavior is a product of our own individual character inclinations and how nature and nurture can then amplify both for either the better or worse of our society.

As such, where one man may kick and scream his way through life, another may prove himself as gentle a caregiver as any devoted mother. The same is seen in the wild where a battle-scarred tomcat may act as a dedicated nanny to a litter of kittens in a feral cat colony.

However, in the aggregate, we can state that women are the reason why our human race continues to exist whereas men are the reason why our existence is constantly being threatened. And this leads us to consider the ultimate question raised by this book, which is:

What are we going to do about all of this senseless male violence and social combat so that men do not completely destroy our world in the coming years?

After all, it seems that any time we make a few strides forward in our social progress, some gang of heavily armed thugs comes along to tear it all down again. In fact, as these words were being written, men in the Ukraine and Russia are engaged in killing one another while leaving a trail of civilian casualties and destruction that are the hallmark of every male-sponsored war for dominance. And once they return home, they will leave a mess for others to clean, including the land mines that will continue to kill children, pets and wild animals long after their latest glorious war for peace has ended and they train for yet another.

...

All of this represents a predictable pattern of male behavior that will ensure a constant tearing down of our societies in men's never-ending quest to prove themselves superior to other men. This will also leave our conscious and social evolution in a perpetual holding pattern as we are made to wait after each new war for our male occupiers to rebuild our cities and get our electricity and water systems working again just so we can break even as a civilized human being with indoor plumbing and an electrical stove.

In reality, we rarely push far ahead before we are forced once again to dig ourselves out of the rubble of human warfare. Nor are we often rewarded with greater social freedoms. Instead, we most often inherit a new male ruler to order us around and take from us as he wants.

But how much longer can our species or even our planet tolerate these militarized and politicized death marches toward cultural inertia before we run out of time or the support of an otherwise benevolent planet on the verge of ecological collapse?

Unfortunately, this is not something men typically would consider in the heat of battle nor in preparing for another economic or military strike against "the enemy." And so, while we are heard yelling "Enough is enough!" on behalf of humanity and our planetary ecosystems, those leading the victory charge will instead be heard yelling what they have always been yelling throughout the ages:

"Let us fight to the death!"

And in doing so, they will often care far too little whether the rest of us live or die. As such, we, the majority, have always been forced to surrender in a centuries old tradeoff between misery and death.

CHAPTER 2
What is Bio-Psychology?

Now that science has become the predominant investigative tool over superstition, we are better able to understand various aspects of our natural world. For instance, when an earthquake strikes, we now know that it is not because someone's God is angry, but because there has been a shifting of the earth's tectonic plates.

But given our convenience-oriented mode of thinking, we may still prefer a more simple explanation for the things we encounter in life, be it in the realm of science or religion. For that reason, we may also dismiss the sight of two men fighting as just a symptom of their having too much "testosterone" in their bloodstream. However, such a simple, one word answer won't explain the root cause of their altercation any better than the word "evolution" explains the root cause of life. Nor will our reluctance to pursue the matter give those men the intellectual tools they will need to curb their violent behavior in the future.

As such, we must gain a deeper understanding of male conflict if we are to eventually break out of our historic cycles of warfare between bursts of quarrelsome social progress.

...

The term Bio-Psychology does not currently appear in commercial media or school textbooks. And yet, it is one of the most important topics we can learn about in seeking to live a life of joyful contentment rather than one of tormented misery. Such torment is a common feature among hyper-competitive men and is parodied by the lead character in the popular film, *American Psycho*, as his competitive envy drives him to obsess over the better quality of his peers' business cards.

As for the term itself, it came to me while working on my previous book, *Clearing a Path to Joy*. After thinking I'd found the perfect term for my branch of study — "Bio-Psychology" — a quick online search revealed that others were already using it. For this reason, I want to clarify that *Bio-Psychology*, as I define it herein, is only relevant to my own work and not that of any other academic field of study.

And now, let's begin this insightful journey of discovery by defining first what I mean by "Bio-Psychology" in context of this book:

> *Bio-Psychology refers to a broad range of thoughts and behaviors working in the interests of our biological instincts to survive and procreate. That is to say, these two needs of our body trigger our mind to engage in certain thought processes, which then trigger our body to fulfill those needs. As such, our mind is not the point of origin for our actions concerning survival and procreation. Instead, our body is in charge. Hence, it is the psychology of our biology.*

To understand how this process works, let's imagine that our body is low on energy. As a result, we will feel an instinctual urge to eat as our body creates the sensation of hunger. This in turn warns our mind to seek food energy, which may then lead us to hunt and gather food in the wild, or perhaps drive to the nearest fast food restaurant.

Although we are choosing to eat, the impulse to act is itself triggered by our body's fear of dying from starvation. In other words, we are simply obeying our body's unconscious orders, even by choosing how to carry out those orders. In short, we have little choice but to do as our body says if we want to stay alive.

Sexual desire also originates from our body's biological impulse to procreate. Here, our urge to mate will trigger sexual thoughts about a potential mate we may encounter. This in turn leads our body to make social contact with them. And although we may also engage in sexual activity as a conduit for spiritual communion or recreational pleasure, the triggering of this impulse is primarily the function of our body's instinctual urge to create offspring — no matter how we interpret it.

...

Our urges to survive and procreate are further administered by three sub-urges that manage how we attend to our basic needs. They are part of a biological values system being triggered by our want for *comfort, convenience* and *control*. Moreover, all species share this values system, which we can refer to as our *Physical States of Being*.

To understand how these sub-urges influence our behavior, we need only recall the last time we put on a warm coat when the weather was cold. In feeling cold, we sought to resolve our discomfort by keeping our body warm. Further influencing our behavior is a want for mental comfort, which can have us refusing to talk about or believe in those things that may cause us emotional discomfort — perhaps by learning that a trusted friend or leader has betrayed us.

As to our want for convenience, this has us trying to save time and energy in accomplishing any task. We may then choose to buy fast food to avoid cooking; take a shortcut to avoid a longer drive, or cut corners when drilling an underwater oil well in the Gulf of Mexico.

Our quest for control has us trying to influence the circumstances that can affect our survival and procreation success. This also causes our social domination behavior as we seek to control anything from our spouses to our employees or government in an effort to ensure that all aspects of life side in our favor. Over time, men have found many ways to control their own circumstances, from rigging governments and banking systems, to invading other countries if their leaders refuse to surrender control of their land and natural resources.

The *Physical States of Being* are part of a system for analyzing human behavior that I developed in *Clearing a Path to Joy* and refer to as the *The Six States of Being* or C-SIX. This includes three *Spiritual States of Being* responsible for engaging our feelings of joy and purpose in life. I recommend this book for those interested in a deeper understanding of our pursuits of happiness and personal freedom. However, for our immediate needs, we now have some basis for understanding how our physical sub-urges can influence our decision-making as we tend to our primary biological urges to survive and procreate.

Knowing this, let us then introduce the single greatest cause of most of our human social problems, which is mother nature herself.

Nature's War Against Life

When asked to describe nature, we may think of it as a remote location far removed from the concrete jungles in which many of us now live. We may also think of its beauty, its diversity, its plethora of colors or the lush greenery of some undisturbed natural habitat. And although death is a necessary part of maintaining its life cycles, we typically see nature as a benevolent force whose purpose is to maintain the balance of life here on Earth.

Subsequently, the idea of nature being at war against life itself may seem counter-intuitive and absurd to us. After all, why would nature go to war against its own creations? It just doesn't make any sense.

Or does it?

Actually, it does. And we can find the reason for it in the competitive behavior of animals all throughout our world, including among human beings and other primate species.

For example, in order to procreate, a roaming male lion must take over another male lion's territory to gain access to the female pride. He may even have to kill that resident male if he refuses to surrender. Here as well, just as among human males, the fear of losing to a rival acts as a powerful incentive to keep on fighting, even to the death.

In having defeated that resident male, the conquering intruder may then also kill any cubs sired by his opponent in an effort to bring the females into estrous. And so we see that by nature's own direct orders — in acting upon his biological instinct to compete — that male lion is being guided to destroy life, including that of the helpless cubs. And therein lies a genuine source of confusion unless we can find a valid explanation as to why nature would allow, let alone *encourage* this kind of senseless killing behavior to become part of her cycle of life.

As an aside, and for purposes of scientific accuracy, lion prides may be overseen by a coalition of males, who must then be defeated by an ever more powerful coalition. But either way, such transitions of power between male lions are typically a violent affair when their primal lust to dominate has been triggered.

As for what would cause a male lion to engage in a brutal murder spree against his own kind, this has to do with genetics and — most ironically — the greater good of its species. For instance, it is best for the future well-being of any species if only its healthiest candidates are allowed to reproduce. This seems obvious in that unhealthy offspring are more likely to die as a result of illness or predation. Hence, they are already born ill-equipped to survive in the long term.

For this reason, nature has declared her preference for healthy mates as opposed to weaker, sickly or aging ones. And this includes elderly male lions who may no longer be a suitable candidate for the siring of offspring or defending the home territory of the pride.

...

To further promote her "survival of the fittest" values system, nature has also created safeguards to prevent conception among animals too weak or otherwise unqualified to conceive young.

For example, if a female black bear enters hibernation underweight, she will not be allowed to conceive cubs due to the inferior condition of her body. This makes perfect sense because she needs fat to produce milk for her cubs and keep them warm. In this way, nature avoids the risk of weak cubs emerging from a winter den to a mother who cannot properly care for them.

The same safeguard exists for women with eating disorders who will stop menstruating to prevent the birth of a malnourished child. While not a foolproof system, it helps to discourage physically unfit women from giving birth. In that regard, this should also give us grounds for concern about how our bodies may be weakened by constant exposure to industrial chemicals in our food, water and air.

While nature may prefer that only healthy specimens mate, there is no system in place to prevent weak, sickly or unhealthy animals from mating — especially when it involves achieving a sexual orgasm, which may be the most powerful sensation of pleasure that any animal can experience, perhaps even insects. In response, nature has developed an additional safeguard to keep weaker candidates from mating, or to at least reduce the risk of their contributing to the gene pool.

Here, nature has devised a clever solution by inciting males to fight for sexual access to a female — thereby producing a *qualified* winner. Thus, if the invading male lion proves himself "fitter" than the resident male, then it can also be assumed that he is genetically superior in having defeated his rival. In this way, nature can then reward him with an orgasm for having successfully won the right to mate with the females of the pride.

...

In creating this contest for genetic supremacy, nature has also found a simple and thoughtless way to automate animal reproduction among most species by rewarding males for "good behavior" — defeating their rivals for dominance. Ironically, this means that the best candidates for reproduction may also be those best at dominating or even killing their own kind — an uncomfortable realization in considering men's own tendency toward violence. But at least now, it all makes sense.

Unfortunately, by creating this often brutal system for determining the best candidates for mating, nature has also made it impossible for the males of most species to live in peace within their respective herds or animal societies — including those of human beings.

And this is why we encounter so many male-sponsored problems within our own societies. Moreover, nature's process of elimination to select a single male inseminator is counterproductive to any quest for democracy in that it would require our male dominators to share their governing power and winning status not only with other adult males, but also with females. Yet when and where has this ever happened?

As such, we should not expect to see men rushing to create any new form of governing system that promotes greater equality. Instead, they will instinctively move in the opposite direction by rigging our systems in their favor and taking ever more power and freedom away from us.

If in doubt, we need only refer to any current government that uses orbiting satellites and other remote surveillance technology to ensure that *everything* is under their control, most importantly, its citizens.

Proving Grounds

Given the complexity of this topic and its many potential offshoots, let us revisit the two most critical aspects of reproduction to understand the objectives of Bio-Psychology in governing our bodies:

1) Nature wants only the genetically healthiest members of each species to procreate as a safeguard against future extinction from weakness or disease.

2) Nature typically determines genetic health using an automated qualification system that triggers males to compete for dominance via physical combat or displays of their supremacy over other male rivals.

However, to more fully understand how humankind arrived at its present state of psychosocial dysfunction, there are some other crucial pieces of information that we must also absorb. The first has to do with the contest for domination itself.

Had humankind remained in the wild as hunters and gatherers, we would have continued competing for dominance based on each man's physical strength, hunting and gathering skills, or his ability to build a better shelter than his tribal peers. These are the natural determinants of superiority in the wild and therefore also benefit nature's plan to bring out the best in us in context of such competitions.

Our troubles began in transitioning toward a "monetary ecosystem" wherein we no longer depended on hunting and gathering to survive but on trading symbolic energy in the form of money, which ideally represents the time and effort we invest toward earning it.

However, this notion is immediately problematic in that anyone can steal a fortune instead of earning it, thus putting a thief in a position of dominance over countless others. And that is the standard by which many dysfunctional societies function today by allowing the wealthiest to have the most sway over our collective lives and future.

While a blessing at times, money can therefore also represent a curse in that it allows men of inferior stock to masquerade as our best simply by controlling the flow of money into our lives.

For example, poor people are poor because they have no money, not because they are genetically inferior. Conversely, rich people are rich due to having lots of money, not because they are genetically superior to others. After all, what skills must one demonstrate to inherit their family's fortune? In fact, all that may be holding someone poor from rising up in our world is those wealthy individuals competing against them. And even if that poor person is proven physically, intellectually or creatively superior, our social values systems attribute little value to the lives of those at the bottom of the economic hierarchy.

This social disparity between rich and poor is how the domination game is played by humans in most societies. This is mainly achieved by keeping money out of the hands of rivals and taking money as much as we can from others to prove ourselves the winner.

The result of this new way of gauging dominance has an unfortunate impact on our genetics in that it is no longer determined by natural parameters such as strength or dexterity, but rather by artificial values, such as economic or military might. As for who gets to represent us as our top alpha male sperm donor, that is now largely determined by the size of a man's stock portfolio or technological ability to bomb the rest of us into submission in what truly is a "new" world ordering of life.

Ultimately, our economic systems and the values they promote have compromised the integrity of nature's genetics-based survival system as well as that of our ancient tribal communities, neither of which arose to keep us in a state of poverty and powerlessness.

Meanwhile, our history books overflow with hard evidence that this orchestrated economic exclusion of the many by a privileged few is a long-standing social problem that began once we no longer needed to prove our genetic dominance but simply display our wealth.

...

In considering this problem of the greater majority of society being excluded from power by its male dominators, we need to recognize the importance of our formerly functioning tribal societies. Herein, the two most critical factors in determining our fate were the opposing forces of selfishness and sharing; with each form of behavior proving to be critical to our long-term survival.

As mentioned earlier in this book's introduction, a familiar example of selfishness is the behavior of newborn kittens as they fight to gain access to an available nipple. This is a perfectly natural attitude and one that is also critical to our survival. Yet in stark contrast, the mother cat ensures the survival of her young by sharing not only her milk, but also her time and loving attention. In short, she cannot afford to behave selfishly to succeed as a mother. As such, the act of sharing represents a natural expression of nature's wisdom to ensure the survival of most animal species, including our own.

And so we have an obvious social dilemma because men are highly competitive by nature in seeking to become the dominant inseminator of future generations of offspring. As such, they have every incentive not to share except with those who can elevate their status. Hence, the popular expression "rubbing shoulders with the rich" whereas there is no such expression as "rubbing shoulders with the poor."

Women, by contrast, are known for sharing due to the importance of such behavior to the survival of their children. And here again, we see another reason why women must win political races given that we have seen how things turn out when men are selfishly grasping at the nipples of power.

Why should women lead our societies? That reason is clear once we consider the contradictory aims of capitalism and democracy, which the economic alpha males of society oft claim to be mutually inclusive. But let's question their wisdom by studying the dictionary definition of each style of governing and its implications:

> ***Capitalism:*** *"an economic and political system in which a country's trade and industry are controlled by private owners for profit, rather than by the state."*

> ***Democracy:*** *"a system of government by the whole population or all the eligible members of a state."*

Here we see that each system opposes the other in that one allows for private interests to determine our collective fate (in regards to food, shelter, mobility, etc.) while the other seeks our collective involvement in society's decision-making process. In other words, merging both systems into one creates a political paradox of cross purposes based on the impulses of selfishness versus sharing, the fallout from which will also be addressed throughout this book.

For this reason, the democratic governing systems wherein we now vote act more as Plutocracies where wealthy capitalists determine both the future course of our societies and their purpose. And clearly, if their goal is to claim it all for themselves, they cannot have our societies functioning as a protective sanctuary as nature intended if they are to use them as a competitive proving ground in their wars for status.

Moreover, given that men still largely control our societies, we have no reason to expect anything but an endless state of social warfare with no prospects for peace in sight, let alone a ceasefire.

Winning the War for Status

How does one win a global war for status? It depends on whether we want to win symbolically or genetically, as nature intended. If the latter, then we must do as Germany or England once did, by going to war against its male rivals in distant lands. However, only hand to hand combat would be allowed as the use of weapons proves nothing about the supremacy of one's genetic traits. As such, since men first began to use weapons to determine dominance, we have also been subverting nature's rules for judging those worthy from those not.

But since our dominators want to enjoy the spoils of their victory, most opt to engage in symbolic warfare to avoid an early grave. This is done by amassing symbolic equivalents of power such as wealth and land as a psychological weapon to intimidate others into submission. A familiar example finds a wealthy family threatening local politicians to carry out its selfish demands, perhaps by defeating a social equality initiative that would diminish their own status and power.

The earliest stirrings of symbolic warfare would have occurred in tribal societies with a shared values system by which dominance could be judged beyond mere bodily assets. While skills such as hunting and pottery making would have been highly valued, there was often a form of currency used in trade; something portable like sea shells that would be easy to carry around. Today, those sea shells have turned into virtual numbers in a bank account, yet they still wield power in representing something of value in trade.

Ironically, when we were hunters and gatherers, we valued people of true merit who could help us to survive. Today, by stark contrast, our values system has us admiring men for their ability to earn large sums of money. Sadly, this may only prove a man's dominance as a swindler of the public. However, given that money is the basis for world trade, those amassing the most will win this symbolic war to bask in the company of the world's wealthiest men. But surely not the happiest.

Here again, wealth is not an indicator of a man's genetic supremacy or leadership potential, especially if his gains were ill-gotten. However, it does give them the symbolic power to influence and even control the future course of our societies — for better or worse.

...

The importance of symbolic dominance becomes clear as we begin to identify its use within society as a substitute indicator of one's genetic dominance. That is to say, while our Bio-Psychology urges us to prove our physical status, our body may fail us in that regard. And so, to make up for this shortfall, we may instead use money, cars, jewelry and any other symbolic indicator of personal power to fool an available female into seeing us as a top candidate for mating. And if she seeks only a good provider — a geriatric billionaire perhaps — then victory is within that man's reach. But if she also seeks a genetically dominant sperm donor, then she may have to slink over to a nearby sports field for a better selection. While this may appear a joke, it is not inaccurate in depicting genuine human behavior, even it if fails to conform to our cultural norms. What we want and what nature wants are not always conveniently aligned. But that is a whole other matter.

A further important detail of symbolic warfare is that a man cannot carry with him huge bags of money to prove his financial dominance. As such, to make public boasting of this kind more practical, we began to give value to portable items that could only be purchased for large sums of money, including designer watches or clothing. We also began to offer items for competitive display in our homes, from chandeliers to rare paintings by long-dead artists. Today, some men buy yachts the size of a small island to boast of their being *a better man* than those sending mating calls out from smaller craft. But here again, this is all just a ruse; a way of bluffing our way to the top of society's dominance hierarchy without ever having to prove our true genetic worth.

...

In earlier times, keeping up with our rivals in any symbolic war for dominance was easier because we only needed a cave with fewer bats to win the tribal championship. As things began to escalate, so did our symbolic contests until they evolved into one man — typically a king or emperor — ruling over vast numbers of people and their lands while forcing them to pay tributes and comply with his every whim. This is how the global war for status came to be played and continues today in various forms, including by way of banking cartels that hold entire nations hostage via massive debts and globe-trotting looters of oil and minerals who take as they want by paying the rulers of any exploited nation a share of the spoils. And all are hoping to reach the summit of economic power, if only to avoid losing to someone better.

Today, we have all manner of private interests vying for the kind of symbolic power that none can challenge. And facilitating their harvest is greed, an obsessive urge to hoard money and valued material assets as indicators of one's supremacy over all challengers. Nor can this war ever end with each new generation of men vying to prove themselves.

Furthermore, all men are affected by this biological urge to win and dominate, which compels many to engage in these symbolic wars for status at any income level. This is often done by way of mimicry — namely copying the behavior of those of a higher social status, whether monarchs, business leaders, sports heroes or rock stars. Subsequently, such mimicry has not only shaped what we value as a society, but has also made selfish hoarding seem an acceptable purpose in life.

Today, men and women at all levels of society are using material gain as an indicator of their dominance over others. While only a theatrical bluffing game to attract more attention to themselves, many have now embraced *hoarding* as a substitute form of dominance display.

Such material displays of dominance also create many problems for our planet's wildlife and natural habitats. For instance, in competing for retail dominance, early traders took a wealth of goods from foreign lands, including the feathers of egrets in the Florida Everglades so that European aristocrats could wear them in their hats — a show of vanity that pushed these birds to near extinction in that region. Some other popular vanity imports included African slaves, who acted as proof of a master's status in not having to work so hard to earn a living.

All such assets, be they human or otherwise, were treated as status symbols and purchased by people of means to prove they were indeed people of means. This is the human version of displaying our plumage like a peacock to show off what others cannot afford — be it a crown of jewels, a stuffed lion's head, or a personal house slave to serve us.

Today, our material wars for status continue in the behavior of men like Donald Trump, whose life has been spent naming everything after himself to create the illusion of deserving special access to women and power. However, like most wealthy men, he has yet to prove his genetic worth through any physical display of his alpha male virtues. Instead, he keeps himself in the public eye by displaying the symbolic plumage of his wealth, where it has even won him the US presidency.

In recognizing the importance of symbolic display, we can then see why the burial of Egyptian pharaohs demanded pyramids to be built to ensure no one mistook their remains for those of the poor. They also insisted that slaves did all the heavy work to prove their victory over the struggles of the ordinary. And yet, it was all just a game; a symbolic form of bluffing to prevent anyone from seeing them as equal.

Naturally, to supply our modern social gladiators with the symbolic weaponry to compete for status requires a constant harvesting of raw materials. This leads to further disparities of power as child laborers are forced to harvest diamonds in African mines, and land is stolen from indigenous S. American tribes to let transnational fast food companies graze their cattle. Elsewhere, men are drilling ever more wells in our oceans in competing to be the world's dominant supplier of oil. And all of this leads to two major problems that have also long plagued humankind and our planet, and they are:

1) An excess demand on natural resources used for symbolic displays of power.

2) A competition for dominance among suppliers of such symbolic weaponry, thus creating a constant demand for more profits from natural resources.

In concluding this introduction to the meaning and consequences of our human Bio-Psychology, let us consider one notable casualty of men's competitive pressures upon our planetary resources, which is the rhinoceros. Here is an animal on the verge of disappearing as men use their horns as a symbolic indicator of wealth and a superstition-based cure for a subdominant penis. Yet with everyone busy competing to win, we fail to see that our human race may soon share the same fate.

Ultimately, we are witnessing men's inability to manage their natural competitive urges while their fear of losing will not allow them to stop long enough to evaluate their reckless behavior. And in succumbing to both the fear of losing and the obsession to win, men have turned a once natural biological urge to compete for genetic dominance into a global suicide march toward a planetary wide extinction of all life.

CHAPTER 3
The Very Best of Our Worst

Bringing forward the previous chapter's primary insight, we can state with great confidence that men's urge to procreate is what makes them highly competitive as this is how nature expects the males of many species to prove their suitability for mating. We can categorize such behavior as "glory-seeking" in that it is a display of dominance for the purpose of public acknowledgement or recognition through any kind of contest, be it hand-to-hand combat, economic warfare, or climbing the world's highest mountain. Ultimately, the manner of contest is of little significance as long as it provides a means for men to compete.

This urge to compete affects all men differently depending on their character, temperament and biological adversity to risk. Subsequently, while some men are highly fearful of death and injury, others seem to revel in putting their lives at risk. In modern parlance, we often refer to such risk takers as "adrenaline junkies."

Men's adversity to risk is a major determinant of their social success. For instance, a man who is more willing to risk injury is more likely to win a fist fight, whereas a man who is more willing to risk rejection is more likely to strike up a conversation with an attractive women. In the extreme, a man who is more willing to risk his life for the sake of glory is also more likely to engage in dangerous challenges, whether riding angry bulls, or taunting wild stingrays, as did famed Australian thrill-seeker, Steve Irwin, in filming his last-ever wildlife episode.

Despite a person's willingness to engage in various risky behaviors, biological necessity also requires us to be "comfort-seekers." In that regard, we all must eat, stay warm, and avoid danger in order to survive. Yet men's urge to procreate drives some to seek glory over comfort in the hope of proving themselves "the better man."

This mindset is most evident in adolescent males who suffer from far higher rates of death and injury in taking greater risks to display for their peers and now also for their internet audiences.

In addition, the prefrontal cortex of men — that part of the brain responsible for decision-making — does not mature until the age of twenty-five or later. As such, young men often fall victim to their own competitive urges until they reach brain maturity. This benefits those governments that use young men to fight in wars as they are both more eager to win at that age but also less averse to taking life-threatening risks due to a limited capacity to self-regulate their own behavior.

Although we are all comfort-seekers and glory-seekers by nature, we tend to side more with one impulse than the other. Subsequently, we may find the majority of people choosing a life of comfort over one of risk. This is also why risk takers gain more public notoriety and media attention than those choosing to stay at home and play it safe. As such, societies tend to celebrate men who challenge themselves rather than cling to a life of comfort and security.

...

It is when coupling a man's risk-averse glory-seeking behavior with his procreative urge to dominate that we see a relationship between those who rise to become leaders versus those who remain as followers.

For instance, a militaristic dictator who is willing to kill millions of his own people is far more likely to succeed in becoming our leader than a man who heals the sick and wounded. And while a concerned caregiver is far more qualified to lead our societies than any murderous psychopath on a quest for power our history clearly shows that such villainous glory-seekers often win control of our societies. And while seen as "winners" from a domination perspective, they often prove to be losers in leading others to success. In fact, a tyrant's life may revolve entirely around oppressing others to protect his ill-gotten seat of power. This also explains his dependency on militarized police forces and covert spy agencies to ensure that the needs and ambitions of the many do not threaten his own all-consuming want for control.

Subsequently, this also brings into question the role of society itself, whose founding purpose was to act as a sanctuary from the dangers of the wild, including roaming predators. After all, what use is a society that puts our lives at even greater risk due to the selfish ambitions of a tyrannical leader with an insatiable lust for power?

Logically, it makes no sense to turn blood-thirsty human predators into leaders. And yet, it seems that the very best of our worst often end up ruling over us, whether in politics, business or even religion, where many a psychotic dictator masquerades as a holy man. As a result, our society may barely function as a sanctuary in having become a source of even greater threats from within.

Today, we can find glory-seeking politicians and crooked lawyers in any nation working to steal our votes or civil liberties by rigging our social systems against us. We also find industrial leaders who willfully poison our food, water or air in competing for greater profits, while the false prophets of religion shamelessly steal the meager savings of the elderly and poor to enrich themselves. On the fringes, we find the kind of men who delight in raping, killing and otherwise dominating the innocent for the sheer thrill of proving their power over others. And the more risks these sociopaths and psychopaths are willing to take to win their selfish-serving contests for glory, the more they put the rest of us at risk.

But given our inborn comfort-seeking nature, we may choose not to fight back against the tyranny of others for fear of being injured or losing our access to a warm bed and a steady income. Instead, we often remain quiet and keep our eyes to the ground hoping for better times ahead that never seem to come. Moreover, as history clearly shows, our human tendency to cower has never put an end to the tyranny of our dominators, nor to the decline of other species or our planet's natural resources. In this light, our fear to act can put us at even greater risk.

The Winner Takes All

In having attained a position of prominence and power, glory-seekers are often heard singing their own praises by dispensing platitudes that justify their self-serving ascent. Among those we have all heard is that "Competition brings out the best in us." Yet if this were even remotely true, then why are so many star athletes caught cheating? Instead, what competition also brings out in equal measure among great athletes is their own desperation to win at any cost.

But cheating is not only limited to sport. As such, in addition to any athlete or sports official demonstrating the very best of their worst behavior, we also find widespread cheating in politics, religion, finance, industry, medical research, school exams, and anywhere where people are willing to break the rules to gain a winning advantage.

Cheating also takes many forms. For example, cigarette companies once claimed that smoking was cool, sexy and glamorous while fully aware that their product was killing people. Also cheating to get ahead were food companies sprinkling sugar on breakfast cereals to keep kids loyal to their brands. Even adding nutrients back to factory-processed food is a form of cheating if such processing destroys what is naturally present upon harvesting. It's all just a matter of degree.

Yet the lure of cheating is understandable given that we all do not have the same winning potential. And if the stakes are high and the field crowded with competitors, then it's obvious why some of us will be tempted to cheat our way to the top rather than risk losing to fair play. This makes it doubly ironic if those same cheaters are then asked to offer advice on what it takes to be a winner — dishonesty, for one.

Perhaps in some ideal future world where lions and gazelle can sit down to share a hearty vegetarian meal on the African plains, we may finally see the kind of fair-playing society promised to voting citizens. In the meantime, competition only tends to bring out the best in those who want to play by the rules, which excludes anyone willing to risk our lives and future in shoving their way into the winner's circle.

...

Men's competitive quest for dominance also makes it difficult to know who is on our side. Criminal prosecutors, defense lawyers and police officers, for example, are often caught cheating to win cases and may cheat even harder to avoid losing them. Given this kind of behavior, it would not come as a shock if a defense lawyer sought to win a serial killer's release because the bodies of his victims were found through an illegal search, thereby making them inadmissible as evidence. While this example is exaggerated for dramatic purposes, it highlights how men's urge to win can often defeat the cause of justice itself.

In a similar example, after the Exxon Valdez tanker caused a massive oil spill along Alaska's pristine coastline, killing countless orcas, seals, otters, salmon and other wildlife, the company went on the offensive by suing the US government and Coast Guard, ultimately holding up court cases until they were obligated to only pay 10% of the original fine for polluting. Decades later, much of the coastline remains tainted by aging oil while Exxon has made a near-clean getaway from taking responsibility for its reckless actions against the Alaskan wilderness. In this way, it revealed the very best of its own worst behavior.

Sadly, minimizing losses to maximize profits is a common behavior among companies competing for dominance. This may also explain the low investment in oil spill cleanup technologies to guard against future ecological disasters if such R&D costs are interpreted by oil companies as a greater loss to them than the destruction of our planet.

At the core of such aggressive competitive behavior is the fact that our fear of losing is greater than our lust to win. This is because the fear of losing is tied to our survival, while our glory-seeking urge to win is tied to our procreative urge to display for dominance. As such, our fear of losing takes priority. Furthermore, the combination of both urges to *keep winning* and *never lose* explain why the male-dominated world of business is so ruthlessly destructive in its pursuit of economic glory.

Here again, we see our competitive Bio-Psychology being directed in ways that undermine the protection of our societies and the natural world, whether by engaging in endless wars for profit or refusing to put safety first, as in the containing of toxic waste from gold mining.

And on it goes, with countless daily infractions against humankind and life itself arising from men's inborn lust to always win by ensuring that they never lose. Unfortunately, this puts unfair pressure on those who play by the rules to lower their own standards in competing against the kind of businesses whose unspoken slogan is: "We cheat to win."

Killing The Good Guys

In observing men's competitive behavior throughout the ages, what is clear is that it typically brings out the worst in us rather than the best. Moreover, it appears that we knew this from the start.

Case in point, the Christian bible may not be an accurate account of human history, but it is certainly an accurate accounting of the worst of human behavior. This includes the story of Cain and Abel, which acts as a cautionary tale that we cannot even trust our own siblings due to such competitive rivalry. In this case, after having killed his brother, Cain did as any self-serving perpetrator of a crime does by denying his guilt to avoid losing his community status and privileges.

But a far more significant cautionary tale is that of Jesus Christ, the hero of that same book. While his existence remains debated, the value of his most practical advice is incontestable. Ironically, the lesson best learned from his gruesome death is about the fate that awaits those who attempt to reform the self-serving competitive urges of men for the benefit of the greater good. In short, the bad guys have a habit of killing the good guys for getting in the way of their bad behavior. And if we follow the course of human history, we see that this killing of the good guys is a long-standing tradition among the worst of us.

In fact, while editing this chapter, future presidential candidate and anti-corruption crusader, Fernando Villavicencio was assassinated in Ecuador. Did a foreign nation kill him to gain control of Ecuador's oil fields? The country also has a history of catastrophic oil spills in the Amazon jungle — a tradition that would be threatened by a new leader with a mind toward cleaning up oil industry practices. As such, the suspects are many in that all had something to lose by his winning.

His is just one more name on a long list of dead do-gooders; heroic individuals who sought to elevate the human condition at their own peril by confronting those who wanted to keep others out of their race to the top. Among those dead are many famous people, including Dr. Martin Luther King, Mahatma Gandhi and countless others who will never be known to us. But most significant about their deaths beyond predicting a similar fate for any future hero to come is that, due to the competitive actions of our very worst, we can never know to what heights our world might have risen under the enlightened leadership of the very best among us. Their execution at the hands of those who cheat to control our social, political, economic and religious systems denotes the public execution of our hope in that a superior individual of any kind will ever lead us while cabals of self-serving men continue to conduct themselves according to the very worst of their impulses.

Even today, in a world boasting of its modernity, many nations still kill, imprison or harass citizens for speaking out against their leaders to defend the greater good of society. Or, as happened in the case of Julian Assange and Edward Snowden, for exposing governments that were cheating to win greater control over our lives.

As such, whether it's the fabled young Abel, the prophet Jesus, social reformer Martin Luther King Jr., or the modern day messengers of any inconvenient truth delivered to our world, it is clear that tyranny will likely always win given that the very best of our worst also happen to be those most pathologically determined to win at any cost. Moreover, it proves once again that competition does not bring out the best in those who have no intention of playing by the rules.

...

This trend of killing the good guys continues in many countries today, whether we hear of it or not. People are framed, blackmailed or simply made to vanish, suggesting that Adolf Hitler's Nazi regime never truly left us but was simply woven into the fabric of governments wherein the spirit of burning books and smashing store front windows informs their own crazed aggression in seeking to dominate those who dare to speak the truth — or question their lies.

Yet through every malicious act of violence or plot against us, the very worst of those leaders who engage is such behavior also reveal themselves to be absent of the moral and ethical qualifications that are required to lead society — lest it take the form of a concentration camp. This also explains their constant reliance on mental terrorism and bloodshed to keep unhappy citizens in a perpetual state of fearful submission. Some will even build walls to keep us from escaping their cultural prisons by suggesting that they keep our enemies out.

As such, this combination of killing of the best among us as well as the very best within us poses a major obstacle in raising our collective standards of living and quality of life. Clearly, we must demand a more trustworthy and open system of democratic governance that allows us to create societies that reflect the better qualities of our humanity as opposed to the worst of our savage competitive impulses.

This begins by rejecting every self-serving psychotic or narcissistic sociopath who seeks to control our society by portraying themselves as our savior. After all, history proves that they will only betray us in the end. And if all they have to offer is lies, threats and secrecy, then it is a clear admission of their inability to lead us anywhere but to the lowest reaches of their own grim potential.

The Killer Instinct

Returning our gaze to the controversial glory-seeker, Donald Trump, here is a man who will likely be remembered by history more for his competitive vanity than his dealings in commerce or politics. As one who is seemingly desperate to win by any means, his well-documented public behavior acts as a warning why male competitive thinking must never inform how we govern our nations.

Case in point, during one particular interview, Trump congratulated himself as being a man with "the killer instinct." And perhaps this was one of the very few true statements he made that particular day.

After all, most men would not want to be associated with the term "killer" because it suggests psychosis; that in the heat of competition, he may become so reckless in his desire to win as to lose all regard for the lives and well-being of others. Hence, this is not a character trait that any politically ambitious person ought to be advertising if he hopes to be elected as the guardian of a nation. Yet his boastful statement is also helpful in revealing the mindset of men whose blind obsession with winning can do great harm to a society. As such, let's consider the value of Trump's claim by comparing it to some real world standards.

For example, let's imagine that a husband and wife are applying to adopt a baby when we, as the interviewer, ask: "So what makes you uniquely qualified to adopt this child?" to which the husband proudly replies: "I have the killer instinct." Clearly, we would put a quick end to any process involving the adoption of a child by someone boasting of such an inappropriate character trait.

As a further example, imagine if a nurse was applying for a job at a hospital and wrote "I have the killer instinct" on her resumé. As the administrator, we may even quietly begin an investigation into how many patients had mysteriously died under her care at any previous place of employment.

In other words, the real world has no use for those who brag about having an anti-social and potentially psychopathic mental disposition.

On the other hand, if applying to become CEO to a major industrial polluter, the use of such language might guarantee a second interview. And in a pro-business world guided by broken community ethics and a strategic apathy for the sanctity of life, this *killer instinct* seems to be guiding the opinion of many a misguided business leader that human societies also ought to be run like a business.

But what business model should inform a nation's trade in its citizen products? The stock market? An oil company? A brothel? A factory chicken farm? A dollar store? Clearly, there are a good many options to choose from in terms of how we might govern our nations.

And while taking such an approach clearly represents a bad joke in any real world setting, there are wealthy men of endless ambition who believe that the success of a nation ought to be gauged by the value of its shares rather than its role as a protective sanctuary for humankind.

Under such competitive circumstances, might we then see mothers being encouraged to charge their infants a fee for each breast feeding? Or letting "the market" decide whose child may live or die, basing its need for medical treatment on its projected future earnings?

After all, *business is business.*

Sadly, such irrational ideas for organizing society represent more an admission among selfishly competitive men that they have very little awareness of the actual needs of human communities beyond what serves their own interests. Subsequently, their skewed perspective on managing our lives sounds more like a joke without a clever punchline offered by someone who may not have any experience in looking after others, let alone treating them as respected equals. And with history as our witness, those who rule society with such a crucial deficit in their understanding of life are destined to lead us into a state of social and moral bankruptcy.

What we do know from experience is that treating the protection of human life and society like a stock-dependent enterprise guided by the male killer instinct is behind the current worldwide destruction of our nations, communities and ecosystems. And if we continue to allow the very best of our most pathologically ambitious men to take charge of our collective destiny, then we will remain on this downward trajectory that will see us becoming like the rhino: a species lost to the ignorance and reckless greed of our world's most successful poachers.

And so, in concluding this chapter, what should catch our attention is not merely that those leading our societies are commonly the worst possible candidates for the job, but also that the best qualified among us may never rise to power in not having the same obsessive drive to dominate — which is what men's Bio-Psychological urge to rule our collective political and economic territories is all about.

Instead, the very best of our worst will continue to engage in these meaningless symbolic races for glory that serve none but themselves. And like anyone too busy running toward the finish line, they will have no time to slow down and reflect upon who they are or where they are going — let alone where they are taking the rest of us.

CHAPTER 4
A Special Kind of Stupid

Nature appreciates her dominant males, rewarding them with greater access to females and other privileges. Yet she does not discriminate as to who can aspire to this coveted position. Instead, she encourages all the males of various species to enter this contest for genetic supremacy by triggering their Bio-Psychological urge to compete against each other. As such, she also leaves them little choice but to act upon these selfish, competitive impulses.

When triggered in human males, this urge to compete causes men to engage in contests to prove themselves *the top man.* In return, those who prevail are also awarded greater sexual access to females and other advantages for proving to be worthy of alpha male status — which is a designation that we now typically measure through material wealth or popularity rather than superior genetic traits as nature intended.

In calling all males to compete for dominance, nature gives everyone an equal chance to become one of the chosen among the many called. Yet despite her massive recruitment drive, there will always be those who show early signs of becoming a top contender in any chosen field, be it sport, academia, or even the musical entertainment industry.

In a real world example, those closest to rock guitarists Edward Van Halen and Randy Rhoads during their teens already sensed they were destined for musical greatness — it was that obvious. And so it is for the dominant in any field whose physical attributes or superior skills may already set them apart early in life and have us expecting them to become "a winner" in whatever future contests they will have entered.

This would suggest that some of us are seemingly destined to play a leading role in society for which we may also be well-rewarded. But what about the rest of us — those closer to the mediocre end of the dominance spectrum? Are we destined for a life of standing at the end of the line waiting for our share? Probably so.

As such, we must each learn to make peace with our station in life, no matter what level of success — or failure — we might attain. And while there are ways to further elevate our social status, we also cannot deny reality itself. In that sense, it is not unlike getting plastic surgery to alter our appearance while our unflattering genetic traits continue to be passed down to our children — there's just no escaping the truth. As such, we must accept that we may never be a champion in any field, let alone a leader of others simply because the odds are against it. And for much of society, that is the reality of our predicament.

Yet what the reality of our modern times failed to take into account is that nature has implanted each men with the urge to compete for dominance. And so, at the constant urging of their inborn, procreative lust, men are endlessly driven to enter all manner of contests to prove themselves superior, regardless of their actual qualifications.

This urge to compete for dominance also causes an inner desire to feel "special" — which is how our mind translates the urge to stand out among the crowd. And since we all can't be winners, we may then feel resentful toward those getting special treatment for their achievements while we must settle for less or even nothing at all.

This exclusion of the majority from positions of power and privilege also leads to a predictable consequence in all societies wherein groups of the downtrodden huddle together to heckle those at atop society's dominance hierarchy. Here, to elevate our self-esteem, we may look for flaws in our leaders or other prominent figures, even delighting in their downfall and suffering. Moreover, since the urge to compete does not leave us, such competitive envy can become a lifelong obsession for those to whom "winning" is beyond reach. In this way, if we cannot actually compete against the dominant of society, then we can at least put them down with insults or by praying for their ruin. This also helps to explain the popularity of tabloid media full of celebrity gossip about those who we may both loathe and admire for having risen above us.

This uncontrollable urge to win among the unqualified introduces us to the main theme of this chapter in that we can then anticipate within all societies the presence of men who feel the competitive urge to take a leading role despite lacking leadership credentials. To some, only the brutish laws of nature apply, thus putting them on a constant collision course with those in power as they seek to claim their rightful share of the kind of special treatment to which they may feel entitled.

Once again, given that nature plays no favorites as to who can enter her race for genetic supremacy, this also puts our societies at risk from weak-minded individuals fighting for dominant status over the rest of us. As such, we may at times encounter men of limited potential who feel emboldened to lead courtesy of a competitive state of mind that might best be described as "a special kind of stupid."

Would You Believe...

Although "stupid" may not be the most accurate term for the occasion, it does offer some comic relief in approaching a rather serious topic. For one, it is highly flexible in its use as an insult by both the dumb and the wise should we dare to disagree with either one. In addition, all of us have made *stupid* mistakes, most often as teenagers where a lack of wisdom and an undeveloped pre-frontal cortex may have had us making decisions that we would later regret. Yet as we began to reach adulthood, we may have learned from our mistakes of the past and left our childish ways behind us. In short, we will have grown up.

But not everyone succeeds in making this mental transition. Instead, some people remain trapped in the mindset of a self-indulgent child both intellectually and emotionally. Coupled with a competitive urge to dominate, we can then anticipate the problems we may encounter in having to negotiate with such a person. The end result is as famed writer Charles Bukowski once mused: "The problem with the world is that the intelligent people are full of doubts, while the stupid ones are full of confidence."

As competitive beings, we may snicker at "the stupid ones" to boost our own self-esteem. Yet even smart people can behave in ways that leave us wondering if anyone is truly sane. In working our way through this maze of mental chaos, let us then begin by first considering our mind's relationship to belief itself.

...

Regardless of our level of intelligence, we are all generally quick to defend our beliefs, no matter what they are or whether they ultimately prove useful. This is because the primary role of our consciousness is to serve the needs of our survival and procreation. Subsequently, our habit of developing simple, repeatable patterns of thinking and social behavior allows us to serve those needs with greater efficiently.

Unfortunately, some of these patterns can be self-defeating and may even endanger us. And yet, we may continue repeating them simply for fear of losing control of our predictably scripted lives.

This fear of losing control is also what makes us stubborn to change our ways given that what we believe helps us to meet our body's needs for *comfort, convenience* and *control* — those Physical States of Being alluded to earlier. And so, even if our repeating a self-defeating pattern of behavior may seem illogical to others, it might make perfect sense to us given that our beliefs also keep us alive based on our relationship to the world, whether its knowing what is safe to eat or who to trust. Subsequently, given that our minds hold a vast store of such life details, we cannot simply surrender them on a whim just because somebody else thinks we're being stupid. In fact, most of us want others to change their way of thinking to ours just to make us feel more comfortable.

In addition, our beliefs act as a first line of defense against our fears of the unknown. A belief in the afterlife, for instance, makes us feel less fearful of dying, while a belief in our superior status makes us feel more confident. As such, any attack on our beliefs can also feel like a struggle for life itself, no matter how misguided our beliefs may be. This would explain the difficulty people have in convincing members of a religious cult to leave an imaginary world that has been specifically designed for them to escape the objective one in which we all must live.

In addition, those who are struggling to think at a "normal" level of intelligence not only have a greater need for such repeatable patterns of thought and behavior, but also for simple patterns that are easy to follow and remember. Moreover, such patterns may apply not only to their daily survival, but also to their beliefs on such matters as politics, religion, family life and morality. And while some beliefs might seem stupid to others, they may help that person to function better in their daily life. Moreover, all minds function this way to help us meet the rigors of existence, including those of wild animals who also develop such daily life patterns. Yet knowing this doesn't make it any easier in dealing with an angry stupid person who insists that the rest of us have gotten it all wrong and only they know what's best.

...

Let us now reorient ourselves to the fact that this book concerns itself with the ill-effects of male social competition. And as expected, this often confusing array of individual and group-based patterns of belief is also used by men as a premise to compete for social dominance. As a result, not only do we defend our beliefs as a matter of life and death, but also as a matter of competitive pride.

This was evident during Hitler's reign over Germany as hordes of fanatical Nazis strutted around like they were something special after having adopted a belief in their own genetic superiority. Sadly, such self-aggrandizing beliefs are common to group thinking, which is why we can find them everywhere, whether among religious followers or anti-government militia groups who believe themselves heroes in their own group's narrative about the meaning of life.

Also, as many will have seen, when men argue over beliefs, each will typically believe he is right, regardless of the actual merit of his various convictions. This forces us to address that proverbial "elephant in the room" in that we all cannot be right about what we believe. And yet, our selfish Bio-Psychology does not seem to care much about the truth as long as we're fighting to win. As such, the truth is of no consequence to those intent on having us surrender our beliefs, right or wrong. This also makes it challenging if they are not clever enough to realize that winning is not meant to keep us from learning.

...

The *Dunning-Kruger Effect* describes a mental paradox wherein those less competent in any activity may believe themselves more competent than they are — or at least above average. While this makes no sense logically, it makes perfect sense to our competitive Bio-Psychology in that we must feel confident in going to battle to prove our worthiness. And the less we know of the values or standards of what we are doing, the more we may believe we are doing it right for lack of real world feedback. This is why a person of lesser intelligence may also believe himself to be a genius out of a defensive need in confronting anyone who truly is mentally superior. But luckily, not everyone reacts this way, otherwise our world would seem to have gone mad altogether.

This counter-intuitive state of mind also suggests that we can expect a greater resistance to logic from those with higher confidence in their illogical beliefs. This is borne out by anyone who speaks with authority about knowing the mind of God or having knowledge of conspiracies without direct experience thereof. In the realm of social competition, those claiming authority on any matter often hope to draw attention to themselves as having leadership status. This is further demonstrated by their dismissing of rivals to bolster their self-esteem. We may even recognize some of their most popular putdowns, including "Sheeple" to imply the stupid, herd-like mentality of others. Yet if we listen to such people talk, we may find them both inarticulate and poorly versed in provable facts. What they are, however, is determined to win.

Complicating matters further, sociopaths often pretend to believe as we do to win our trust. We see this among charlatans who gain power over their victims by pretending to side with them. Such people embed themselves in the worlds of politics, religion and finance, where they use our shared belief patterns to divide us from our sanity and conquer our lives.

When Stupidity Wins

Given our reliance on belief and our urge to compete, let us use these insights to help make sense of the chaotic events that occurred in the USA during the Trump presidency which also stand out as some of the most stupid to many a thinking person in that nation.

Given their competitive urges, we can understand why many men also treat politics as a venue to fight for dominance. This urge to reign supreme can infect entire groups, giving rise to "culture wars" wherein angry tribes of voters clash over shallow ideological differences while ignoring all they have in common over some absurdly rich politician.

This divisive group-based mindset also helps to explain much of the politically-motivated mayhem during the COVID-19 pandemic.

At the time, people also started to adopt questionable beliefs that did not stand up to logical scrutiny, whether promoted by President Trump himself, or shady internet entities such as QAnon. Ironically, few who adopted these questionable beliefs seemed to care about the truthfulness of that information as long as it could be wielded like a weapon against one's perceived enemies on the opposing side.

Sadly, what many true believers failed to realize is that this was all a counter-intelligence plot by members of their own party to divide and conquer millions of fearful conservative voters into running away from the *liberal* bogeyman, just as Catholic priests have long been doing by wielding an imaginary devil against their followers.

This domestic war for social dominance was a full-spectrum effort by well-funded conservative institutions and corporations, all of whom hoped to sway the minds of those too naive or trusting to question the deeper motives of those in the upper tiers of wealth and power. In one example, FOX News told its viewers that rigged voting machines had caused Donald Trump to lose the 2020 election; a lie for which they had to pay $787M in damages for defaming the company that made those machines. During this time, we were also reminded about how dictators train citizens to believe that the truth is a lie, as happened when information on COVID-19 was wielded as a political weapon rather than as a means to prepare the nation for future outbreaks.

In hindsight, we might even speculate that the COVID "alternative facts" debacle was born out of a selfish attitude within the USA's highly competitive culture, which tends to favor the wealthy over the greater good of the many. This includes a profit-driven health care system that typically forces cancer patients to sell their homes to pay for their care. For this reason, the nation was ill-prepared to serve those among the working class who couldn't afford a costly health insurance plan, let alone a lengthy stay in a hospital ICU.

Evidence of this economic divide was seen in the USA's death rate from COVID-19, which outranked even the poorest nations. And so, to hide this gaping hole of apathy in its economic system, those who sought to defend profit as a way of life needed a way to distract citizens from the reality of their dire predicament. As the leader of the nation, Donald Trump initiated this mindset by declaring that COVID-19 was "nothing to worry about" while mocking infectious disease experts and trying to keep the working poor at work, sick or not. Many took the bait, perhaps out of loyalty to their president. And soon we began to even hear that this pandemic was just a big hoax staged by "them."

In addition, perhaps hoping to reap future financial rewards from a cure, COVID testing technology from Germany was rejected in favor of funding its own — a decision that caused delays in public testing due to shipments of faulty test kits arriving at hospitals.

Meanwhile, talk of a government-sponsored vaccine had conspiracy theorists up in arms about their mass-extermination by the elite. In the interest of exploiting an existing anti-establishment sentiment among right wing voters, some predatory grifters began to claim that simple, off-the-shelf miracle cures were being suppressed to protect the profits of vaccines makers. In short, they were playing history's time-honored mind game of divide and conquer by masquerading as the heroes on the side of the greater good. And then they took their money.

Atop the list of social media approved treatments was Ivermectin, a drug meant to prevent malaria — a parasitic infection. It is neither safe to use nor designed to treat viruses. Yet seemingly in defiance of reality itself, right wing pundits and influencers began promoting it to treat

COVID-19, perhaps to avoid filling hospitals with people who could not afford their stay. As expected, experienced medical professionals began to speak out against using unproven treatments, which created the desired reverse psychology affect among the already-suspicious by acting as proof of a top-down conspiracy to kill the poor with vaccines or by denying them access to a cheap cure.

In short, stupidity took control of the healthcare narrative.

...

Understandably, the onset of the COVID-19 pandemic was a time of fear for many of us, as was the economic fallout from forcing people to stay at home. In the USA, a culture already at war within itself, this created a convenient excuse to blame outsiders, proving that Hitler's strategy to rally the hate of the masses had not lost its charm.

In keeping with stereotypical stereotypes, hatred was directed at the Chinese, at "big" government, at non-caucasian female politicians, at a Jewish billionaire who funded liberal causes, and seemingly at anyone who had gotten a higher education. In the midst of a losing battle, at least this kept the finger of blame from pointing at Donald Trump or the ideologies that helped to perpetuate this medical, economic and political crisis within the nation.

Adding fuel to the fire of peoples fear and anger was a proven history of top-down social oppression courtesy of everyone from the Egyptian pharaohs and European monarchs to white slave owners of western nations. As such, rather than being a conspiracy theory, the selfish exploitation of human beings is a genuine and chronic social condition that we must constantly guard against in our world. Yet in times of social unrest, our fear of being conquered becomes a political weapon that can have us working against our own best interests — perhaps by voting for the worst political candidates or buying drugs from online grifters whose medical experience is limited to the use of bandages.

Beyond providing con artists with the basis for a shameless feeding frenzy, political opportunists also used the pandemic to further drum up anti-liberal/anti-establishment hatred among conservative voters. The vilification of medical experts and those of a higher education also undermined the USA's ability to respond to the pandemic as devious minds incited ill-informed citizens to terrorize doctors and nurses for simply going to work to do their jobs. Subsequently, one great irony of that time was reading about people who had died from COVID-19 after having declared it a hoax — or who were then later treated with kindness and compassion by the same medical professionals they had been so loudly and proudly condemning in social media posts.

Sadly, when societies stop functioning as a protective sanctuary to become just another symbolic territory over which men can battle for dominance, then we can expect little progress as each side focusses on building walls of exclusion rather than bridges to understanding. And as one battle ends, another must begin to keep this futile game in play that has all sides losing together in the end.

What we saw unfolding in the USA was the beliefs and competitive vanity of the gullible being manipulated as a platform to elevate other men, whether politicians like Trump, or grifters selling fake cures to people who were scared of dying. But is this "every man for himself" social attitude one we should be embracing to create a better world? Or is this just a convenient shortcut to our total destruction?

Ultimately, such behavior only further demonstrates how men's urge to compete is causing all of us to lose. And in a final ironic nod to that era of reckless stupidity, then-president Trump addressed the violent mob that had scent marked the sacred halls of the US capitol by telling them exactly what they had always wanted to hear:

"We love you, you're very special."

Playing Stupid

Albert Einstein once claimed that people liked him better when he was silent. This is the plight of many a deep thinker who points out the reckless stupidity of others to their own detriment. Einstein also felt regret in having helped to build the first atomic bomb once he saw its devastating consequences. Yet the deadly fallout from that detonation pales in comparison to the death toll from gun violence in the USA as innocent people are killed each day by men having no intention to lose to anyone, be it their government, a dissatisfied wife, or a black man sleeping off a long day's work in his parked car.

Here again, we must keep in mind that the USA is host to a highly competitive culture. Yet to be a true winner requires having not only a winning attitude, but also the strength, skill or intellectual might to defeat one's opponents. And since most of us don't have what it takes to battle our way to the top, our next best option is to defend ourselves from greater loss — perhaps by bringing a gun to the negotiation table. And given our prevailing competitive mindset, a purposeful amplifying of our fear of losing can quickly have us taking countermeasures, be it by increasing our insurance coverage, buying a vicious guard dog, or starting a small gun collection for when "they" finally come for us.

...

We can better understand the gun violence problem in the USA by referring back to the negative consequences of a young man entering adulthood with an as-yet-undeveloped prefrontal cortex while feeling nature's competitive urge to compete for dominance. Already being at a mental disadvantage due to age and a surging male biology, if that young man is also born with a dysfunctional mind, then he might even be tempted to bring his gun to an intellectual debate for lack of having the necessary mental weaponry to win against his opponents.

In one such case, a boy of seventeen travelled with rifle in hand to a public protest (against police shootings of black men no less) to keep unruly protestors from becoming a danger to others. He even walked past police vehicles before finally killing two young men and maiming another under the pretext of self-defense. Obviously, the best form of self-defense would have been to stay home instead of driving all that way to put himself in harm's way. Furthermore, if all he wanted was to give peace a chance, then he should have brought flowers, not a gun. Later, crying for the court's mercy, it was ironic to note that in seeking to control the violent behavior of others, he failed to control his own.

...

As a highly competitive culture, the USA is also the center of the internet's "attention economy" where those who gain the most public notoriety win the most glory. This creates a further deadly consequence as young men use their newly purchased guns to compete for status on social media. This economy includes mass shooters showing off their cache of weapons or boasting of how many "kills" they plan to make in some future shooting spree.

This kind of attention seeking also incites "copy cat killers" to ride the coattails of celebrity mass murderers by trying to "one up" their psychotic heroes to win public attention. It's a strange state of mental affairs but as the saying goes, "Records are made to be broken" — and that applies not only to athletes competing in the Olympics, but also to killers seeking to break body count records during a massacre.

The combination of youthful competitive lust, low intelligence and easy access to guns also creates a social media culture wherein guns are being used to shoot at targets for which they were never intended, such as propane tanks or other combustibles. This kind of reckless depiction of gun ownership further perpetuates a mindset wherein guns are seen more as a toy for all ages than a deadly weapon. In addition, some rural parents treat shooting a gun as a right of passage in preparing their kids for life as a gun-toting adult.

As a result of both competitive social attitudes and the lax standards surrounding gun ownership, we are also seeing a greater frequency of shootings by mentally unstable young men acting out their urge to win against those against whom they could otherwise never compete. Here as well, a loaded gun becomes the great equalizer for any weakling on a quest to defeat his rivals — whether face to face, or as an anonymous strangers in a premeditated public proxy killing.

Gun violence of this kind has lead to a further destabilizing of US society as news stories grow about young men shooting their way to infamy inside public schools, nightclubs or shopping malls. Some even smile while sitting in court, seeming to revel in the notoriety they have achieved as someone "special" in the public eye, perhaps as a murderer of a classroom full of helpless children. So much winning.

Beyond fueling competitive envy among budding psychopaths, such events also trigger a great fear among gun manufacturers and elected officials paid by defend gun makers from losing their privileged status in the upper tiers of the US economic food chain.

Yet in defending against such enemy attack, these manufacturers of war weaponry take a much less violent approach than what they may prescribe for their gun-toting customers in standing their ground.

And so, rather than coming out with guns blazing and a "fight to the death" air of defiance, both gun manufacturers and politicians alike opt instead for the more reliable defense strategy of playing stupid by just pretending not to understand the problem. So much so that they even recommend selling more guns to stop all the killing.

Clearly, they must think that we're all pretty stupid.

...

In having come to the end of part one, we have established a strong foundation for understanding male competition and the damage done when we treat our society as a battleground for alpha male domination and display rather than a sanctuary to protect us all.

In the coming chapters, we will consider the negative consequences of such competition to many aspects of social life, from the governing of our nations to our negotiations for power within relationships.

Ultimately, we will realize that our various competitions for status hinder the creation of a truly civilized world in bringing our selfishly competitive nature into a closed system wherein we no longer battle for genetic supremacy but for social and economic privilege.

Moreover, we will continue to explore how willful ignorance and blatant stupidity keep our societies from progressing toward a higher ground wherein we all might enjoy the best of what technology and personal freedom have to offer. And although we cannot defeat nature, including our own, perhaps by gaining a deeper understanding of how our biology influences us, we can ultimately tame our selfish impulses to where they no longer pose a threat to others — or ourselves.

PART TWO
Keeping Other Men Out of Power

CHAPTER 5
Leading with Fear

Prejudices and stereotypes are often used to inflate us with a false sense of superiority over those against whom we discriminate. Yet they also offer us a convenient way of predicting how others might behave. For instance, we may use them to predict how a smart person would behave versus someone who is stupid.

Yet even the smartest among us are prone to bouts of stupidity as a result of mental blindspots — those aspects of our thinking that may only see limited use or have been downgraded in their importance to give other aspects of our thinking a higher priority.

To demonstrate this prioritizing of our brain activity, we would not, for instance, be able to write romantic poetry while being attacked by a vicious dog. And although we may never find ourselves in this odd predicament, it demonstrates a tendency to make fear a higher priority in that it is our first line of defense against injury and death. And given that the urge to survive is the highest priority of any life form, this has made *the fear of losing* a constant presence in our lives given that it has historically meant dying from predation or for want of food.

Subsequently, many of our personal life decisions are based on this nagging fear of loss, including *the fear of missing out* that retailers use to torment us into buying their goods. As a countermeasure to our fear of losing, our mind may then develop an obsessive urge to always win. But while it may be easier for animals to act on both impulses in a wild setting, doing so in context of any human society can be a complex and even dangerous undertaking.

A familiar example would be choosing to risk doing harm to others to avoid losing out on buying a popular item during a *Black Friday* sale. Here as well, our fear of losing incites a fierce battle to win possession of something that may prove of little value to our life. And yet, we may risk trampling others to death in a bid to claim it for ourselves or to simply avoid losing it to some other equally-determined shopper.

Given that our minds are already agitated by an instinctual urge to compete for dominance, we are then further burdened by this urge to prevent others from causing us to lose. Subsequently, whether we fear being defeated by a stampeding horde of bargain hunters or losing our job to a wave of highly-ambitious immigrants, our thoughts may be so preoccupied with fear and defending ourselves that we have little time left for anything else, including our pursuit of happiness.

Noteworthy is that such fears are more prevalent among men and for good reason. After all, women have always been too busy doing the important work of society, such as caring for children, thereby leaving men with far more time for their competitive inclinations to transform our societies into a battleground for dominance or a paranoid prison colony of lethal restraints to keep others from defeating them.

This has led to many familiar expressions of male-sponsored fear among our world leaders. A common symptom is the building of walls along national borders to suggest that its resident alpha male is feeling much too vulnerable to write romantic poetry — let alone to allow his captive citizens to run free.

This prioritizing of fear in competing for dominance is a common blind spot among leaders in politics and business in that it causes them to lose sight of the joys of living, including the pursuit of a far more meaningful goal than the mere exercising of power over others. As a result, we also find many a smart man acting rather stupidly in having lost decades of joy to the fear of losing and a compulsion to win.

But such epiphanies often come to us only in times of crisis or when pondering our list of regrets as death nears. Subsequently, the future survival of our world remains on its current downward trajectory due to leaders endlessly fighting over nation-sized prison compounds that were designed to keep other men from competing against them.

This makes it all the more ironic when we hear our political leaders cheerfully promise to create a more open and democratic society given that most want to hoard more power, not share it. And once seated, those reluctant to surrender that power might make death, destruction and dishonesty their top mental priorities in an all-too-familiar style of governing wherein we all lose under the failed leadership of a man besieged by the competitive urges of his own Bio-Psychology.

Trust No One

In approaching the topic of leadership through fear, let us first make a critical distinction in that *leadership* and *domination* have nothing in common beyond being ways to influence the behavior of others. And whereas leadership is meant to inspire and empower, domination seeks to suppress. As such, we can expect leadership behavior among social visionaries and school teachers, whereas domination behavior is more commonly seen among invading soldiers, rapists and wife-beaters.

This distinction is important given that a political tyrant is not a genuine leader but rather someone who uses fear and force to suppress other people's access to power and independent thought. As such, even though he may appear a "leader" for exhibiting alpha male domination behavior or traits, such a tyrant often inspires in us little more than fear and an urge to flee from them. Subsequently, tyrants must also live in constant fear of being overthrown by those they are oppressing.

If we were to assign a personal motto to the mindset of a tyrannical male-dominator such as this, it would be: "Trust no one." And therein lies that man's own great misfortune in having condemned himself to a life of endless suspicion wherein he cannot even trust those who may prove themselves a genuine ally.

Ironically, the reason for his chronic fear of losing is a symptom of his suspicion that everyone else harbors the same self-serving impulses as he does. And so, in suspecting everyone of wanting to engage in the same selfish behavior, that tyrant then sets out to gain control over his potential rivals at every turn.

Such paranoia is common among unfaithful couples where the one cheating becomes suspicious that the other may be doing the same. Likewise, a leader who is plotting against us behind our backs may accuse us of plotting behind his. In the USA, for example, a politician may wax patriotic over the freedoms offered by the constitution of that nation while secretly plotting to steal those freedoms from voters who might side against him in future elections. And if he loses, he may even accuse those politically emancipated voters of having cheated.

Returning to our tyrant, to further neutralize the threat of our doing unto him as he is doing unto us, he may govern over our lives in ways that ensure we can never pose a threat to his reign of selfishness.

As part of his defense strategy, he may want to know everything we are doing or thinking to identify any potential threat to his hold on power. This fear has given rise to government surveillance programs in most nations so that leaders can keep us under their control as they serve their own interests. Nor can we expect such leaders to admit to a self-serving agenda as such information is classified "top secret" — which has necessitated the rise of WikiLeaks and other organizations that help expose the unsavory truths about political leaders who are secretly plotting against us behind our backs.

And once a leader's next of kin or accomplices inherit that empire, they also inherit those safeguards that protect this governing system against the threat of unruly citizens who have come to realize that the system was not designed to help them, but rather to exploit them.

...

In addressing matters of political tyranny and social oppression, what also becomes apparent is how our fear, a once natural survival instinct, has begun to rage out of control since we began to migrate from the wild into our artificial concrete landscapes. And where once we had to face legitimate dangers from the wild, today, the dangers we face are not so much directed at our immediate survival but at our freedoms of choice and independence of movement as global citizens.

In that regard, our modern surveillance societies have implemented security measures that make sci-fi films about dystopian future human slave colonies seem almost within reach.

Today, in watching any forensic crime-solving show, we will notice an increased reliance on surveillance technology whose omnipresence we now seem to take for granted.

For example, many of us use electronic credit cards instead of paper money when we go shopping. And although invented to make bankers richer by having us pay high interest on borrowed money, these cards offer the side-benefit of allowing us to be tracked like collared animals, thereby exposing our lives and activities to many other prying eyes.

Another surveillance aspect of society now taken for granted are the growing number of "security" cameras on our streets. And so, if police officers need to solve a crime, they simply seize footage from a nearby camera to identify a perpetrator. Conversely, if a corrupt officer needs to hide his crimes, he may seize that same evidence to protect himself from justice. In this way, a dishonest defense lawyer can also introduce the absence of footage as evidence to dismiss a case. One real world example was the death of Jeffrey Epstein, a billionaire sexual predator with deep political ties whose death by suicide was dismissed as a mere coincidental lapse in all prison safety protocols. Hence, no video.

But perhaps the most important new weapon to control the masses in a surveillance society is the cell phone. Here again, if we watch any forensic crime-solving show, we see that, aside from security cameras, a suspect's cell phone records are a crucial piece of evidence used in the solving of many crimes.

For example, in a recent high profile murder case, prosecutors could show the jury in which room disgraced lawyer Alex Murdaugh stood at various times of the day in question. Such tracking is possible using satellites and "pinging" phone signals off transmission towers. In fact, much of our technology is vulnerable to outside tampering by anyone from hobbyist hackers to spy agencies. And although we can justify in part why others may need to invade our privacy at times, it proves that someone may always be watching us, just in case we try to undermine the power of those in control — whether by breaking an actual law, or by joining a local activist group to demand clean drinking water.

Subsequently, this presents us with a problem in regard to the limits of our personal rights and freedoms, a concern also voiced by former intelligence agency contractor, Edward Snowden, who exposed his government's illegal spying on citizens without reasonable cause or suspicion of their having engaged in any form of criminal activity.

Snowden's fate as a vilified exile proves that even in nations that claim to uphold the rights and freedoms of its citizens, there can exist an undercurrent of fascistic abuse to protect its inner circles of power from losing control of their lucrative taxpayers.

As such, just like a cheating spouse, a government's inability to trust its citizens may just be a reflection of its own untrustworthiness. After all, a well-respected citizenry has no need to overthrow its leaders; a fact that every political dictator should take to heart.

Dividing The Conquered

Logically, not all leaders are brutish villains, yet they all face the same challenges in needing to defend their seats of power against revolt. Subsequently, under the constant threat of being overthrown by angry mobs, most leaders are careful to keep us under their control.

Leadership in this light reflects the motto "Keep your friends close, and your enemies closer" to ensure that one always knows where one's potential rivals are lurking — including citizens demanding to have competent leadership or long-awaited political promises delivered.

Many political leaders begin their careers as a candidate running for local office, which involves telling voters what they want to hear in order to win. Yet once in power, their true colors may begin to show, as well as our disappointment if they prove incompetent. As such, a leader may resort to various mind control tactics to distract us from their selfish grasping for power or inadequacies as a leader.

Among those tactics is a "divide and conquer" strategy that has long protected tyrants from angry mobs by having citizens fight amongst themselves instead as a form of distraction. But humans were not the first to use other people's mental chaos to their advantage. Instead, that strategy has long served various predators in the wild.

For this reason, a qualified expert of the divide and conquer strategy is any feral cat hunting for food. If it hears two squirrels quarreling in the distance, it will silently move in their direction knowing that when animals are fighting over food or territory, they may be too distracted to notice a predator lurking in their midst. And unless a crow sounds the alarm from above, one of them may become an easy meal.

Similarly, many nations are divided along conservative and liberal party lines that are also constantly quarreling while the apex human predators of society calmly feast on the labor forces and land resources of our nations from high above.

On the liberal side, leaders may offer a more equal-handed, *sharing* kind of governance that attracts women and those marginalized by a history of male domination. Conversely, the conservative side focusses largely on issues of patriarchal self-preservation often to the detriment of women and the exploited. As such, this "every man for himself" approach also attracts those kinds of men who enter politics to serve only themselves. Yes, we all have selfish impulses, but the inclinations of our character often guide us to choose one party over another.

Ironically, our body's Bio-Psychology is also divided by these same opposing traits of selfishness versus sharing. We feel compelled to be part of a protective community while often working against its greater good due to our status-seeking selfishness. This splitting of our inner values explains not only the slim 50/50 voting margins so often seen during elections but also the tendency among men to advocate for a more openly selfish style of governing for lack of a woman's capacity to act as an unconditional caregiver — as nature has inclined her to be for the sake of her children. This helps to explain why social services for women are often cut by men exemplifying the competitive social ideology of a patriarchal system wherein women's needs are treated as having lesser importance — whether her health, or her orgasm.

Given this insight, we can then predict various behaviors on either side of the political aisle. On the conservative side, for instance, we find a more openly aggressive stance in support of the selfish impulses of men's competitive nature, including the "fear of losing" wherein we feel that our status is perpetually under threat by outside forces beyond our control — like aging male lions clinging to power. For this reason, this fear of losing is often used by conservative politicians to incite voters to reject liberal values or solutions by presenting them as a threat to their fear-adverse lives of comfort, convenience and control.

In a very real sense, conservative values are often focussed more on ensuring our basic survival — a selfish endeavor. As such, there is little need for a more articulate plan for our future beyond "Me first!"

During election campaigns, we may then hear right wing politicians mocking alternative social values or condemning a kinder approach to governing as a sign of weakness, whether caring about immigrants, or showing a willingness to compromise. As such, conservative politics also tends to be more about domination than inspired leadership.

While this stereotyping of conservative political values may obscure some of its benefits, it does hold up to scrutiny in predicting the lack of a future vision among its politicians beyond living in a world with fewer taxes, fewer immigrants and fewer rights for women. And to put a mask on this trend toward patriarchal selfishness, leaders may try to distract voters with fear to control our thinking and behavior.

For this reason, it has long been a tradition in the USA, Canada and other multi-party nations that prior to an election, some form of crisis must be declared; some looming threat from which only conservative values can save us; be it rampant crime, moral depravity, an invasion by blood-lusting foreigners, or hoards of liberated women armed with birth control and an equal day's pay.

This is not to suggest that liberal politicians are flawless because they may also be driven by such self-serving impulses. Instead, all of this is simply a reminder that we can never truly know the motives of those seeking to dominate us via our political systems. And the more selfish a politician tends to be in their words or deeds, the more we need to worry about our own fair share under their future leadership.

But if there is any doubt as to the voracity of this comparison, we need only ask the women of any oppressive nation where conservative patriarchal values are the standard fare — and the only choice.

While our own conflicted biological needs for status and communal protection help to explain this ongoing ideological warfare between pro-sharing and pro-selfishness political parties, what we also learn from this two-sided approach to governance is how we are being kept divided by manipulating our fears and competitive urges as opposed to appealing to our basic human intelligence or desire for peace.

By keeping us divided within ourselves and from one another, the apex predators of society can then sneak off with our money, land and civil rights as we frantically search for danger in various misguided directions. In this way, our downfall is all but assured at the hands of those who want to discourage our strength in numbers lest we attempt to overthrow their tyranny. And all it takes to divide us is the same old fear-based mind games that have long been conquering us since this kind of top-down mental tyranny began.

Making matters worse, we may then see both sides of the political aisle feasting from the same trough by taking legal bribes and direction from wealthy industrialists, bankers and institutions who secretly steer our nations in whatever direction best serves them.

The Loss of Our Humanity

The fear that divides us is also one that we must learn to contend with in a world where our survival depends on consuming the life of others. As such, animals in the wild must live in constant fear of being eaten or attacked by those who can overpower them. Yet they seem to get used to this way of living, as seen when gazelle graze within striking distance of sleeping lion prides. Yet in always having to be alert in case of attack, their own natural behavior is forever altered in never being able to fully let down their guard, day or night.

Turning our attention back to human society, we can then anticipate the damage being done to both our individual and collective lives by having to also live in a constant state of fear of being attacked.

The source of such fear is the predatory threat from the alpha males of our societies expressing an urge to dominate just like any ambitious male animal in the wild. Here as well, their ancient biological instincts have them eagerly competing for status and even using our laws and the threat of police violence to keep the rest of us under their control. And this is how most of our nations work insofar as they all originated from one man's or one male group's urge to dominate and subjugate all challengers who stood in their way. Hence, the birth of our nations.

But such safeguards against the unruly masses are never enough to calm the fears of tyrants wielding illegitimate power. And so they build elaborate defenses to protect themselves on an ever-narrowing road that leads to fascism. And like those gazelle living in constant fear of attack by lions, so must we as citizens surrender parts of our humanity in societies designed to keep us from becoming a threat to those in power. A prime example is the use of mental terrorism by any religion to inhibit our sexual or intellectual freedoms of self-expression.

Such restrictions not only inhibit our human potential but can also have dire consequences for our mental health by obstructing our path to joy. In this way, our society can become the cause of a widespread depression or suicidal tendencies among those losing hope.

This is self-evident given that fear inhibits our ability to function as a complete human being. Gone are any hopeful dreams for our future; our seeking of simple pleasures, and our ability to appreciate a perfect moment in time. Instead, we will be on constant, fearful alert against the threat of displeasing our leaders or making ourselves suspect for not following the strict rules of our oppressive regime. In other words, we will be living in a purposefully induced state of mental terror.

We can also not expect any leader driven by selfish motives to think about anything but his own self-preservation — especially if he lives in constant fear of being overthrown. As such, both sides ultimately lose in having been divided and conquered by a fear of each other.

Human social competition is also a selfish endeavor in that it often demands a constant gaining of power to stay on top. Subsequently, the most successful alpha male predators of human society must always be taking more for themselves to prove their winning status. This can be observed by the removal of social protections and safety nets to limit our power as citizens and escalate our feeling of need and desperation.

As such, a decline in social programs also represents a decline in our humanity and the community values that once ensured the well-being of our ancient tribal societies. All are now being overrun by values that best serve the lone male predator on his selfish quest to gain the most for himself. As a result, we have created societies wherein we stand to gain the most as individuals by weakening everyone else around us.

In competing for personal power and glory, leaders may also disrupt the peace of our communities or even threaten our lives by engaging in armed conflicts to increase their territory. And as is true in any war torn country, the greatest losses are incurred by civilians while those who start wars are often sequestered safely at a distance from the life of fearful deprivation that they have forced upon the rest of us.

Today, greed is the primary expression of a man's urge to dominate in our money-based societies; a compulsive hoarding of the symbols of economic supremacy. And as one man ascends, others feel compelled to surpass him, thus turning our communities into a war zone where wealthy men engage in subduing all rivals with their weapons of mass economic destruction.

As for the rest of us, we are not unlike the gazelle grazing in fear of losing to the alpha lions of society as they battle nearby and likewise feel no intrinsic desire to see us getting ahead. To them, we only exist to be eaten.

CHAPTER 6
Dominating the Human Mind

Fear may play a critical role in protecting us against danger, yet there are times when fear alone cannot save us. Earthquakes, flash floods and hurricanes, for instance, can strike at any time to remind us of just how vulnerable we remain despite our valiant technological efforts to evade the natural threats of this world. As a result, we also have a long history of seeking mental comfort in beliefs that offer us some sense of control over the uncertainties of life and the greater unknown.

Knowing this, we can better understand our widespread human trait of seeking out mystical seers and embracing faith-based myths to help us make sense of what would otherwise make no sense at all, including the reason for our existence upon this planet.

And so, whether we pray to an invisible God or await our spiritual salvation at the hands of cosmic beings from another realm, what all such beliefs prove is that we are not only prone to being superstitious and steadfast in our faith in what others claim, but that we also depend on our beliefs to counteract the fear and confusion of finding ourselves in a dangerous world without context of either a beginning or end. And as we each attempt to fill that void of missing information as to our origins or purpose in life, we also tend to fill it to favor ourselves. A Christian, for instance, may believe themselves to be a heroic savior of our world, while a Scientologist may believe the same of themselves in having adopted an entirely different mythology. And this holds true for all such group-based belief systems, including those with an overtly anti-social or sinister intent. In short, we all want to play the hero.

As a result, our minds can often exist within a reality that mentally separates us from the objective one in which we must live. Herein, we can escape to a place in our imagination that helps us to face life with greater courage by making us feel special or important. And if this was our only reason for creating such an elaborate inner fantasy life, then it would probably be harmless and perhaps even therapeutic. But what if the citizens of an entire country believed themselves to be heroes as part of a dominant "master race" that is entitled to rule the world?

We have already seen the tragic results from this kind of misguided thinking and its predictable road to war and societal collapse. And yet, many continue to believe in their own racial superiority as though such self-deluded beliefs have never been put to the test.

As with Hitler's Nazi regime and its own belief system, our adoption of an alternate interpretation of reality typically involves the influence of a charismatic leader who creates a "mental empire" through which he can control the minds and actions of his followers. In doing so, he will also create an enticing myth that puts us at the center of a glorious plot to save the world and/or enter into paradise. And in return for this promised reward, he will demand our lifelong faith and loyalty, which typically also involves offering our free labor, money or sexual services. In other words, the typical fare on the pricey menu of any cult.

For the most ambitious of sociopathic narcissists, creating a mental empire is a proven strategy for amassing great power over others. In knowing this, we can then easily identify these mental con artists as they set out to exploit others through various adopted belief systems in the domains of politics, religion or business.

Logically, common sense should protect us from this kind of mental manipulation. Yet our mind's defenses are undeveloped as children and some of us will have been indoctrinated by our parents to live in the exploitative fantasy world they adopted. As children, utter dependence has us trusting parents who may then put us in harms way by offering our lives into the service to some mentally deranged cult leader.

Unfortunately, such mental racketeering is a long-standing part of our human story, as is the accumulation of great wealth and power by those who excel at it. These are the dominant alpha males of various mental empires that still exercise such absolute control over their loyal followers even now. And yet, all but the most self-deluded of leaders knows it is all just a mental game. Yet to reap the many rewards of their parasitic existence, they must keep the minds of their unsuspecting victims in the dark by promising them a path to a glorious future life — just as all mental and/or political cults tend to do.

...

In 1998, Canadian film actor and comedian, Jim Carrey, introduced us to *The Truman Show*, a movie about a man who was being exploited in the service of a long-running Reality TV show and its creator. Born in captivity on a television sound stage, every detail of his life was being broadcast to a worldwide audience as a form of entertainment — all carefully orchestrated by one man whose power depended on keeping Truman from discovering the truth about his captive life in an artificial world of hidden cameras, fake sunshine and fraudulent friends.

Today, the minds of many people throughout our world are dwelling in some version of that Truman Show — some interpretation of reality that was created for them by others. This also makes any discussion of mass mind control a sensitive topic because our leaders have taught us to believe that only we see things as they truly are, whereas those living outside our mental compound are either self-deluded or living a lie.

We can easily prove this by asking a devoutly religious person if they hold any mental biases against non-believers or the members of other religions. If honest, many will claim they feel superior as a result of their adopted beliefs about themselves. In other words, beliefs systems of this kind not only cater to people's desire for inner peace or to enter a blissful afterlife, but also to feed their Bio-Psychological lust for status by adopting beliefs about their own social supremacy.

Many people sincerely believe in what they believe, while others just pretend to avoid persecution. Yet whatever our beliefs, they would likely pose no great threat to anyone but ourselves as long as we didn't force those beliefs on others. Yet the quest for status is built upon the gaining of power over others. As such, leaders are often driven by their own competitive hunger to expand their mental empires. And this they have always done by turning their legions of loyal followers into conquering armies on a quest to "save" the world.

But whereas swords and rifles had long been a traditional choice, the most effective weapon of conquest by far has proven to be imposing a belief system on the defeated. After all, whoever controls our mind, controls how we think and behave. And if we believe we should pay our leaders 99% of our income as a tribute, then that is what we will do. Hence, the ultimate form of human domination is from within.

This threat of mass mind control was explored in my book, Clearing a Path to Joy. Herein I introduced the term "Mental Empires" to define a scripted mental containment system through which leaders control and exploit us. Such mental empires can be as small as a secluded rural cult or as large as a nation. And if we never leave the confines of that cultish bubble of scripted illusions, then we also remain unaware of the greater reality that exists beyond its imaginary mental borders.

Here again, the harm caused by such mental empires would remain confined if those self-serving rulers did not lust for more power as a sign of their dominance. Insulated by that bubble world, status-hungry young men can also be more easily recruited to kill by promising them alpha status upon their triumphant return — or in the afterworld.

The danger of coming under the influence of such nefarious mental forces is both real and constant because of our tendency to rely on faith and mythology to get our bearings in life. Moreover, if we fall under the spell of someone with sinister intent, we may even find ourselves becoming a hater of the kind-hearted, or a patriotic defender of a nation that openly engages in crimes against humanity.

As such, our best defense against the threat of exploitative mental empires and their destructive beliefs is to understand the mechanics of mind control and tribal thinking. In this way we can avoid becoming just another unwitting actor in someone else's Truman Show.

The Folly of Group Thinking

Given the worldwide distribution of mental empires, their presence suggests that there is more at work here than just mind control. This introduces another problematic aspect of our Bio-Psychology in that we are inclined to form human groups for the same reason that many animals form herds in the wild.

This is an understandable urge, given our body's inferior design for both durability and self-defense. As a result, we find both strength and security in numbers due to our shared vulnerabilities. And this creates opportunities for selfish manipulators to exploit our human herding instinct for selfish gain. As for evidence, we need look no further than to politicians, marketers, religious charlatans and fascist dictators, all of whom target groups of people for the purpose of exploitation.

As already stated, such exploitative social groups often form around a charismatic male who claims to have special powers or qualifications that make him appear a natural born leader — historically these were often monarchs or priests. In this way, that leader could gain control over the individual lives of members by having them adopt a common regimen of group thinking and behavior.

As these groups form, we may begin to see the stereotypical signs of favoritism and abuse, such as young women being recruited for sex with top level males, while others are forced into slave labor. And this is all made possible by creating a myth about the group's special status and future reward potential for dutifully obeying its leader.

Given their predictability, it is surprising how effective these group recruitment and manipulation techniques remain. Yet we may join for any number of reasons that range from a quest for status or romance to communal protection or even seeking new business contacts.

The goal of our social manipulators — or "mental emperors" — is to create an isolated form of society governed by a belief system that puts them first in line for all privileges. This is also why some communist countries ban religion, teaching us instead to worship a political leader or his ideology the way others worship God. In this way, both politics and religion merge into one system, like a theocracy. This prevents rival systems of belief from subverting the dominant empire and its rulers.

...

Admittedly, we cannot save everyone from themselves, including aging widows who send their life savings to religious grifters, or young men who engage in acts of terrorism to please their God. Sadly, such people often don't want to change their way of thinking, not only because it is difficult, but also because it would be frightening to navigate this dangerous and uncertain world without some belief to guide us.

On the other hand, we also cannot just stand by as parasitic mental empires ravage our societies. But this battle for the mind has never been an easy one to win — we need only recognize how difficult it can be to change our own minds. As such, our best offense is a strong defense by arming ourselves with precise knowledge as to how these mental empires form and function.

In recognizing the mental mechanics of these mind control systems, we are not only able to better protect ourselves, but also to keep others from falling under the spell of sociopaths who masquerade as saviors. And if we are currently the member of any exploitative group that has us doubting our own sanity or common sense, then we can use this information to break the mental chains of their hold on our lives.

And always, when in doubt — *question everything.*

...

Mental empires typically control our lives by exploiting our fears and competitive vanity. As such, the beliefs we adopt are often meant to increase our fears so that we seek the group's protection — as many religions do by using our fear of evil or eternal damnation to keep us praying and obeying. In addition, the group also inflates our sense of importance to make us feel special for belonging to the group. In short, they appeal to our Bio-Psychological urge for status.

In the interest of opening a public dialogue on humankind's mental control systems, I will introduce **the IPSFA Sequence**, a mind control template that I discovered while unraveling the mysteries of thought. Surprisingly, it has been in use for thousands of years worldwide as a means to gain control over groups of people in the realms of politics, religion, finance, and elsewhere.

As presented here, the IPSFA Sequence works as a visual aid to help us understand the process of how ambitious manipulators form social identity groups that can be mobilized to do their bidding, be it as a nation, religion, terrorist organization, or a citizens advocacy group.

The generic structure of the IPSFA Sequence allows for its easy adoption by groups seeking to maintain their unique identity and way of life. It requires only that its five elements be defined by various rules and parameters that dictate how the group should think and behave.

The structure of the IPSFA mental control system is also simple in that the acronym itself identifies its five elements as follows:

(I) **IDENTITY:** The social group identity we are asked to adopt.
(P) **PROMISE:** What we are promised for adopting that identity.
(S) **SCRIPT:** The rules we must follow to prove our identity.
(F) **FEAR:** The punishment we face for disobedience or leaving.
(A) **APATHY:** What we must ignore to remain in the group, from our own private suffering to the harm we cause to others.

In identifying the IPSFA Sequence structure and its requirements, we can then invent our own hypothetical social identity group to see how this process of mental control works in a real-world setting.

In our case, we will create a hypothetical social identity group whose name will be "The Extra Specials." This will help us to see how each of the five IPSFA elements are used to this day by political and religious governing systems. This allows us to chart how all group identity are formed and maintained by those controlling them. More importantly, it offers us a simple and easy way to analyze the intent of such groups and even show us how to escape their scripted hold upon our minds

Let us now invent a hypothetical social group identity and see how its scripted elements help to build the invisible walls of a newly formed empire within our minds.

- (I) **IDENTITY:** *The Extra Specials* (a religious cult).
- (P) **PROMISE:** To enter paradise or live a life of greater wisdom and privilege than our perceived rivals in this world.
- (S) **SCRIPT:** ; Keep our leader happy by following his rules and doing as he instructs; never question his wisdom.
- (F) **FEAR:** Being caste out or reprimanded for daring to question our leader or the group's values, beliefs and mission.
- (A) **APATHY:** Having to pretend that our leader represents the best of humanity; believing that the group's divisive views can lead to a better world; having to sell our home or abandon our family to prove our loyalty to the group.

Going forward, the IPSFA Sequence shows us how we are all being controlled, whether as citizens of a nation or devout believers of some religious cult. Indeed, such mental racketeering is a long-standing and global phenomenon. As such, our leaders may deny knowledge of such mind control systems even as they use them to control us:

- (I) **IDENTITY:** *Canadian* (a nation-based social group identity).
- (P) **PROMISE:** To enjoy a better quality of life than in many other nations around the world.
- (S) **SCRIPT:** Keep our leaders happy by following their rules and doing as they instruct. Above all, pay our taxes.
- (F) **FEAR:** Being caste out or reprimanded for daring to question our leader or the group's values, beliefs and mission.
- (A) **APATHY:** Having to pretend that being Canadian magically transforms people's lives for the better.

While offered with a touch of humor, using this example of being a Canadian proves that cults and nations share the IPSFA Sequence's mental scripting structure. Like DNA, it is universal.

The IPSFA Sequence can also be used to "deconstruct" any kind of group identity to identify aspects of its script that may potentially be working against our best interests. In this way, we can keep our leaders honest in delivering on their promises while also ensuring that people's membership in that group is not causing them more harm than good.

Better yet, if harm is being done, the IPSFA Sequence allows us to sit down with a pen and paper to analyze and eradicate any negative aspects of a group's scripted identity. In this way, group members can suggest removing mental obstacles that may be impeding their ability to live a more joyfully contented life. And if the right to make such progress is denied, then it may also confirm that the group's true intent is to exploit us by keeping us in a state of mental imprisonment.

Bugs In the System

Like the DNA sequence, the IPSFA Sequence is incredibly flexible in regard to what kinds of identities it can create. Yet for our purposes, it will be most useful in revealing the mental structure of social identity groups that may be undermining the well-being of our society.

In that regard, not all social identity groups share the same agenda, meaning that there can be vast differences between the scripted values of one group versus another. For instance, we should not expect trouble if the Local 48 Dew Worm Pickers Union comes marching into town. On the other hand, given that the billionaire Koch Brothers founded "American's for Prosperity" in 2004, we can suspect that the group itself was formed with their own prosperity in mind.

Common sense tells us that whenever men of great economic power form an alliance, the urge to dominate is behind it. Here, at the top of the economic food chain, wealthy men may seek an increase in their financial status and power by dominating government leaders, who are seen as the alpha male dominators of a nation. As such, this exposes a common "bug" found in many social action groups whose members are actually undermining their own status under the misguided belief that they are elevating it. In this case, in the name of "prosperity," they may well be fighting against the kinds of government oversight that would otherwise protect their interests as citizens from the selfish exploits of greedy billionaires. After all, paying higher union wages, safer working conditions and family leaves of absence cuts into one's profit margin. As such, what could be better than having one's own employees fight the government to get even less for themselves? Also, as the second largest public company in the USA, one may suspect that profits were very much on the minds of the ultra wealthy Koch Brothers as they formed a citizen's action group to assist the unwealthy.

Keeping in mind that wealth is a widely accepted tool for measuring male dominance, let us then invent an imaginary advocacy group to lessen the struggles of poor billionaires in trying to control our world. Adding to the irony, let's name it "Rich People For More."

- (I) **IDENTITY:** Rich People For More (an advocacy group).
- (P) **PROMISE:** To get even richer by using ordinary citizens to pressure their government to make legislative changes on behalf of the wealthiest of society.
- (S) **SCRIPT:** Fight to eliminate unions; minimum wage incomes; taxation; non-profit medical care; limits on pollution or the amounts of money that can be used to bribe politicians.
- (F) **FEAR:** Losing our dominant social status to democracy.
- (A) **APATHY:** Advocating for a society whose quality of life is diminishing so that its wealthiest can prosper even more.

Although the RPFM is a fictitious group, we find its equivalent in the real world efforts of the powerful to claim ownership of ever more political influence, natural resources and wage-dependent slaves. And should we doubt their existence, we need only refer to any history book not already banned or censored by advocacy groups that reveal a long historic list of exploits by the wealthy and their political facilitators.

...

The Bio-Psychological urge to dominate arises in any group setting, be it a rock band or a political party battling for control of their nation's government. This introduces another type of system-wide bug wherein group leaders are reluctant to admit to their flaws or weaknesses for fear of losing their perceived position of dominance over others. This is also a common feature among narcissists who fear being exposed as the inferior beings they often are. A such, a leader may do whatever is necessary to keep their flaws or weaknesses hidden so that we cannot use them as leverage to negotiate for greater power or to demand their resignation so that someone better qualified can take the lead.

The Catholic Church offers a prime example of both systemic bugs. First, it has a history of dominating human minds, including those of the native cultures of other continents. Secondly, to protect its hold on power, it has long-denied a history of abuses against humanity. As a result, many followers were shocked to learn of the ungodly treatment of native children in Canada by abusive nuns at Catholic missionary schools, or the widespread molestation of children by sexual predators masquerading as priests. Sadly, the reality that the angry parents of those children faced was that the leaders of a social identity group that claims to represent an all-loving God chose to protect its most sinful members of high rank rather than their child victims.

Trapped by an unquestioning faith in a belief system that its leaders clearly refused to uphold, many parents unknowingly facilitated these sexual assaults, which may well number in the millions given that an estimated 6% of Catholic priests commit sexual crimes without ever being held accountable. As to why God allows children to be raped by these supposed holy men — their victims still await his official word.

This introduces yet a third bug within such mental control systems which is the fear of losing our privileges or status by questioning the integrity of the group or its leaders. As a result, we may force ourselves to live in denial of our group's criminal transgressions or crimes against humanity to protect our own membership and its promised rewards.

If we refer back to the IPSFA Sequence structure, we find the source of such mental conflicts in the "FEAR" and "APATHY" categories, which detail the truths we may be forced to deny to maintain our faith in any social identity group and its way of life.

For example, investigators found that many devout parents refused to report their child's sexual assault (APATHY) to protect their faith in the Church or avoid being shunned for making accusations against a local priest (FEAR). And so, to protect their own selfish interests, their children were made to suffer, sometimes for many years.

In addition, other devout members of the group may "gaslight" us by pretending that our perception of reality is at fault rather than the group itself or its crimes. We may even have to gaslight ourselves if our group is exhibiting behaviors that fail to align with our values. In this way, we protect our need for comfort, convenience and control by not having to change our way of life or thinking. Yet this fear of change is also a common cause of chronic frustration and misery.

Subsequently, in an illusory human world where even the criminals claim to be "the good guys," it is not easy to know who to believe or even what is true anymore. Ultimately, we must rely on our instincts to make our way through any mental maze of contradictions or lies in dealing with social identity groups who pretend to be one thing yet often prove themselves to be something entirely different.

Rejecting What Simon Says

Leadership comes by way of a person's experience and authority on the matters needing to be governed. As such, it is not determined by one's physical might or the decibel level of their boasting. However, with so many contenders fighting to lead us, we are often challenged to know who is truly best qualified for a leadership role in any group situation.

Recognizing this dilemma, let us recall "Simon Says," a game that many of us played as children. Here, the goal was to follow only those instructions that began with the phrase "Simon Says." And if we then followed any instruction that did not begin with "Simon Says," we would lose the game and be "out." Yet oddly enough, no one ever told us who this Simon person was or why we must follow only *his* orders. After all, what if Simon was a psychopath — or an arrogant dimwit who might have led us all astray?

Clearly, we needed to ask more questions about this Simon fellow and his assumed leadership qualifications — yet no one ever bothered. Instead, we all just did as Simon told us to do.

Looking back, we can interpret the purpose of this game in several ways, yet it clearly trains us to follow orders by a mysterious authority figure rather than act independently of our own accord. And as we entered adult society, we soon began to understand who Simon was.

Simon is the leader of our government, our religion, or any kind of social group; Simon is anyone with the authority to tell us what we can or cannot do. And if we follow anyone else's instructions, they would be deemed invalid and we might lose our freedom, job, reputation, etc.

Oddly enough, what was missing from our childhood was any game that would teach us to listen to ourselves. Now isn't that odd?

And so, aside from teaching us to pay attention to whoever is in charge of instructing us, the Simon game is also teaching us to become obedient followers of the many Simons in charge of our world.

But with so many of them in charge, how do we know which Simon to listen to? Nor will any of them admit to not being Simon but simply an imposter who is trying to control us. As a result, we may one day put ourselves in danger by listening to what the wrong Simon says.

To give us a more enlightened perspective on what all of this means, let us imagine ourselves walking into a mental health clinic and telling the attending psychologist — Simon, of course — that we feel as though we are being constantly watched and judged every minute of every day by an invisible entity whose existence we cannot even prove. How might this particular Simon's assess our state of mind?

In asking this question, what it will demonstrate is how each mental empire interprets reality based on its social identity script.

To prove this, by walking into such a mental health facility, we would likely be diagnosed as suffering from some variation of schizophrenia. And yet, if we were to cross the street to speak to the priest at our local church — another Simon by any other name — then he might instead tell us that we are showing signs of becoming a good Christian. After all, that is what his religion teaches us to believe — that we are being constantly watched and judged by an invisible God whose existence we cannot prove. So which Simon should we believe?

Ironically, these real world examples of mental empire programming prove how twisted and confusing life can be under the influence of so many Simons all competing to control our minds by inviting us to live inside their subjective bubbles of reality.

And lest we forget that Simon is also compelled to win by his own instinctual drives. As such, he may sacrifice the truth to protect his continued reign over a mental empire under the control of the most formidable Simon of all — the selfish urges of our Bio-Psychology.

As this ultimate of all Simons is telling us to form groups to protect ourselves from harm, he is also telling us to fight for control of our group. As such, we can never be sure if someone is trying to help us through their leadership of that group or just keep us trapped within the imaginary walls of our own version of *The Truman Show*.

And with that in mind: Simon Says: "Proceed to the next chapter."

CHAPTER 7
Yachts, Hookers & Blow

Consumerism has become like a faith-based religion in its own right in that many also believe that their salvation or happiness depends on what material goods they will one day possess. In addition, the power of leaders has historically been displayed through their material assets. As a result, this combination of cultural influences has led to a rather predictable form of social display behavior, especially among men.

What we can therefore predict is that any wealthy man who buys a yacht costing millions of dollars is not doing so merely for recreational purposes. Instead, he is signaling his economic dominance to female onlookers in search of a life of luxurious ease while also signaling to any man owning a yacht of lesser value that he has been defeated.

In response, those men bested could either choose to buy an even more expensive yacht, or sheepishly concede their defeat to Mr. Big.

While materialistic grandstanding of this sort is so transparent that it is has become comical, it has nonetheless been with us since before the first pharaoh demanded a pyramid-sized tombstone to mark his glorious passage into the afterworld. Moreover, nature's law of sexual attraction teaches us that the more female attention the male can draw to himself, the less he leaves for his rivals, thus ensuring his biological victory in monopolizing the reproduction for his species. At the very least, he may draw the interest of our wives, daughters or girlfriends.

Here as well, our human Bio-Psychology makes its presence felt by causing men to prove themselves a winner. But rather than showing their genetic superiority through feats of strength, dexterity or skill, our societies have largely replaced such real world indicators of male dominance with symbolic representations of his masculinity. And for much of our history, a common symbolic indicator of alpha male status has been material wealth in the form of gold, gems, land, etc.

Ironically, this has also led to some bizarre mating consequences in that the owner of that obscenely oversized yacht may well be a wrinkly old man who requires medical assistance to rise from his deck chair or achieve a viable erection. And yet, here he floats, a man nearer to death than his prime, but still able to outperform any virile young man by the merit of his financial supremacy. And if our ears could detect it, we might even hear mother nature cursing.

…

As stated earlier, our modern societies now function less as a protective sanctuary than a proving ground for ruthless men to take as much as they can for themselves. And with the blessing of equally self-serving accomplices in government, they can amass great fortunes if willing to share their spoils with political policy-makers. This has turned many societies into an adult male venue for materialistic showboating.

Yet in reaching this pinnacle of symbolic power, many a successful man has arrived only to realize that nothing more awaits him beyond this point. In having been driven to outperform other men throughout his life by the obsessive urge to dominate and win at any cost, what he and many others now lack is a genuine sense of purpose in life. And so, while arriving at the summit of economic power fully enriched, he may remain spiritually impoverished for lack of a meaningful vision to guide his future steps. And often, there also awaits a dark night of the soul for those who have everything, yet seemingly nothing at all.

In reaching this crossroads, a man can either turn back to find what he may have lost in his rush to get ahead. Or, he could simply keep going in the same direction, hoping that something might change for the better beyond the balance of his bank account.

But if joy doesn't arrive as planned, then he may hope to fill his inner void in that distracting world of *yachts, hookers and blow*.

Ironically, this lifestyle choice does make biological sense in that it simulates a dominant males having won sexual access to females. But in this case, money and a day full of drug-enhanced sun-tanning on a yacht are responsible for making those females receptive to the man's sexual overtures, not the appeal of genetics. And given that she is a working girl, she will offer an award-winning performance of feigned sexual delight to make him feel like the biggest of all winners.

As for the cocaine, it can help to make the treadmill of hedonistic material hoarding seem virtuous or at least it temporarily disrupts the feeling of emptiness in having to rent one's sexual partners and friends while never knowing which of them can actually be trusted.

Yet the sellers of yachts and cocaine would not want the faith of the next generation's male glory-seekers to be undermined by revealing these sullen truths that await them on the path to self-indulgence.

As for those working girls, they will deliver the same services to any man at a price, including the scurvy-ridden captain of a tug boat. After all, they're just in it for the money, too.

And so, while my previous book, Clearing a Path to Joy, was written for those choosing to turn back, this chapter highlights the destructive fallout from those who have failed to make that turn.

...

Greed and its feverish demand for more have been the topic of many a Hollywood movie or scandalous news story. After all, conflict sells. And while men's desperate grasping for more can offer us something to snicker about, we must not lose sight of the fact that for every big winner, many more losers are needed to ensure their oversized victory.

For example, in the course of earning billions, a wealthy industrialist may have to poison the water supply of thousands of working class families. And if he enters politics hoping to transform the government into a for-profit enterprise, then he may do as one former governor of Michigan did, by poisoning the citizens of Flint in trying to privatize its water supply. Today, many residents still live with toxic levels of lead in their bodies while the politician responsible avoided paying for his crimes, as is typical for the wealthy or politically-connected.

And so, as we applaud the material excesses of our ultra wealthy, we should not lose sight of the fact that there is a price to pay whenever anyone wants more than everyone else. Unfortunately, that price is often paid by those who can barely afford their bills, let alone move to a location where reckless industries cannot poison their children.

However, as in the wild, the attention of society is not upon its losers in any competition for dominance. And so, instead of being alerted as to the lowering of our quality of life by another's random act of selfish gluttony, our media mostly focusses on praising the stellar material acquisitions of our glory-seekers on their aimless quests for more.

In this regard, the behavior of many such men mirrors that of any gambling addict who moves from table to table to get his adrenaline fix through his symbolic conquest of others. To them, how they earn a living matters less than the conquest. Moreover, if not for this blind obsession to win, many wouldn't know what to do with themselves.

In perpetuating this social domination game, our role as citizens is to keep our heads down low and remain silent, lest we interfere in what others insist we are not smart enough to understand, such as why our government makes it so easy for economic predators to loot our society or to put us on a path to chronic illness, poverty or homelessness. And if we behave as expected, these men can afford their new private jets thanks to tax cuts given under the pretense of creating more jobs for those having to take the bus to work.

Yes, this is the world that awaits us, wherein far too many men still run around like unsupervised schoolboys to taunt and terrorize others out of sheer savagery or a budding biological urge to prove themselves. As a result, many people must live in fear for their daily survival as a direct result of those having the luxury to ponder what color of trim to put on their newest yacht. But rather than drink or drug ourselves into pretending that all of this is normal and perfectly fine, let us instead look at these dire social issues and conditions under the heady influence of a pure, uncut logic.

Short Selling Our World

In approaching the topic of unchecked greed and its dire influence on society, we will find no simple answers but only a bird's eye view of a world seemingly gone mad to facilitate the mindless quest for power among hyper-competitive men. As such, let us instead shine a light on the socially destruction aspects of various economic war games that allow men to win a fleeting place of prominence as society's symbolic top breeder — even if they remain entirely oblivious of the biological forces driving their competitive behavior.

On the absurd side of male social combat, we find a stock market that allows men to temporarily buy ownership in a company for which they never intend to work. And even if that business has not sold a single product in years, it can still produce massive financial returns for its sellers based merely on rumors or the telling of a good lie. In other words, there need be no actual substance or good that comes from any stock purchase, as long as it gives men a premise to gamble and win.

Even more absurd is the idea of short-selling, which allows men to profit by betting on other men's failure. But most absurd is that those who create these imaginary games of economic chance create nothing of usable value while making vast fortunes by overseeing the spending of other people's money, just as banks do. And in a demonstration of what society values most, they can earn more in a day of trading than most people make in a lifetime of creating tangible goods.

Short-selling reveals how unsustainable the male-dominated world of finance has become in that men can grow rich from loss and failure, which might even cause them to encourage it. Making things worse is that many respected institutions engage in high-risk gambling activity of this sort by investing our retirement funds and future well-being as though they were mere toys in the hands of a spoiled child.

Here as well, scripted social identity group thinking plays a critical role in how men interpret their actions in risking other people's lives. Furthermore, the self-congratulatory nature of tribal thinking ensures that our questioning the reckless behavior of the stock market or its founding ideology will be met with ridicule for being out of touch with how "the real world" really works. After all, gambling is what sustains much of human civilization — whether its gambling on a new president, on our religion's faith, or on some mystical seer at the stock exchange whose predictions affect what happens in the business world and the private lives of others. And whether we win or lose, the sellers of stocks keep earning commissions while often knowing little about what they are selling, beyond hope itself. And the dream that many share is to one day also be able to afford yachts, hookers and blow.

...

Economic predation and the thinking that justifies it is responsible for many devastating social collapses and the ensuing loss of people's jobs, homes and lives. Such was the case when millions of innocent citizens were victimized by the global economic collapse of 2008.

According to testimony by those responsible, it all began with banks offering mortgages to those unable to afford them, then reselling those bad debts as *securities* to brokerages. Tipping the scales of sociopathy, those brokerages bundled those bad mortgage debts as investments, with some even taking a "short" position by betting they would fail, as they ultimately did. As a result, the more investors lost, the more these two-faced brokerages profited from their losses.

Here again, we saw a prime example of how the protective aspect of society is being sacrificed by greedy men so they can use it instead as a game board for their competitions for symbolic dominance. Did any of them care that children would be coming home to empty supper plates — or that their homes would soon be a tent in a nearby park? No. Their minds were only on winning by making more money.

Clearly, the kind of men who would endanger the lives of others and the very economic foundation of their society are the embodiment of pathological selfishness. And here again, the obvious rears its head in that many traders are young male warriors not only eager to win, but also not fully-developed in their mental capacity to understand the consequences of their reckless actions against our society. And leading them are greedy old patriarchs with a kill or be killed attitude akin to that of a military recruiter enlisting young men to risk it all for glory.

As citizens of a top-down parasitic society, we are left with the sad realization that those preying upon our world economies are also being entrusted to gamble with our future, using people's pension funds and other lifelong earnings as gambling chips.

Teachers, trades people, and public servants have a different attitude toward money than those willing to risk it all. A wealthy brokerage owner, for instance, might spend as much on a rare oil painting as what a working class couple earns during their lifetime. Clearly, they do not share the same values or perspective on life. And yet, the money being put aside for their future is dragged onto the economic battlefield of men willing to sacrifice it all for a fleeting moment of adrenalized glory and a good week's pay. Surely, as brokers were earning massive commissions from the selling of bogus mortgage derivatives, they had the opportunity to warn their clients that this was all just an illusion.

Here again, economic crashes and their chaotic fallout prove what happens when men are allowed to use our societies as a male proving ground for dominance. In this case, through displays of financial and material wealth. And if our systems are rigged to accommodate their self-serving ambitions, then little to no thought is given to providing a protective sanctuary for those not engaged in these economic battles for dominance in our midst. "Get over it, snowflake", they will say.

And as they back-slap each other after each devastating blow to our society, economy or ecology, they readily dismiss their actions with the mantra that "boys will be boys." Subsequently, it should once again be clear why women must take over to clean up this mess.

...

In considering the parasitic attitude of our greediest social dominators, this also extends to having others clean up after them. After all, what could be more profitable than to do all the reaping while having the losers do all the sweeping? And this unfortunate pattern of behavior is often seen among those who feel entitled to more than the rest of us.

Take Charles Keating, for example, who had denounced Larry Flint, owner of Hustler magazine, as "immoral" while having tax payers pay for his $3, 000,000,000 in losses after he recklessly gambled away the money of his clients at Lincoln Savings and Loan Assoc. More absurd even, he blamed the US government for his crime. In fact, government deregulation made it easier for men like Keating to commit financial crimes against the public. In other words, the government was on his side, not against him as he claimed.

To demonstrate the sociopathic nature of Keating's business empire, an internal sales memo advised staff to "remember the weak, meek and ignorant are always good targets." And that is how many in the world of finance see their customers — as ignorant suckers.

The same "sweeping up is for the poor" attitude was in evidence after greedy Wall Street investment houses had caused countless people to lose their savings in the 2008 economic crash. Here again, it was the American tax payers who were forced to clean up, many of whom did not earn enough to gamble with — yet their money was taken away.

While no concrete tally of the damage done to society by Wall Street fraudsters remains, the tax money paid out to banks and institutions is estimated at $500,000,000,000 or approximately 16,129,032 years of working as a cashier for Walmart at current 2024 income rates.

Nor did citizens paying for this financial cleanup have a democratic voice in where their tax money could better be spent — whether to improve infrastructure, create an affordable healthcare system, or to upgrade inner city schools so kids have a better chance to succeed

Flush with an infusion of cash, those who gambled away everyone else's money offered not a "thank you" nor apology to the American public. Instead, hefty bonuses were paid and surely spent on a lot more yachts, hookers and blow — and the silencing of witnesses.

Beneath such sociopathic debauchery is the continuation of nature's violent struggle for dominance as played out in the venues of modern society. Today, it is no longer tribes of blood-thirsty savages but men in expensive suits engaged in monetary acts of territorial pissing who have won control of our nations and economies. As such, we must also give up any hope that such sociopathic predators will ever come to our collective rescue, let alone give up their selfish games for the greater good. Most only care about being recognized as a winner.

Where the Criminals Run the Courts

For the price of admission, Hollywood was quick to retell the stories of how the 2008 global economic collapse unfolded. This inspired the making of several films and documentaries that recounted the various aspects of a reckless stock gambling debacle that shook the world.

While some set out to identify the cause, others sought to capture the mindset of the perpetrators, including rogue tricksters like Bernie Madoff, the reigning champion of shameless economic grifting.

Ironically, the film "American Psycho" had been released eight years earlier, offering a clear warning about the shallow world of pretense wherein beta level male stock brokers vie for alpha male status through various measuring games of their symbolic might. This included the already mentioned judging of another's business card or their ability to make a reservation at a restaurant known for catering to the successful. Although meant as a parody, the film offered an honest portrayal of just how absurd the world of youthful male competition at the corporate trading level can be. However, what the film did not delve into was how these young men also control entire nations by their influence upon how and where investors spend their money. Have they any idea what destructive power they wield as selfish young glory seekers? Or does it even matter a fraction as much as yachts, hookers and blow?

Some documentaries about the 2008 crash alluded to a criminal conspiracy between Wall Street and the US government to protect the guilty from facing justice — thus victimizing crash victims further by undermining their faith in the legal justice system. This was even more evident when bankers were being jailed in Iceland for their crimes while only one senior executive was jailed in the USA. Clearly, each country has a different value system.

Even more absurd than white collar criminals avoiding prison time while being given a taxpayer bailout was the offering of high-level jobs in the new Obama administration to oversee the US economy. In other words, rather than doing time for causing a global recession and the loss of millions of jobs, they were given even more privileges and financial rewards. What better reason for citizens to become cynical?

This patriarchal Wall Street show of power is reminiscent of another tragic incident that occurred in India recently where a man had raped a teenaged girl and left her pregnant. But rather than punish him for his crime, India's patriarchal judicial system demanded instead that he marry his victim. In this case, rather than choosing to protect the rich over the poor, that government chose to protect a man over a woman.

Sadly, such miscarriages of justice are common wherever men are in charge of our government and social institutions. Likewise, the crisis of 2008 demonstrated an equally incestuous favoring of wealthy white collar men by allowing the equivalent of an economic gang rape of society to be committed by its highest ranking financial leaders.

Also worth noting is that fines nearing $150 billion were repaid by some, yet their $700 billion in ensuing profits ensured that those fines would not become a deterrent to their future bad behavior but simply the cost of doing business at the top of the economic food chain. In fact, their punishment proved that crime does pay, and rather well.

...

Admittedly, dredging up the past can be painful and tedious. However, what we can establish from such events is that the dominant males of the US economy and government rigged the entire economic system to favor themselves. And so, when caught red-handed, both sides were protected by ensuring that the punishment would not extend beyond a few fines whose proceeds would flow upward rather than to victims.

In addition, the crisis was facilitated by the questionable advice of respected economists who had also filled their pockets by sanctioning the committing of these economic crimes. And seemingly after a few reassuring words by a charismatic new president, all was forgiven.

Yet most of us cannot afford to forgive and forget each time we are victimized by our economic dominators. Instead, such events should have us asking: *What is the true purpose of society; why does it exist?*

Is it there to protect us and should it serve as a gambling house for men to game away our collective lives and future as an exciting form of entertainment? We had better decide before we all lose.

"It's a Wall Street Government"

The mortgage derivative scam of 2008 had a huge economic impact on many people by causing them to lose everything in the aftermath. Yet the real tragedy is that little was done to address the cause of that crisis or curb a social values system that allows men to shamelessly plunder the lives of others for excessive — and needless — personal gain.

And such gain surely is needless. After all, once we are able to afford a yacht, we have likely acquired all we need financially. But if we then continue to amass ever more wealth, we risk becoming as a rudderless ship aimlessly adrift for lack of a meaningful destination.

As for the citizens of a reckless gambling nation, what is there to protect us from even greater losses in the future? Natural disasters and global pandemics already present us with sufficient threats without our having to worry about the future of our nation being gambled away. Ultimately, our only protection is in government regulations under constant threat by those seeking to engage in a reckless free-for-all.

At the core of the issue is our collective vision as a species; what we aspire to be in making our way through life. Are we there yet?

For some, yachts, hookers and blow are the final destination, after which no others have been charted. And this would not be so terrible if we didn't give those men the power to determine our collective fate. As such, we exist as unwitting pawns in their private wars for public significance. And so, in their constant attempts to elevate their status, we become as meaningless stepping stones because our lives matter far less to them than does winning. As to what they win…it has no actual value — all of it is just a transient, symbolic illusion that neither makes them more dominant physically, not happier in having been declared the latest winner in a race that never ends — that for existence itself.

And always in their ear is a voice playing on their fear of losing. But if the competition is too great, they will find a way to make winning easier by rigging the game. In this way, they are assured victory and may even take greater risks knowing that they can never lose.

And this explains the statement made in the documentary *Inside Job*, which declared that "It's a Wall Street government!"

Clearly, this states what we already know, which is that those on the inside have our systems rigged to favor them. And here, the trick is to keep on winning while making sure that no one finds out they're being cheated before the cheaters can run off with their loot.

In the meantime, they must feign ignorance as to why people want to overthrow their system of government — or why police look more like soldiers in a fascist regime as they beat down angry protestors for demanding honesty and fairness from leaders who can afford neither if they are to keep on winning.

CHAPTER 8
Always Just Out of Reach

Nature being nature and biology being biology, men will continue to feel the urge to compete for dominance, even if they don't have the qualifications to win in a fair fight.

In addition, men have taken nature's battle for genetic dominance into the symbolic arena of wealth accumulation where the richest men can pretend to be winners without ever needing to prove their genetic supremacy as the males of other species must do. Nor are they deterred from cheating as long as they can pay those in key positions to assist them in their cause. In short, it's *business as usual* for humankind.

But what is puzzling about this new symbolic combat arrangement is that a man's social victory, according to natural law, was never meant to last beyond a winner's physical peak — or one mating season. And we can be even more sure that it wasn't meant to last for centuries as happens with monarchy or other dynastic domination rackets where a leader is not chosen for his merit but by tricking others into believing that he represents the best among us based on his family bloodline.

For this reason, life in human society is not unlike a trip to a carnival where awaits many a game of skill and chance, each one rigged for us to lose. And what keeps us playing is that we are tricked into believing that we have a chance to win when in fact those games were purposely designed to keep our victory always just out of reach.

The low level tricksters who operate these rigged carnival games are known as "carnies," and once we leave their amusement park, we will find others of their kind waiting to trick us at all levels of society. But instead of wearing faded blue jeans and a t-shirt, they may be wearing an expensively tailored suit or a large ornate hat to appear as someone special and worth listening to.

Born into this human carnival environment, it is therefore best that we keep a close eye on our money and legal rights in the presence of any top level carnie who invites us to try our luck at his game.

...

The over-taxation of citizens is a prime example of a top-down carnie grift by many governments. Although taxes can provide for a far more sophisticated form of society that also assists those most in need, they tend to show their true purpose whenever those of the lower class dare to rise up in economic rank or popularity.

A well-documented example took place in the 1970's as the Rolling Stones, a famous rock band, were forced to surrender up to 90% of their band's income to the British government. As astute businessmen, they responded by escaping to greener pastures to avoid having to pay their fair share to keep the lights on at Buckingham Palace.

In another example, Austrian pop singer Falco once declared that he had paid the Austrian government $50 million in taxes for his right to live in that country. Oddly enough, his government never helped him to write songs, drive equipment to gigs, or contribute in any way to his creative success. Instead, it held out its hands as if to say: "Pay me, or else!" Yet what value could it offer in return for such a hefty tribute?

And so, while taxes can serve a useful purpose if managed fairly, they also appear to act as a form of suppressive punishment for competing against our mighty government by rising in our economic stature; the more we earn, the more we are punished for earning it.

Here too, power seems to purposely remain always just out of reach of those not among the ruling class. Moreover, the competitive envy of working class citizens only helps tax collectors as we chant "It's only fair" for the wealthy to pay more — even if it means pillaging 90% of their income. Clearly, this is an unfair way to level the playing field and may even dampen our entrepreneurial spirit if all that awaits is a loss of our wealth in the end. It also explains why many feel a need to cheat on their taxes — or hide their money in offshore bank accounts.

In that regard, there is also no small amount of irony or hypocrisy in the behavior of those who expound the virtues of doing our patriotic duty. For example, at least one Canadian prime minister had his bribes safely deposited in a Swiss bank to keep them out of reach of his tax department and the justice system — according to the man who made the bribes. Another Canadian prime minister registered his cargo ship enterprise in African to avoid paying the high rates of his own country — as ordinary citizens were being expected to do.

Hence, it appears to be true what many say, which is that the rules were made for those who follow them.

...

Extraordinary success belongs to those willing to take extraordinary risks. Those prepared to forego personal comfort in the pursuit of some all-consuming dream or personal goal are best positioned to succeed and even change our lives for the better in doing so; whether a daring young musician from the ghetto, or a scientist who defies convention to reinvent the proverbial wheel. As such, tenacity and endurance are also prerequisites for those hoping to achieve a notable success in life.

Yet risk takers represent only a small portion of humankind, whereas most of us are comfort-seekers in wanting to know when dinner will be served each night. But even comfort-seekers can get bored with just working and paying taxes all their lives. As someone in this category, we only want what everyone else wants, which is to feel happy or just less miserable. In short, we want a reason to live.

This yearning for more among the risk-free masses also represents a wealth of opportunity for the carnies of mainstream society to exploit us with their empty promises and offerings of false hope. The signs of this are everywhere, including the selling of lottery tickets.

In this hopeful state of mind, yet unwilling to risk our comfortable life of routine, we are certain to encounter many such grifters who will try to take our money or power under the pretense of helping us to attain a success that may also remain always just out of reach.

In *Clearing a Path to Joy*, I introduced "The Physics of Psychology," which allows us to better understand human behavior by seeing our lives as single atoms and our social and personal interactions as energy exchanges of various kinds, including symbolic, kinetic and more.

The significance of this interplay is that when we lose energy in any form, we feel compelled to replenish it to regain our lost sense of inner balance — just as hunger causes us to do. And this requires taking that energy from others. Our need to seek revenge is a prime example.

Let us then further preface what is to come by stating the obvious, which is that money does not offer a cure for personality disorders nor men's chronic urge to compete against one another for dominance.

Subsequently, despite his great wealth, a glory-seeking billionaire may still feel an emotional deficit in his life that constantly causes him to take the energy of others in a futile attempt to regain his own sense of inner balance. And like feeding a drug addiction, this can become a chronic behavior. This also goes a long way toward explaining what is happening in our homes, communities and nations as people feel the same compulsion to take our energy from us, often without a genuine need for it — whether a billionaire who constantly demands more, or a narcissistic politician who constantly demands our attention.

Given this additional perspective on life, we can then consider some of the typical behaviors among those atop the dominance hierarchy of our society as they push us down while tempting us with promises of attaining what is also being kept always just out of reach, which is our feeling of balance in relation to our survival and personal freedom.

The result is an energy dynamic that appears common to any society wherein those at the top feed off those at the bottom while keeping them hoping that they will also be among the top feeders one day. This is also the essence of a political carnie grift wherein those seeking to gain power over others promise us our own fair share in the future in return for our vote. But as with all such promises, it remains pending.

Scamming the Poor

The worst kinds of leaders, including fascist dictators and self-deluded religious visionaries, have no genuine desire to help others rise up in status or power. As such, they often mock those below them as being worthless pawns to be tricked and bullied into a state of obedience.

It is therefore a tragic sight to see millions of poor people voting for a wealthy man whose elitist lifestyle makes it obvious that he has no desire to be in their company except during elections. And so, while he lives a life of luxury insulated from their kind, his voters often exist in the worst of living conditions as they wait for that promised ladder of opportunity to be lowered so they can all rise up to join their leader in his pampered lifestyle of ease and comfort.

But that ladder has never been lowered, nor will it ever be within their reach as it goes against the very nature of men's competitions for social dominance. As such, it's just a typical lie told to the needy to win their votes and voluntary subordination in any top-down system.

Poor, under-educated and often naive as to how the ruling class has been waging war against them, all they see is a man of means who is finally treating them as though they matter. But this is all just amateur street theatre to trick them into sacrificing even more of themselves to enrich this latest version of a promised messiah come to save us.

And later, he will snicker at them for being such gullible fools — just as the carnies do when we walk away empty-handed.

...

This offering of false hope is a prevailing theme in "democratic" nations wherein the wealthy and other elites run for political office by making promises to the working class majority that they never intend to keep.

For their part, voters often believe they are in better hands when guided by someone with a proven history of wealth accumulation. And yet, they would do much better choosing a leader not given to a lust for money or power. In fact, a street sweeper would be a more eligible spokesperson for the masses than an elegant liar whose main concern is for himself and keeping his fleet of private jets up to date. In short, neither side has anything in common in terms of their future needs.

Here as well, the Physics of Psychology comes into play as those in a dominant social position gain power by taking it from others — not by sharing it. And so, in setting his sights on that goal, the last thing any aspiring dominator wants is to put more power into the hands of those who may want to compete against him. That would be akin to a victorious male lion helping an injured rival to continue fighting; it would never happen among those to whom winning is all that matters. And that is what we can also continue to expect into the future from all men under the influence of their competitive Bio-Psychology.

While social competition among humans has long been studied, it tends to remain off limits as a topic of serious public debate. This is understandable given that the wealthy own the media and it does not serve their best interests to confess their selfishness to working class audiences looking to be distracted from the harsh realities of life.

In addition, no commercial media empire that relies on advertising revenue would vilify its most valued customers in politics and business by suggesting that we are being led by selfish, greedy men.

And so, the truth must never be told, at least from the standpoint of our social dominators. As such, most of us will never know the extent of the social influence being wielded by the worst of men with access to political favor, even if only because fictionalized dramas and beauty contests draw a bigger viewing audience than fact-based journalism.

Thus, our widespread ignorance on the matter helps to ensure our continued victimhood at the hands of society's dominant male grifters as they play us for fools with their rigged games of skill and chance.

Lessons from the Unsinkable Titanic

As this chapter was being edited, news came that five people had died aboard a submersible vehicle on its dive to the sunken RMS Titanic. Their fate mirrored a critical lesson from that ship's own sinking in that we must always put safety before ambition. And if women were in charge of our societies, this would be more the rule than the exception as oil, chemical and nuclear spills continue to assail us due to men's far more reckless attitude in playing their symbolic measuring games for public recognition and personal glory.

Here, the gender differences in our attitudes become evident as men are invariably more willing to risk the lives of others in pursuit of their self-enrichment. In the case of the Titanic and the Titan submersible, the ocean clearly sided with the experts that passenger safety was not being properly addressed. And so, whether as a doomed passenger on a speeding ocean liner or a citizen working in an unsafe environment, we all live in constant danger under the leadership of the kind of men who risk putting their personal ambitions before the public's safety.

As a gentle reminder: men are still selling cigarettes to teenagers.

...

It is no revelation that society favors the wealthy for having a higher reward potential in the human energy trade than the poor. In other words, a person with lots of money and power is more likely to help us rise in status than someone poor. Subsequently, the rich also attract those with lofty ambitions. As such, the sinking of the HMS Titanic offers a perfect allegory for the social conditions we face as citizens under the influence of this bias that has long prioritized the needs of the wealthy over those of the poor.

As with all stories concerning human competition, the Titanic's also began with the helpful urging of male Bio-Psychology. In this case, the men of the Northstar company sought to build "the biggest" ship in what would be equivalent to nature designing the biggest male lion so that it could never be defeated. Here again, it was business as usual in the world of male posturing for social dominance.

Instead of an iceberg, it was the urge of company owners to compete for glory that was responsible for the loss of so many people's lives on the Titanic's fateful first voyage — a claim long proven by witnesses.

As expected in any social class system, this story also involves three layers of consideration wherein the rich on the upper class deck were given priority over those on the lower decks. As a result, once the ship began to sink, those below were not immediately alerted of the danger. But equally appalling, their escape routes were sealed to prevent them from competing against the wealthy passengers for the scant number of lifeboats available. As to who made saving women and children the highest priority — that was mother nature calling out the orders.

At greatest fault in this tragedy was the posturing of male company owners to win dominance in their industry. This forced the captain to run the Titanic at full speed to impress reporters with an earlier than expected arrival time. Also, the ship held only 25% of the lifeboats that it needed so as not to impede the sightline of wealthy passengers as they strolled upon the upper decks. After all, why would an *unsinkable* ship need lifeboats? And wouldn't that just create an air of suspicion around such a claim? As such, those company owners even saw having a full compliment of lifeboats as a liability to the winning image of its premier passenger ship.

Putting further blame on its prioritizing of winning over passenger safety was a critical oversight later discovered by scientists studying the metal content of rivets used in fastening the Titanic's hull. Here it was discovered that Northstar chose to use a cheaper grade of rivets for the part of the hull torn open by the iceberg. In other words, had they not cut corners on rivets to save extra time and/or money, the ship may not have sunk. In essence, a minor flaw in its strategic thinking may have ultimately had the greatest impact on the ship's fate that night in April, 1912 — an event that tarnished the company's reputation for failing to protect its passengers in a selfish haste to cross the finish line.

As for the company, it denied using those lower grade rivets, which is an expected reaction for anyone protecting their public image and its accompanying revenue stream. Yet denial has never helped to push us forward in our technological or social development. However, that part of the story seems destined to remain unsalvageable.

Not surprisingly, we can find the same attitude among many leaders in government and business, wherein they also take no responsibility for their wrongdoing for fear of appearing weak or inferior. And this same attitude continues to cost far more in terms of human lives than what was ever lost on the RMS Titanic.

Yet as citizens of a nation, we are also like trusting passengers, with our government as the shipping company and its governing system as the great ship that is also claimed to be mighty and unsinkable.

Here as well, the wealthy are favored for buying the most expensive tickets to keep the company financially buoyant and moving ahead. As such, this symbiotic economic relationship leaves those on the lower decks of society last in line for consideration or rescue.

Moreover, those atop the dominance hierarchy of our society must always blame their failures on those below. In this way, their captains and crew can be thrown to the sharks as the company pushes full speed ahead toward its next intended conquest.

Eat Your Chitlins

Keeping our gaze on those roaming the upper decks of life, beyond the bane of taxes and strict government regulations, the greatest threat to the wealthy is the middle class, whose economic might is sufficient to shape social policy on behalf of its own greater good. Yet given that many among the middle class aspire to higher positions of power, they also tend to favor the wealthy as better equipped to serve their needs than those of the working poor below.

Here again, it is only common sense that if we feel hungry, we go to where food is plentiful. In short, our human selfishness follows proven energy routes to survival. And here, the path of least resistance to our future success is to go where the money flows rather than trickles.

This claim that the upper class feels threatened by the middle class is long proven by its history of union-busting and migrating once high paying jobs to poorer nations where slave-labor is better tolerated. In this way, not only do wealthy manufacturers cut costs like the owners of the HMS Titanic did on their rivets, but they also force a majority of the middle class back down into steerage with the rest of the poor by eliminating their higher paying jobs.

Down in third class, where life is often harsh, many are happy just to have food on the table rather than a thoroughbred in the stable. In this way, by causing social conditions of near desperation, they lessen the threat of upsetting the imbalance of power held by the so-called 1% and the upper 1% among them who rule our world.

...

All of this presents a problem in our presumed democracies wherein we constantly hear the message that we will all soon be rising with the tide in our nation's ship and sailing off to a better world. Yet that port always seems so far off in the horizon that we have yet to see it.

In reality, those at the top don't want us competing against them for social power and privileges. They want to win by default. And so they find ways to discourage fair play to ensure that they never lose.

Consider for instance the "catch and kill" strategy employed by large companies that buy startup businesses threatening to compete against them for marketshare. Lured by sudden wealth, small business owners may sell a company only to see it dismantled so that it can never again pose a competitive threat to that industry dominator.

Here again, we see the hypocrisy of those claiming that competition brings out the best in us when so many of them resort to cheating.

Greed is the culprit, an insatiable hunger whose appetite is linked to measuring ourselves against those with more and mimicking the same hoarding behavior. This is why even billionaires cannot rest while an economic rival has a single dollar more to flaunt. For this reason, there can be no end to such competition, nor any satisfying of one's appetite for excess among those competing for dominance in symbolic form. That is also why our species may be doomed as we run out of unspoiled land and raw resources with which the greedy can measure their social dominance over one another. That is, unless they search for those assets beyond our planet — as some billionaires are now plotting to do.

This contest to out-perform one's rivals through hoarding explains our decline in planetary resources and the plundering of incomes and people's civil rights to feed the insatiable hunger of those competing at the top of the social dominance hierarchy.

Such behavior is not theoretical but a historical fact as embodied by the treatment of black African slaves who labored on plantations in the USA for centuries. Their plight, as that of anyone marginalized by society, is symbolized by having to eat "chitlins," a primary food given to slaves for having worked all day on behalf of their masters.

In this race-based interpretation of dominance, the white master and his family ate the best of the pig while leaving the worst of it, the feces filled intestines, to the black slave family. Hence, "Chitlins," a name likely associated with the origin or smell of that food.

For this reason, if we consider someone's past behavior a predictor of their future behavior, then we can predict that those now controlling us from above have no intention of setting us free or letting us eat at their table. After all, that would require us to be treated as equals rather than as subhuman prey for opportunistic social predators.

Subsequently, any hope of living in a democracy is unrealistic lest we find a way to govern that cannot be undermined by those wanting to maintain a lop-sided balance of power that favors their enrichment. In the meantime, our nations behave more like a Plutocracy; governance by and for the wealthy class.

A similar reckoning faces women, given their historic oppression at the hands of patriarchal governments and religions that also treated them as lesser beings. We can then also predict, based on past behavior, that it will not be greedy men in high seats of power who will fight for a woman's right to social equality, especially in those nations where she is openly persecuted for wanting any rights at all.

As such, the promise of a democratic world of gender equality is yet another carnival game played by the kind of patriarchal governments that also oversee lotteries wherein we try to win our freedom back from a lifetime of daily toil and taxes.

Sadly, we can find many such games of chance being rigged with the promise of false hope. Yet if our unsinkable nation's ship were to start sinking, there is little hope in our being rescued by those on the upper decks. That's how *the system* — that of men — has always worked. We are not as travelers on a holiday cruise but as unwitting servants on a well-camouflaged slave ship. And for those on the lower decks, the service is even more deplorable.

PART THREE
Keeping Women Out of Power

CHAPTER 9
Follow the Loser

Nature compels men to compete for dominant mating status and not for leadership of our society. That men do compete for such leadership is an unconscious expression of their wanting the power to control all others. As such, when a military dictator takes over a nation, it is only to serve his selfish urges. Moreover, there is nothing in men's biological inventory to suggest that they were designed for a mentorship role in the life of others.

Women, on the other hand, give birth, making them natural born leaders in having to mentor and organize the lives of their children from the moment they are born.

Moreover, she may have many children, depending on her bodily constitution and the culture in which she was raised. And all of this is by natural design to ensure the survival of our species. In other words, women were born to be in charge of the lives of others to assist them in rising up and succeeding in this world.

We encounter those same circumstances in the wild, where the male lion does not fight for leadership of a pride but only for mating access to its females. And this only requires him to protect the territory where those females are hunting and raising young. But when the lioness is ready to give birth, she does not consult with that male. Instead, she distances herself from him in a remote place where she will raise her cubs until they are less vulnerable. And as those cubs grow, she will also be the one teaching them to hunt and care for themselves, not the male lion — whose presence may even have a negative influence on the cubs if he has an aggressive, anti-social disposition, as some fathers do.

The same is true of African mountain gorillas. Here as well, we can romanticize that the male silver back is an altruistic beast on a mission to protect his troupe. Yet in reality, he is simply protecting his status and privileges as the dominant inseminator, using his brute strength to control and protect his clan from all external threats. And here as well, the females look after the young, as nature intended.

This gender-based behavior among lions, gorillas and humans gives us first-hand knowledge of what genuine leadership looks like, which is a mother caring for her offspring until they have learned to fend for themselves. And for many species, the father is either absent or a mere bystander in watching this leadership process from the sidelines.

...

Animal behavior in the wild is an important consideration for our own approach to leadership given that humans are the only species whose suspiciously male gods and governments insist that men must lead our societies and thereby also its women and children. As such, despite any formal training or biological inclination to assume such a critical role, we have long been conditioned to believe that "the man of the house" knows what is best for both *his* wife and *his* children.

But what if that man is the town drunk, the village idiot, or a violent psychopath who favors fists over wisdom? And what if all three traits reside in the same person? Furthermore, given that women and their children are still treated as a husband's "property" in many cultures, to whom can she turn for protection from the tyranny of a man with little to offer her beyond a life of abuse? Certainly not to any masculine God or male-dominated government. And if living in the kind of culture where women are still traded like livestock, then her parents may have already sold her as a child bride to some aging patriarch to elevate their own economic status. Hence, to divorce him would bring "shame" to those who seem to have no shame in selling their children into slavery.

Sadly, female disempowerment is a persistent global problem that leaves many women with nowhere to turn in a world whose national governments, religions, legal justice systems and economies all remain male-dominated with few exceptions. And since those systems were rigged to favor men, they also have no motivation to seek solutions to the problems that women encounter under their patriarchal rule. Nor has the passage of time elevated women's low standing among men who believe themselves entitled to a leadership position over the entire female gender, not by virtue of their merit, but in having the upper fist.

Hence, a woman born in England during those worst of times when Charles Dickens was penning his epic novels about social oppression would have found her male-dominated government passing The Great Reform Act of 1832, which forbade her from voting. Subsequently, no matter how poorly her country was being run by men, she had no say in any matter; nor did her "queen," who was stripped of all legislative power in 1689 to become a mere mascot for the aristocracy.

And had any woman been born in the United States in more recent times, her struggles for independent power would have also been met by the ire of the nation's most televised male religious guru, the late Pat Robertson, who's 1992 fund-raising letter warned followers that:

"Feminism is a socialist, anti-family political movement that encourages women to leave their husbands, kill their children, practice witchcraft, destroy capitalism and become lesbians."

But karma came calling for Pat Robertson because, contrary to his "holy man" facade, he was later outed as a greedy capitalist for spending ministry donations on transporting drilling equipment to his diamond mines in Zaire. Clearly, he worshipped the god of Wall Street above all and even sought help from Zaire's violent military dictator for his venture. Yet despite his costly fall from commercial grace, he and other false prophets of his era paved the way for women in the USA to lose their legal right to abort an unwanted fetus in 2022 — although such laws do not deter women from seeking abortions but only force them to take even greater personal health risks in unsanitary backrooms.

...

Humankind's long history of gender-based social oppression has led us to this very moment in time, wherein men are still the presumed rulers over women's lives in many parts of our world. And based on the false assumptions about men's leadership abilities by their suspiciously male Gods and governments, we are also being forced to pay a growing price to accommodate this grave error in men's self-assessment.

Yet in having always had ultimate power on their side, men's selfish impulses were allowed to prevail so that even today most households, businesses, industries, governments and nations continue to be ruled by a gender whose main leadership qualification is having a penis. And predictably, this has left many women in the same position as those living under a fascist dictatorship wherein she has no power or means to escape her oppressor beyond hiding in various forms of addiction, whether it be television, alcohol or mood-altering prescription drugs. As such, addiction remains a lingering problem for women trying to cope with feeling socially or spiritually imprisoned.

Not surprisingly, such addictive distractions are far more available to her than are public debates or practical solutions to her predicament as these would require a monumental shift in our male-centric social systems and their competitive priorities. Here as well, few men would qualify for so selfless a leadership role in the service of gender equality, let alone feel any need to change a male-centric social system that has purposely been rigged in their favor under the moniker of "tradition."

Instead, to protect their long-standing monopoly on social power, the dominant male hierarchy of our patriarchal societies will insist that even if putting a man of pitiful credentials in charge all but guarantees our total destruction from war, pollution or the looting of resources, we must nonetheless stand firmly behind him on behalf of our man-made gods or government laws. As such, despite women's superior abilities as leaders in tending to the needs of others, for much of womankind throughout history, this has meant having to follow the loser.

And since we are conditioned not to talk about politics and religion lest we rethink what is being done in both their names, let us defy that polite custom instead by exposing the male-centric bias at their core.

Questioning God's Will

Aside from men's inborn ability to physically dominate women, what has often kept even the weakest, most incompetent of men in power is the implied will of his god. And even if anyone has yet to see this supreme male deity to prove he exists, apparently it pleases him greatly to have women kept socially powerless — at least according to men's interpretation of ancient religious scripture which, coincidentally, was also exclusively written and translated by men.

And while this biased way of thinking was likely met with suspicion by the hard-living women of those times, it has now blossomed into a worldwide prejudice against women acting as leaders in any context involving men. And should we question our faith in this gender-biased arrangement of society, we are encouraged, gently or by brute force, to keep our heads down and do as we're told, or else…

Obedient conformists that we generally are, this is what we've been doing for thousands of years. Yet our fear-based tendency to avoid all conflict is fast catching up with us. Today we can see the damage being caused by allowing our world to be governed by a gender that is not biologically driven to protect life but to fight for personal glory.

Yet unlike the males of other species, we use everything from fighter jets and nuclear arms to cutting down forests and filling oceans with oil rigs to gain an upper hand over others of our kind, often with little regard for the collateral damage we cause to our societies and natural world. After all, cleaning up has long been designated as *women's work*.

As the book, *Silent Spring*, by marine biologist and conservationist Rachel Carson made clear, it often takes a woman to remind men of how reckless their behavior is becoming in trying to rule our world. Moreover, in moving toward a post-fiction global mindset, we can no longer plead ignorance in watching men prioritize their war industries, gambling casinos or sports arenas while demoting public education, daycare services or women's health in their order of social importance.

And wherever women require specific services, they are often under threat of being privatized by men seeking to profit from their demand. Such threats can even be to life itself, as we are reminded again of the handiwork by former Michigan governor, Rick Snyder, to force the mothers of Flint Michigan to unwittingly poison their children with lead laden water. As the hometown of Michael Moore, he brought this greed-fueled political crime against humanity to the public's attention in his documentary, *Fahrenheit 11/9.*.

But Moore's hometown is not unique in its social decline by men's competitive greed or its being left in a state of disorganized chaos in their aftermath. Meanwhile, aspiring dominators in other developing nations copy the reckless behavior of our first world sociopaths as they also stage their own parades of personal power through the endless displaying of their material wealth and symbolic dominance.

...

Returning to the God that many of these men claim to worship, what is most confusing in all this reckless destruction by men is the silence of God *Himself.* Where is this all-knowing man in the sky who seemed so eager to tell everyone how to live only a few thousands years ago? Why has he mysteriously disappeared from sight, with his existence kept on life support by way of legend and blind faith?

The less trusting among us may suspect that men actually invented God, or at best, had re-interpreted his intentions to award themselves undeserved power, especially over women. This might also explain the glaring contradictions of reality in various religious texts, including that womankind was born of a man's rib when scientific research has proven that human life begins from a female template — which is why men are born with non-functioning nipples. As such, no "real man" can ever hope to outrun his inborn femininity.

Would a truly supreme being make such a glaring factual error in penning a book about our origins? Nature surely knows where babies come from and which gender can be trusted to raise them to maturity. As such, women are far better qualified to nurture and protect the people of our societies, if only men and their male gods would allow them to take the reigns. But this would also require men to take a more *submissive* role, which goes against their nature. It would also require not pressuring women to devote all their attention to pleasing men so they can do a better job of keeping society in working order.

As the past collides with the present, there are seemingly no answers as to why men's masculine God is absent — does *He* even care that they are killing each other in ever more violent ways while destroying his once pristine paradise? Why has he not yet intervened or at least nulled our most remorseless troublemakers as he was said to have done with great zeal in ancient times? Instead, he allows psychotic warlords and greedy industrialists to run amok as though our species matters not at all to him. Something just doesn't add up.

Moreover, what is he waiting for now that it's almost too late for a miraculous intervention from above?

Ironically, the only otherworldly beings who seem concerned for our well-being these days are those that many claim do not exist. These are the controversial "extraterrestrial" beings whose visitations to groups of school children in Africa, Australia and Korea are well-documented in offering dire warnings about our self-destructive ways. If anything, at least they seem to care enough to make the occasional appearance.

…

Clearly, the silent indifference of any of men's various god's suggests that these problems we face are humankind's to solve and that we will either live or die by the decisions we make in regard to our future on this planet. Should we invest more money into building casinos and fighter jets, or would our efforts be better served by cleaning up this mess that we've made?

In that regard, we must wonder why it took a teenaged boy from the Netherlands to consider cleaning up the plastic pollution in our oceans rather than those industries who manufacture it. Lucky for us, Boyan Slat and *The Ocean Cleanup* team acknowledged this problem and are now removing vast quantities of discarded plastic and fishing industry debris recklessly dumped into our oceans by people who care not to see the problem so they can avoid having to do something about it.

Perhaps if more of us stopped waiting for *the end of the world* and chose instead to work toward a new beginning, then we might feel the same enthusiasm to care about our planet's future as Boyan did. After all, there is no future in waiting to die — nor any life worth living.

Clearly, in the interest of evolving our current systems of governing, finance, social services and spirituality, we must put more women in charge of such institutions given that they are not inclined by their nature to turn every aspect of society into a profit-based competition for feminine glory. We must also abandon this impulse by men to design our societies as a reflection of their fight for dominance rather than our quest for personal excellence. After all, Muhammad Ali may have been a great fighter, but he's no Eddie Van Halen.

And if anyone's God has a problem with this approach, he should come out of hiding to offer a better idea to save us from ourselves.

The Wanderer

Anyone with adult life experience knows that women do not surrender all their power to men. Instead, they leverage their unique strengths to gain some semblance of control over any man who wants to always be in charge — especially a self-absorbed or pushy husband.

A woman's most basic use of power is through her sexuality, which is demonstrated by controlling men's access to her vagina; the primary interface for men to achieve sexual pleasure beyond masturbation. And since wrapping one's calloused work hands around one's penis is not nearly as pleasing as entering the soft, wet folds of a woman's vagina, it serves a man's best interests to get along with the proprietor of that vagina to ensure his future access to her sexual favor.

However, the presence of rapists and wife beaters proves that some men are not amenable to making fair trade agreements with women. Instead, their hostile inclinations make them entirely unsuitable for membership in any peaceful society. And yet, throughout history, it is their kind who has traversed our world to rape and pillage their way into power wherever their urge to dominate has led them. In fact, if we took a historical inventory of male rulers of the past, we would find few of them who did not resort to violence to dominate others.

This introduces yet another cause of relational conflict between men and women in that they often have differing responses to social life.

Women, for instance, prefer to fight verbally rather than physically as this avoids endangering themselves or their children. Such behavior is also present among female chimpanzees and bonobos in the wild, who avoid violent struggles for dominance within their own societies. Therefore, when an alpha female dies, her daughter or a senior female will peacefully assume her role as group mentor. As such, her role as leader is typically won as an expression of mutual cooperation and respect as opposed to selfish tyranny — which destroys group trust.

In stark contrast, human males dedicate much of their time, money and energy to inventing a premise to compete against one another. As such, our societies have become the symbolic equivalent of a boxing ring wherein men try to beat each other into submission even in times of peace. Moreover, their competitive behavior is so routine that we take it for granted that wherever two or more men have gathered, they will find some reason to compete for dominance.

Ironically, in modern societies where women are freer to compete against men for status, they have slowly been asserting their power by entering the traditionally-held domains of men. This is seen by women building up their muscles, getting tattoos or beating each other down in a boxing ring. This is an understandable trend given that women are forced to reach for power in societies designed by and for men. As a result, to gain recognition, they must adopt a values system that has long been used to determine male dominance, be it through a show of strength, fighting skill, or competitive cruelty. Yet in doing so, women may also be subverting their own nature to win acceptance by men. As such, we may even see them starting wars one day as this is how our patriarchal systems expect their leaders to negotiate with "enemies."

Another significant gender difference and causes of conflict among the sexes is men's natural tendency to "wander." While this may sound like a euphemism for sex outside of wedlock, it refers to an inborn and natural tendency among the males of most species to travel afar due to nature's uncompromising demand for genetic diversity.

Subsequently, we see again how a simple Bio-Psychological urge has become the primary cause of global conflict as armed groups of men invade the territories of other males driven by an unconscious urge to plant their seed in some far-off womb. And naturally, the men who live there resent such intrusions and will fight back equally hard.

Here we also find the true origin of human warfare, whose purpose has long been shrouded in pretensions of a noble cause that demands a man's ultimate sacrifice through violent acts of bravery. Instead, war is but a selfish competition among male social groups for sexual access to females; an unconscious urge to which most leaders fear to confess.

But men are not alone in this murderous urge to defeat their genetic rivals because male chimpanzees also engage in tribal warfare for the same reason — as we shall later explore in another chapter.

...

Once again, nature's wisdom is revealed by causing an instinctual urge in young men to leave their maternal homes and establish a territory of their own. In this way she prevents oversexed adolescent males from impregnating their own mothers or sisters by having them spread their seed elsewhere on behalf of greater genetic diversity.

This notion is supported by similar wandering behavior among male animals in the wild. In Africa, for instance, young male lions must leave their mother's pride before reaching sexual maturity. And as they wander, growing in size and skill, they will encounter opportunities to compete against the dominant males of other regions as they guard their own access to various females. And if he is powerful enough, then that young male will become the pride's newest inseminator — at least until yet another younger and stronger challenger comes along.

The same departure occurs among elephants. Here the young males are also forced to leave the matriarchal herd to embark on a solitary life interrupted only by short incursions into other elephant societies for the purpose of mating with its estrous females. And then he must leave again, unwelcome to stay beyond serving his only purpose.

This also explains why human males were the primary explorers of our world in having been guided not by mere curiosity or noble cause, but by the urge to sew their seed in distant lands. And however such a coupling is achieved, this urge to wander ensures that each generation of men will feel the same pull to leave home in their hearts and loins.

Women, on the other hand, have a homing instinct that is guided by their essential role as the birthers and caregivers of our species. After all, without mothers, nothing else would be possible. And the same is true in the wild, where most females tend to stay in one place beyond the need to gather food. This is also why the females of many species, from chimpanzees to feral cats, will form social groups that serve their common interests by offering a safer, more supportive environment in which to raise young. As such, neither they nor human females have anything to gain from the presence of males constantly growling and lashing out at one another as an expression of their genetic warfare.

And if we should have any doubt as to the validity of this notion, we need only ask the women and children whose lives are under threat as a result of men fighting over various national mating territories, be it the Ukraine, Israel, and any country in a state of chaos as a result of young, aggressive males engaging in militarized genetic warfare.

Honey, I'm Home

Often in stark contrast to nature's own infinite wisdom, religion and commercial media have played pivotal roles in defining our attitudes toward the female leadership of our societies.

In the Old Testament of the Judeo-Christian tradition, for instance, humankind begins with God creating Eve as Adam's helper so that he won't be lonely. Not only does this infer a subordinate role, but she is also then vilified for tempting this lonely dimwit to defy his master — thus subverting God's own alpha status within the Universe.

The symbolic meaning of the apple is in the eye of the beholder. Was God trying to keep humankind obediently stupid and Eve ruined his plans? Was God miffed at Eve for tempting Adam with the pleasures of the flesh — despite his wanting her to go forth and multiply?

Ultimately, it matters not how we interpret this religious myth as it has long ago succeeded in its purpose of creating a prejudice against womankind for aiding and abetting the "original sin" against God. This justified the promoting of a patriarchal value system wherein the lives of women, as the designated servants of men, could be treated as an afterthought. And for many men of faith, this God-given advantage over women seems to suit them just fine.

Women's reputation as social leaders also hasn't fared any better in the media. Here, she has long been portrayed as a one dimensional damsel in distress whose only goal is finding a man to rescue her. As such, her most celebrated strength is her ability to attract men, whereas men are presented as having the power that women lack. However, this is the result of centuries of purposeful tampering by men to ensure that women have no power of their own to wield but their sexuality.

In short, from the beginning, women have gotten the worst of it. And this trend continues as fanatical male politicians feign religious devotion by calling for a continued devaluation of women as having no purpose but to serve their fatherly husbands in the home.

This unnatural imbalance of power between men and women was also evident in family values-based television shows in the USA of the 1950"s. Here, it was typical to see a man announcing his arrival from work with a jubilant "Honey, I'm home!" upon entering the front door. And having been conditioned to accept the artificial limits placed on a woman's life, his greeting also acted as a signal to the audience that she must now tend to her husband's every need in living the life for which she was born, according to her God, or the male producers of the show.

But with God's extended absence and men too busy fighting abroad and on the stock markets, they've all but missed a revolution that will soon interrupt their monopoly on power, which is that "honey" isn't home anymore to greet them. Instead, she's out working in the world, earning her own money and preparing to take the lead in cleaning up the catastrophic mess left behind by a centuries long succession of dimwitted Adams stumbling around in the darkened wilderness of their primal lust and ideological confusion.

CHAPTER 10
Tearing Down the Gender Wall

Organized crime has been with us since the first group of devious men conspired against their own tribe for selfish gain. Nowadays, under the influence of the media, that term directs our thoughts toward Sicily's Casa Nostra, that infamous crime syndicate featured in the *Godfather* movies and known for its global reach into trade unions, gambling and the illicit drug trade.

Yet as all-powerful and intimidating as Hollywood has made these mobsters seem, there exists a far more notorious criminal organization whose influence has an even greater reach. Deeply embedded in every aspect of society and run entirely by men, "the Patriarchy" is without question the association that rules over everything, from crime families to our legal justice systems, intelligence agencies, financial institutions and governments. And it gains its power almost entirely by controlling the lives of women throughout our world and ensuring that no woman ever dares to speak of it — lest she be labelled a "feminist."

Like any mob organization, the patriarchy runs its own protection racket which we can refer to herein as *The Gender Wall*. This involves the partitioning of men and women within every culture and assigning to each side various duties and social obligations based on one's gender. And since men control this wall that divides the genders, it naturally favors them over women, not for any measurable difference in skill or social competence but merely for owning male genitalia and the bodily strength to impose their will upon women. As such, in many parts of our world, if a woman dares to challenge the rule of the Patriarchy, she may well find herself "swimming with the fishes," as movie mobsters like to say. And through this code of silence, the Patriarchy thrives.

...

While this mob analogy makes light of an orchestrated global gender divide that we know to exist, in actual life it casts a dark and dismal shadow over both men and women.

Here, the mere owning of a Y chromosome has become a kind of free pass for men to move to the head of any line where women are standing. And quite understandably, many women resent the unfair social advantages that men hold over them, which are also typically enforced in the home through verbal or physical aggression and within greater society by introducing laws to keep women from gaining equal power to vote, earn an independent living, or in some cultures, to even show her uncovered face in public.

Like any proven form of organized crime or conspiracy, to argue the existence of the Patriarchy and its Gender Wall of prejudice against women is futile given its many manifestations in all aspects of our lives. Yet in having been conditioned since childhood to accept this bias against women as something that is normal, we may never think to question its wisdom or negative impact upon our lives.

In many cultures, this process of mental indoctrination begins with the practice of color-coding boys dark blue, dressing them in pants and treating them differently from girls, who have been color-coded pink and wrapped in dresses. And while these colors and costumes may vary between cultures, what does not waver is that those on the feminine side of the Gender Wall are typically kept from holding any kind of genuine power within society.

Historically, women's exile from power has forbidden them to vote, work for equal pay, or lead their country. Moreover, in some cultures she is still treated as livestock and traded by men as though she has no more value than a milking goat. Even more tragic is that many women fail to recognize their plight in having been mentally conditioned to believe they are destined to be little more than lifelong slaves in the service of their male dominators.

Thankfully, changes are slowly coming to even the most repressive human cultures. Yet there remains a great resistance among many men to tearing down the traditional Gender Wall that has long guaranteed them an unfair advantage over women. In fact, some men even deny that such a conspiratorial prejudice exists, perhaps hoping to delay their own inevitable collision with an uncertain future under a more even-handed social contract between the genders. And so, at least for now, given their traditional stronghold, men's often violent claim to dominance over women remains intact.

Yet never should we dismiss this imbalance of power as something chivalrous or honorable given that it represents a profitable racket that no opportunistic man would want to surrender, especially to a woman of superior intellect or leadership credentials.

And so, from the most misogynistic of fundamentalist politicians in the west to the all-male death squads of patriarchal theocracies, there is a constant effort by men of traditional "family" values to not only defend their unfair hold on power over women, but also to undermine any woman's ability to independently rule over her own life by legally stripping her of such power.

Here again, the USA's reversal of Roe vs Wade in 2022 was clearly not to celebrate the sanctity of life, otherwise all children there would have access to free healthcare and a better education. Instead, it was about removing a woman's power to decide her own fate.

...

Beyond the use of physical violence and government legislation, we can find many signs of this patriarchal conspiracy to subdue the lives of women in various aspects of modern life. An obvious place to look is among advertisers and romantic folklore that have long told us that men are *hard* and women are *soft*, thus implying that men must protect these delicate creatures from a dangerous world — a kind of *big daddy complex* that may explain why some men want women to dress as little school girls during sex. It also explains why advertisers want to instill in young women a pride in her power to sexually please men; this is apparently what she should aspire to and be most proud of.

In addition, the men who created our world religions made it clear that their masculine god wants men to rule society. And by teaching women to fear this all-powerful male supervisor in the sky, they were also taught to resign themselves to a life of ill treatment at the hands of even the most inept of husbands. And naturally, this also suited men in high seats of governing power who could remain unchallenged by any woman of higher intellect or skill, lest she offend her invisible god or those men who claimed to know *his* will.

Unfortunately, this biased regime of twisted male logic with its heavy reliance on gender stereotyping is not easy to overcome when it has been programmed into our minds for thousands of years. In this way, it becomes a normal way of thinking wherein a women may even defend men's continued hold on power over them. Moreover, if we all believe the same, then to believe otherwise is just asking for trouble.

And yet, in those cultures where thinking is allowed, if we were to ask for specific reasons why men hold power over women, we may hear men claim that women are simply too weak or dependent to survive without a man's assistance. And then, in one of humankind's greatest ironies, we see men designing our societies in such a way as to ensure that women remain in a weakened, needy state, whether by forbidding them the right to vote, to get an education, or as advertisers do, by making women feel insecure for leaving home without makeup on or not presenting a clean-shaven body for the visual approval of men, as though to deny her womanhood by appearing as a pre-pubescent girl.

The result is a self-perpetuating culture of prejudice against women that doesn't allow her to rise up and claim her rightful share of power, nor to free herself from the chains of male domination, whether within her own home, or within greater society.

This is the Gender Wall that continues to divide us for the sake of assigning a greater share of power to men. And that is why we must make an orchestrated effort to tear it down to prevent future organized crimes such as these from being committed against womankind.

The War Against Women

The transition toward a more equal world for both genders has been both deliberately slow and relatively new if we consider that it only began in earnest during the early 1900s as more women won the right to vote. In more overtly patriarchal nations, such as Saudi Arabia, that right was not assigned to women until 2015.

Yet despite the various social advances that have been made since the struggle for women's equality began, the systems that govern our nations clearly remain rigged to favor men. And whenever the threat of female empowerment overwhelms these patriarchs, we find them calling for a regression back to a "traditional" values system when men controlled everything, including the lives and choices of women.

And so, even today as independently-minded women are starting to gain more critical ground socially, economically and politically, there remains a constant threat that men will engage in forms of subterfuge or outright repressive violence to push back against the encroachment of feminine values into their long-held, male-dominated territories.

Although modern-day women need no longer fear being burned at the stake for being accused of witchcraft, they nonetheless continue to be subjected to various horrors as part of a purposeful and orchestrated act of female suppression in many parts of our world. As such, in some cultures she may be executed for adultery, or tormented by roaming male gangs of "religious police" for exposing her ankles, whereas men have far fewer such lifestyle restrictions imposed upon them.

Further impeding our collective social evolution is a natural impulse to seek a comfortable life of convenience over one of constant struggle. As such, many people are looking for a more simple-minded approach to life to save them time and energy otherwise spent in confusion. This is the same impulse that can have us voting for a famous celebrity to avoid investing the time to consider a longer list of far more suitable political leaders. Likewise, our quests for comfort and convenience can have us clinging to some simplistic, socially-scripted recipe for life that has us conforming to "traditional" values, including the notion that the male gender must rule over society, and over women.

However, denial is never a path to happiness or empowerment. And that is why so many women now find themselves on a collision course with angry men and even many women who insist that they go back to pretending to be happy housewives and ignoring all those problems created for them by living the life of an impostor.

Moreover, as already discussed, the imposing of a uniform gender identity and lifestyle benefits the tyrants of this world by making us all more predictable and thereby easier to control. This top-down pressure to conform to a social role of limited personal power is inherent in the worlds of politics and religion, given that both act as social control systems run by elite groups of men seeking to control our collective destinies for personal gain and glory — with very few exceptions.

Yet beyond the mental grasp of social mind control, there are also some practical reasons why men might resent the presence of a woman in their traditionally male-dominated sanctuaries. In his place of work, for instance, a man may find it more difficult to openly boast about his most recent sexual conquest if a woman is present. Subsequently, men's "traditional" bonding ritual of defining a woman's value in terms of her anatomy or sexual surrender could inhibit some men in their ability to communicate more effectively — thereby making them resentful of having a woman's intimidating presence in their midst.

Supporting this argument is chimpanzee behavior in the wild where males also band together, making it understandable why human males might then feel imposed upon by a woman in their presence. But then again, male chimpanzees do not keep female chimpanzees as personal house slaves or force them into the bonds of matrimony to trade sex for survival under the watchful eye of an all-powerful ape God.

Beyond protecting their access to male "in-group" bonding through the exclusion of women in the work place, the Gender Wall of western cultures has also maintained various safeguards to ensure that women would have to struggle twice as hard to achieve half the success of men — a claim supported by every male employer who offered women less pay for an equal day's work under the premise that men have "a family" to support. In this way, men's dominant size and strength are no longer needed to keep women from gaining equal power or independence. Instead, they can just cheat by making it harder for women to succeed.

Here again, the USA offers us a working example of a country in the midst of a conflict between two opposing forces. In addition to its *gun profits vs gun deaths* dilemma, it also struggles to reconcile its enduring patriarchal culture with its professed democratic values. After all, even as its founding constitution claims that "all men" were created equal, it makes no mention of women having the same inherent value. As such, despite claiming itself a leader in promoting "democratic" values, it has yet to elect its first national female leader, whereas Germany, India and several other countries have long surpassed this gender milestone.

Equally revealing is that its male-centric Republican party tends to elect the kind of women who defend men's unequal right to rule, be it through patriarchal religious authority or slave-labor capitalism.

That said, the women of the USA do exercise greater freedom within the confines of their own Gender Wall stereotype — which has even allowed them to be depicted as superheroes in film, as long as they agree to wear something revealing to keep male audiences interested.

But while all of this may look promising from the outside, it merely represents a kind of pleasant social distraction, whereas the prospect of a woman ruling that nation continues to remain off limits while men control the media and its alpha-male interpretation of democracy

And this brings us back to the same problem that has been hovering in the background since chapter one, which is the ailing state of our world under the misguided rule of men. After all, talk is cheap and promises cost nothing to make, putting them within affordable reach of any politician's lips. As such, we have long been promised greater equality, social prosperity and an actionable concern for our planet's ecology by our male-dominated industries and governments. Yet those promises may never fully materialize without the kind of street-level protests and mass workers' strikes often needed to force change upon those rigging our systems in their favor. And in all such struggles for power, women have always had it worse in also needing to look after their children while having to fight twice as hard as any man for her equal share of social justice.

But instead of starting a bloody revolution as in the past, perhaps we can simply treat this entire transition process as a global experiment by allowing only women to guide our nations toward what their gender envisions as a better world. After all, men are inherently too obsessed with competing for power through military and economic warfare to treat our societies as anything but a sports arena wherein *the best man* wins. As such, there is a blatant lack of concern for humanity in their battles for dominance wherein all that matters is winning. Women, on the other hand, have children to protect and that alone ensures a more civilized approach to governing that will usher in a more caring and sharing world than what we are used to under our male dominators.

To restate the obvious, this does not suggest that all women are born inherently better qualified to lead than men. But the odds are also far better that we will never see groups of female soldiers cheering one of their own after her "first kill" in battle. It is this male *kill culture* and its recklessly destructive mindset that must change, lest we continue on our ill-fated decline toward a world that is hostile to life itself.

...

But standing firmly in the way of making this logical, gender-based transition of social power is an ongoing war against womankind that gained its early footing among various patriarchal religions. Here, we find ourselves being offered a creation story about the beginning of our world wherein Eve, the first woman, greatly angered an intolerant and unforgiving God who then made her solely responsible for all the countless terrible life conditions with which humans are beset, such as pain in childbirth and men having to toil all their life only to die. That animals in the wild are subject to the same suffering seems overlooked by true believers, yet the myth and its claim of describing humankind's entry into our world provided society's earliest male dominators with a premise to suppress womankind and even turn them into slaves. And while God's part in this plot to suppress women remains unproven, it matters not because we tend to believe as we want to believe. Also, by blaming God, men also had an alibi for devaluing women in this long, oft violent history of prejudice against those born in the female form.

As a result, women's greatest impediment to social evolution is men's lingering attitude of entitlement from thousands of years of cultural conditioning. Believing themselves superior, many continue to treat women as inferior beings undeserving of the same rewards that await a successful man. Even today, there are men who assume they have the right to decide the fate of women, often with the legislative support of their patriarchal legal systems behind them. Again, Roe v. Wade.

Unfortunately, in expressing their biological urge to dominate, men require women to remain in the role of a victim rather than becoming an equal partner in a balanced relationship. As such, the challenge we now face is to counteract such prejudicial thinking to ensure a safer, more equal-handed future world for all concerned. After all, without the influence of women, we are doomed to continue living on a planet wracked by war, greed, pollution and little hope of anything more.

In moving toward that goal, let us consider some historical evidence to firmly prove the existence of this social prejudice against women in the hope that it may inspire the prevention of such injustices in our collective future.

Although wife-beaters and rapists represent the most immediate threat to women, a far more common crime being committed by men on a global scale is their dismissal of women's importance and lifelong contributions to the betterment of our world. Instead, men often seek to promote themselves as the irreplaceable gender by celebrating only their own accomplishments while extolling the virtues of their system of social competition, which keeps all but the most ruthless of male sociopaths from rising to the top. As such, this exclusionary attitude continues to stifle our conscious evolution not only in many modern households, but also in the professional worlds of science and industry, as the following cases will reveal.

Case One — Rosalind Franklin

Rosalind Franklin was a woman, a respected scientist, and the first person to discover the double helix structure of DNA by using X-ray crystallography and a mathematical plotting of the distances between the distinct elements of its two strands.

Unfortunately, and unbeknownst to her, two male scientists from a competing university had been secretly given access to her private DNA research by a male rival in her department. Her stolen research was then used by those men to claim ownership for having mapped the double helix structure of DNA — a "discovery" for which they later won the Nobel Prize.

Sadly, Rosalind Franklin died shortly thereafter from ovarian cancer at age thirty seven without ever knowing that the celebrated Nobel Laureate and Harvard professor, James Watson, and his brotherhood of male scientists could not have made *their* discovery without having gained improper access to Rosalind's own research in that field.

In fact, Rosalind was so trusting of the integrity of these men that she even mentioned the coincidence of her own research supporting theirs — having no idea that those ideas had been stolen from her.

Adding insult to injury in typical patriarchal fashion, Watson then published a book wherein he made sexist remarks about Ms. Franklin's appearance and demeanor to further diminish her status as unequal to her esteemed male colleagues in their pursuit of life's greater truths.

Once their academic crimes came to light, various half-measures were undertaken to avoid negative publicity. This included naming a wing at King's College in London after both Rosalind Franklin and Wilkins, the man who betrayed her. Clearly, the patriarchs of that institution could not allow a woman to stand alone in the spotlight, even if she was long dead and no longer a threat to them.

However, we must not lose our focus on the true crime committed amidst a smokescreen of posthumous posturing to feign remorse. The fact remains that two men took credit and knowingly accepted a Nobel prize for a discovery made in large part by a woman. In short, despite having beaten them to the finish line, she was ultimately kept from standing in the winner's circle by the self-serving ambitions of two men who had neither her depth of scientific knowledge nor academic credentials to make such an important discovery on their own. That is why they needed to cheat to win.

And although Alfred Nobel, an arms dealing chemist whose own scientific discoveries continue to kill soldiers and civilians alike to this day, is also long dead, Franklin was unable to win his paradoxical peace prize posthumously because its judges do not give out awards to dead people. But what if she had lived? Would they have also sided in favor of those two men? In that era, it would have been expected.

While Rosalind Franklin's story is tragic for a number of ethical and compassionate reasons, it serves to remind us that the institutions of government, finance and science still remain male-dominated and that no matter how brilliant or superior a woman might be, there is a high risk that her efforts will either be diminished or overlooked to protect men's monopoly in controlling our world and our shared knowledge of human history along with it.

For the record, Rosalind was a brilliant woman upon whose coattails those men needed to ride in order to launch their own glorious careers into orbit; a historical fact that no editorial revision can change.

Case Two — NASA's Hidden Figures

Our next case of gender prejudice concerns NASA, a world-renowned space agency, and its failure to seize upon a historical public relations opportunity that would have elevated not only the ranks of all women but also helped to counteract the negative racist propaganda that had long been undermining the status of African Americans in the USA.

The nature of that opportunity was documented in the feature film *Hidden Figures*. Released in 2016, this was the first time that many of us even realized that NASA was not exclusively staffed by white men who chain-smoked around sensitive electronic equipment.

The film gives a relatively accurate historical portrayal of the lives of three black women who played key roles in helping those white men get one of their own to walk on the moon. Based on a book by Margot Lee Shetterly, it recounts the story of Dorothy Vaughan, who became the first black female supervisor at the National Advisory Committee for Aeronautics in 1949, as NASA was then named.

The second woman, a proven mathematical genius named Katherine Johnson, was asked by astronaut John Glenn to check the orbital math of her male counterparts before he felt safe to journey into space. In doing so, he openly declared his trust for that woman's mind over the costly computers that NASA was using for such calculations.

The third woman, Mary Johnson, was not only NASA's first black female engineer but also influenced the hiring of more women into NASA's science, engineering and mathematics departments.

In other words, all three of these women were critical not only to the success of NASA itself, but also to the greater mission of the United States to claim its technological superiority over the USSR during the escalating cold war between both countries.

Subsequently, this thrust NASA into the position of being in charge of the scientific exploration of space and also acting as the propaganda wing for the US government's claim of exceptionalism over the rest of the world. And within this dual-purpose public relations role, NASA lost a monumental opportunity to put these three black women in the spotlight at a time when black men were still being lynched by whites for aspiring to the equality promised them by their constitution.

Beyond throwing humble pie into the faces of the racists of that time, such a bold move would also have represented a glorious victory for all womankind by proving them not only highly intelligent, but also likely capable of running the entire space program if need be.

Instead, what happened was akin to the Rosalind Franklin fiasco wherein, almost out of embarrassment, a much-delayed feeble attempt was made to honor these extraordinary black women by putting the name of one of them on a NASA building. Yet this only happened fifty years later and after millions had already seen a film based on a book written by a black female author who brought our attention to the fact that no one in charge had bothered to mention their accomplishments.

Was professional jealousy to blame? Or just the typical male Gender Wall policy of dismissing women in general?

Using this act of institutional oversight by the men in charge, we can then entertain a hypothetical "what if" scenario. What if ordinary men of that time had learned from NASA in 1949 that women held key positions in its space program? Might it have helped to counter the culture's negative stereotyping of women as being only suitable for housework or working as a secretary for her male boss?

And what if millions of white racists had heard that black women were holding these key positions? How might it have countered their self-serving narrative that "non-whites" were less capable or ambitious than whites, as had long been suggested in boastful rants by the likes of Adolf Hitler to anti-hero television character, Archie Bunker?

While such thoughtless prejudices are losing ground to reality today, they continue to sway the minds of those who need to feel themselves above others for lack of any genuine success in their own lives. Hence, NASA's opportunity to elevate the collective status of women was lost.

Yes, we could argue that NASA was created to explore space and not to ease racial tensions or praise women. But it did not shy away from engaging in a symbolic war for political dominance against the USSR via its space race to the moon. Had it felt a similar calling to dissipate racial tensions or men's dismissive attitudes toward women during that same turbulent time, the USA might itself now be 50 years ahead of its current position in terms of gender and race relations.

Given the nature of the male competitive mindset, we can assume that the dominant male hierarchy of NASA simply gave little thought to the women in its employ. And once it did, it seemed more an act of self-defense based on the attention drawn to the *Hidden Figures* book to finally acknowledge publicly the vital role these exceptional women played in its earlier success.

Granted, NASA had no legal or moral obligation to bridge cultural divides where gender or race were concerned. Yet it must have felt some sense of obligation when it announced in 2020 the naming of the Mary W. Jackson NASA Headquarters building in Washington, some 15 years after her death from old age. In it's press release, it all but confirmed its past failure to act as a cultural beacon by stating:

"...we will continue to recognize the contributions of women, African Americans, and people of all backgrounds who have made NASA's successful history of exploration possible."

What they failed to explain was why it took them so long.

...

While incidents such as these pale in comparison to the horrors that are experienced by women in less tolerant societies, they nonetheless point to a well-established pattern among men to dismiss their female counterparts, especially where promotions or opportunities for further advancement are concerned — and competition for both is fierce.

The same is true for greater society wherein the patriarchs in power continue to show less concern for the lives of women and their critical role in keeping our societies running smoothly behind the scenes.

Yet once we finally do acknowledge all that women have done and are capable of doing to improve our collective lives in the future, it will represent "a giant leap for mankind" in tearing down a Gender Wall that continues to force one half of our species to live on that side of the fence where the grass is never quite as green as on the other.

CHAPTER 11
Choking Her Out

WARNING: This chapter contains graphic descriptions of sexual acts and deviant human behavior. Proceed at your own discretion.

...

The porn industry has always had a tentative relationship with reality in that its purpose is to offer our minds a means of escape into a world of sexual fantasy. And now that the internet is the main point of entry into that world, we no longer have to sneak past our neighbors with a bag of rented VHS videotapes or the new edition of Penthouse as we prepare for a long weekend of frenzied self-indulgence.

Today, through that internet gateway, the minds of literally billions of men, women and children gain easy access to every kind of sexual fantasy world imaginable. And sometimes, with a few absent-minded clicks, we may find ourselves in a surreal netherworld of psycho-sexual deviance from which any healthy-minded person will want to make a quick retreat.

Yet even the most benign pornographic content seems determined to give us an unrealistic perspective on human sexuality. Much of that fault lies in its production values, which call for the hiring of unskilled actors to engage in various mechanical acts of bodily penetration, thus making their scripted sexual encounters seem not only contrived and unrealistic, but sometimes even comical to watch.

Adding to this, the attention of internet "porn stars" is more on the camera than on their partners, which only further exposes the farce of these sexual unions as being just a theatrical performance acted out for our masturbatory mass consumption.

As a result, what these scripted porn actors and their audiences lose through their staged sexual antics is a chance to experience the second most pleasurable aspect of a legitimate sexual encounter, which is the feeling of intimacy between two people sharing the sensual thrill of their physical contact and spiritual communion.

But as anyone with long-term relationship experience knows, sexual encounters between even the most loving of couples can begin to feel scripted after a while, leading some to lose interest in their partners. At other times, we may no longer feel attracted to the person if the bonds of love, trust or security have been irreparably broken. And yet, as per nature's demand, we still feel the urge to mate as a result of our inborn lust for sexual pleasure. So what are we to do?

This is where the porn industry comes to the rescue by allowing our minds to indulge in the virtual thrill of a new sexual encounter with an attractive naked stranger or even some other optional engagement that may break various cultural, moral or legal taboos.

Offering staged reenactments of a wide range of sexual fantasies, the porn industry has nothing to gain by presenting an accurate depiction of real world human relationships when our intention is to spend some quality time with our imagination. As a result, what we tend to see in pornographic material is a misrepresentation of how ordinary people interact in context of a sexual encounter.

This misrepresentation is most evident in the behavior of the naked women hired to give an award-winning performance of feigned sexual delight during any scripted encounter with a man. In that regard, it is much like watching someone force a smile during a family photo to conceal their true emotions. For female porn actors, this means having to moan loudly or chant "oh yeah" with near-religious fervor to coax her male partner to ejaculate. In other words, her role in these modern porn videos remains as it has throughout patriarchal history, which is to ensure the man's pleasure — not her own.

And therein lies the truth: like much of what society has to offer, pornography is mostly made by and for men. As such, by presenting sex from a biased, male-centric perspective, the purveyors of porn also promote the fantasy of male sexual conquest over an imaginary female partner who seems far too easy to please in comparison to any genuine woman that one might encounter in real life.

In promoting this biased version of sex, they also commit a further crime against reality by depicting the most awkward of men as having a God-like command over a woman's sexual pleasure. In fact, when it comes to having sex with women, men can do no wrong, it seems.

As a result, this self-serving fantasy world of male sexual domination over women bears no resemblance to the real one being ignored by the camera lens. And if a male viewer of porn does encounter a woman who reacts to his every touch in that same unrealistic manner as female porn actors are taught to do, then it's likely she has also learned to fake it by watching the same videos.

...

In watching the depiction of these sexual illusions, we are reminded of how much of our world is built on a foundation of wishful fantasies. And while most are relatively harmless and even entertaining, such as pulp fiction and pop songs, those fantasies take a turn for the worse in the porn industry's depiction of how women ought to be treated by men in context of having sex.

Here, we often see a disturbing pattern of physical, emotional and spiritual abuse that seems more appropriate for a crime drama about a serial rapist than something for the healthy-minded to enjoy.

Yes, we can choose not to watch, as advocates for free speech might recommend. But what if we stumbled upon such content as a thirteen year old child and were naive enough to believe that such hateful acts of physical or mental abuse were not only normal for adults to engage in, but even something that women would encourage and enjoy?

This need for concern is supported by nature herself because young people look to adults for cues as to what is appropriate behavior. And based on what these merchants of online porn recommend, it appears appropriate for young men to seek out a woman with low self-esteem and no discretion, penetrate her vaginally, then proceed to manually strangle her as though in the process of trying to end her life.

And make no mistake — the choke hold being depicted is intended to signal a disdain for the woman, not a desire to please. In fact, given this book's theme about male domination, we can understand why women are often treated this way in porn videos. We can even verify our suspicions by looking for a porn video wherein men are treated by women in the same manner during sex, whether in having their asses slapped or their throats grasped during intercourse. However, we are unlikely to find such a video because men interpret such treatment as a sign of weakness and submission. In other words, they are depictions of victimhood. And this points to the ugly truth that porn all too often portrays women as victims of sex, rather than as equal partners.

In facing that reality, we are then forced to reckon with the fact that these porn videos act as a form of indoctrination to countless young men on the internet, showing them how to treat a woman during sex to also create the illusion of being dominant and "in control" of the situation. And this may even become a cultural guide for what could be considered having "good sex" from a misguided male perspective.

I Hear She Likes It

Being a for-profit enterprise, the modern porn industry also tries to reach all markets, including those for pedophiles and psychopaths. But since there are legal risks involved in catering to such an audience, they can skirt the issue by offering simulated acts of pedophilia or female torture. And so one may stumble across videos of girls who appear as children or on the verge of being killed by a brutish male attacker. But since these are all just theatrical depictions of criminal male behavior, they create the appearance that no one is being hurt.

However, the reality of the situation is that millions of teenagers still coming to terms with their sexual impulses have easy access to videos that condone the victimizing of women. And if any young man already has one foot in the moral abyss, then these depictions of female abuse may encourage him to continue in that direction in knowing that his dysfunctional associations of sex with violence are being validated by his naked brothers in the male-dominated porn industry.

Also, by reaching a global audience, these misogynistic depictions of sexual aggression against women act as a patriarchal marketing tool to justify the domination of women in all aspects of life. In presenting sex as yet another form of competition, a "loser" must be declared, which is the role that women play in these sexual conquest fantasies wherein ejaculation represents the final act of humiliation.

Moreover, if we pay close attention, we will notice that a woman's only purpose in porn videos is to tempt a man into a sexual encounter through which he can prove his dominance over her. In this regard, it is not unlike any other sporting event in which he is summoned onto the field to prove himself — and here as well, mostly for the sake of the other men who may be watching him for signs of weakness.

Thankfully, not all pornography stoops to such a primitive level. Yet too often men are shown engaging in dehumanizing behavior toward women under the pretense of a sexual act. This includes urinating on a woman, or having two men simultaneously cram their penises into her various orifices, or even ejaculating into her eyes to intentionally cause a bacterial infection known as "pink eye."

In this regard, it is more than half-way to becoming a snuff film, except that the victim is allowed to return home afterward.

As for her own part in all of this, the female victim must pretend that she craves such abusive attention from men by moaning loudly and asking for more. Yet in her voice, we can often detect the sound of someone on the verge of crying in pain or emotional distress, a sound that is ignored by her selfish male conquerors as they celebrate their victory over her dignity and self-respect like triumphant players high five-ing each other after a decisive win against the opposing team.

The take away is that she doesn't matter to these men; everything that they've done is about the need to display for one another, as is the case with nearly all aspects of the patriarchal society men have created for women to live in. And that is why even today, many women must continue pretending to enjoy sex with a man who has no idea what it means to share, let alone fulfill a woman's sexual desires.

Instead, the message in these female domination porn videos is that the man wins by causing the woman to suffer. And given that female porn actors willfully engage is such abuse for money or attention, they also become complicit in the humiliation of their gender. Nor can she scrub off the residue of shame often felt through such encounters. As such, a reckless early life decision to act in such a porn video may haunt a young woman for the rest of her life.

As for men, anyone in a healthy state of mind will find no pleasure in watching a woman suffer. Moreover, in knowing something about criminal psychology, we may see how female porn actors are often used as proxies or "substitutes" for the kind of women that may have caused men to feel hurt, rejected or humiliated — an ex-wife or lover perhaps; an abusive mother, or the entire female gender for making men feel so inadequate at times. And now, its his turn to get even. Subsequently, this is a theme often depicted — an act of revenge disguised as sex.

And should we harbor any doubts, we only have to read the text descriptions for porn videos that invite us to watch a man "destroy the ass of some stupid bitch." Does this sound hateful enough to warrant our concern? One would hope that it does.

Unfortunately, in leaving men's misguided fantasy world of sexual conquest, we return to a real world wherein the same heartless cruelty is being directed toward all women, often in an even more agonizing and mentally disturbing way.

As such, in the interest of elevating the status of women worldwide, let us look at how men, under the influence of various stages of mental derangement, have made the lives of women into a living nightmare by trying to turn their domination fantasies into a reality.

Cutting Her Off From Pleasure

In a busy world full of distractions, it's easy to ignore what else is going on around us, especially in the rest of the world. Moreover, many of us wouldn't want to know as the shock of it may leave us traumatized. But unless we broaden our mental horizons beyond theme parks and beach resorts, nothing will change for the plight of women worldwide.

For example, let us travel with our minds to a remote part of Africa where a young girl's agonizing screams go easily unheard. Held down against her will by other women from her tribe, a sharp blade or stone is used, without anesthesia, to cut away the most sensitive part of her sexual anatomy — her clitoris.

To help male readers better appreciate what is happening, imagine being invited on a fishing trip by an uncle and his friends who then hold you down and cut off the head of your penis, then leave you there screaming in agony as they go back to drinking beer and fishing. This is roughly equivalent to the nightmare of brutality awaiting the young women in cultures where "female genital mutilation" (FGM) is treated as a proud rite of passage into womanhood.

Ironically, a similar kind of male mutilation ritual continues in many cultures as "circumcision" — wherein the God of men demands that part of our penis be sacrificed in his honor. Although anesthesia is used on everyone except babies, it remains a barbaric violation of our bodies and personal freedom that male children are forced to endure for the sake of the religious superstitions of their parents — or a belief in that the foreskin is a harmful part of the human male anatomy.

Yet beneath this savage mutilating of boys by their elders is the fact that the foreskin is designed to protect the head and nerve endings of the penis against injury. In reality, venereal warts and yeast infections caused by poor male hygiene likely had our ancestors cutting off the unwashed foreskins of men as a permanent solution to bathing. And by getting God involved, no male child's penis was ever safe again.

...

Returning to the screaming young girl in Africa, we may be shocked to learn that these sadistic attacks upon a child's sexual organs are still practiced in parts of our world, including rural India and elsewhere. But unlike cutting off the foreskin, there is a far more sinister reason for cutting off the clitoris of a girl approaching womanhood. Although dismissed by its perpetrators as a cultural practice, hidden beneath its screams and bloodshed is the fact that this is a form of female sexual oppression to give men greater control over the lives of women.

This is clear once we realize that cutting off a young girl's clitoris will make her less likely to stray from her husband to seek pleasure in the arms of another man. It also acts as a formal declaration that sexual pleasure belongs to the husband and that a woman must seek pleasure by way of pleasing him.

Studies of our tribal past show that we have always had an urge to deface our bodies, whether it was binding the skulls of children to elongate them, putting rings around our necks to stretch them or even piercing our flesh with hooks to defy our fear of pain. Some suggest that this is also why the Catholic Church still practices a symbolic form of human sacrifice and cannibalism in offering "the body and blood of Christ" to be eaten by followers. Yet the practice of cutting parts of our genitals away suggests a desire on the part of others to gain control of our sexual urges and freedom of access to sensual pleasure.

In the case of circumcision, it suspiciously occurs most often during adolescence when a boy begins to associate his penis with pleasure via manual stimulation. He is then suddenly punished by way of a painful cutting ritual that imprints upon his mind a trauma similar to that of being raped. And given that this assault is carried out by men on a part of his body through which his genetic seed must pass, we may even suspect that this is a symbolic warning by the patriarchs of his tribe that his life belongs entirely to them — penis and all.

As for why a woman's clitoris is targeted for removal, it represents the focal point of her ability to experience sexual pleasure. In fact, many women cannot achieve an orgasm without clitoral stimulation. And if a young bride has nothing left to rub, she will also no longer be distracted by the pleasures of the flesh and can thus fully dedicate her life to the task of pleasing her husband and attending to his needs.

While women can still achieve an orgasm by other means, it cannot be made clearer to any young girl being restrained and mutilated in a dirty grass hut that her right to choose or feel pleasure must not stand in the way of serving her purpose in life — which is to serve men.

...

Perhaps most disturbing about the female genital mutilation ritual is that women are performing it on one another. Moreover, they seem to feel no remorse in maiming young girls for life. Perhaps, if we consider the purpose of this barbaric practice, we can better understand why women who are sexually compromised might fear that a young woman with a full capacity to feel sexual pleasure might tempt their husbands to stray from them. And so, by destroying other women's ability to feel clitoral pleasure, they can better protect their own selfish interests.

Moreover, in contradiction of the goals of feminism, the men of these cultures have taught women to oppress one another as part of the patriarchal quest to dominate all womankind. And sadly, those women may not even realize what is being done to them for lack of access to higher education and greater knowledge of the outside world.

Rape Yes! Abortion No!

Earlier, it was brought to our attention that domination and leadership reside at opposite ends of the intention spectrum. That is to say, a dominator has no desire to lead us to success but only to control us. As we continue in this investigation of female sexual oppression, we are best to recognize that such dominators often rise up through the ranks to become our leaders. This is why we may see incompetence in the governing of our societies or war-mongering religious dictators who demand that we also kill disobedient women on behalf of our faith.

It was also brought to our attention that the gentler types among us are at a disadvantage in confronting those who are excessively loud and aggressive, or otherwise ill-equipped for life in a peaceful society. We may also find among those aggressors "pro-life" zealots who profess a deeply religious devotion to the welfare of unborn children that may have them murdering doctors who assist women to abort their unborn fetuses. Clearly in violation of their God's first-listed commandment — thou shalt not kill — they are the essence of moral hypocrisy in contradicting their self-professed respect for *the sanctity of life*.

This murderous pro-life stance is often a smokescreen used by those who want to control the lives of others. Hence, their professed concern for the unborn is opportunistic, especially if they work for the weapons industry or any other industry that destroys or degrades human life.

Ironically, those obsessed with protecting the life of an unborn child while it still resides within the womb of its mother may show little concern for its life upon entering the economically hostile and selfishly competitive world of patriarchs where greed and warfare cast a morbid shadow over humankind's respect for all life. Here again, that child's future struggle to access better healthcare or schooling exposes what is a widespread and popular form of moral hypocrisy among many.

Ultimately, such overtly selective "pro-life" grandstanding exposes the true underlying intentions of those leading the pro-life movement, which is to control a woman's sexual and social life without having to remove her clitoris.

Let us then turn our attention to the fact that in a male-dominated world, women fear being raped because many men — like predators in the wild — will take advantage of those who appear weaker. And in many cases, she may also be drunk, drugged, or outnumbered.

And while nature may hope that the strongest among us will pass on our genes, there is no contingency for a rapist becoming that sperm donor. As such, how can nature be sure that the perpetrator's DNA is not laden with physical or mental defects? Yet a woman being raped has little choice in this selection process. Her only role is to spread her legs to avoid injury or death. And just as in wartime gang rapes, this can result in a young woman becoming pregnant by her assailant.

As discussed in an earlier chapter, the patriarchal first line of defense is also to blame the woman for what the man has done to her, which is why in some parts of our world women are forced to wear full body coverings to protect innocent men from feeling aroused. As such, most cultures have a long history of punishing women for being raped, often by painting the rapist as the victim of her overwhelming sexual appeal.

What was she wearing to provoke the attack? Why was she out at night in the company of men? "Why didn't she know better?" Such questions are designed to defer blame so that the good reputation of the accused is not needlessly harmed by this "unfortunate misunderstanding."

And so, aside from accusing the victim of luring some poor man into raping her, there is little concern for how this attack will affect her life, including an unexpected pregnancy resulting from that sexual assault. And if she lives in a culture that does not allow her to abort a child conceived by rape, then her life effectively no longer belongs to her, otherwise she would have the right to choose to be a mother.

...

While this may be a rather cynical perspective on women's social rights, it nonetheless rings true in many cultures. Even in the United States there are laws being drafted to put women on "death row" for refusing to gestate a child of rape. Is this truly what is best for both mother and child? Whose interests are being served in giving her no choice?

As with most things in life that seem to make no sense, a closer look at this cruel, twisted form of moral logic reveals more than meets the eye. In the USA, for instance, it is difficult to reconcile one's moral reprehension for terminating pregnancies with selling automatic rifles to deranged boys who can use them to kill children at their leisure. Nor ought such a nation be selling arms to foreign dictators, or letting its police officers get away so easily with murder.

Instead, it appears to be just another attempt by a largely male cabal of legislators to regain lost power by stealing it back from the gender most victimized by men's incessant urge to dominate. However, their misogynistic bias is becoming more difficult to hide in a world where women are rising up from a history of oppression through education, voting rights and opportunities to lead in business and government. And so, the only way to sustain this oppressive pressure on women is to gain perpetual control of the government, which appears to be the goal of the patriarchs who support anti-abortion legislation.

Criminalizing abortion is how our traditional male dominators have kept women socially imprisoned and unable to compete against men for money, power and social status by forcing them to stay at home to look after their children — a commitment of at least sixteen years.

In this way, a woman's maternal inclinations may dissuade her from competing against men for the lucrative social territory they have long monopolized for power and profit. Also, she may invest decades of her life to raising a child that neither her rapist or "pro-life" oppressors are willing to care for. Poverty may also strike at this time if her patriarchal society decides to punish her for a) not being a man b) being pregnant, or c) not having more free time to offer her employer.

In an earlier chapter, we considered the plight of a woman in India who was forced to marry her rapist so he could avoid going to prison. We find a similar favoring of men over women in many cultures, even if they have engaged in criminal acts against those women.

Fortunately, greater access to education is inspiring more women to become criminal prosecutors while more progressive-minded men are recognizing that the archaic mindset of their fellow male dominators is pushing us all back to the dark ages when it was easier to conceal the selfish impetus behind our transgressions against greater humanity.

As for an alibi, men will claim that God wants them to act this way toward women. Yet religion is not so much to blame as is men's want to dominate and control. In this sense, religions are not much different than South Africa's former fascist Apartheid government which used racial rather than gender profiling to dominate its citizens. As such, the problem is not the systems we create but the urge of men to create such systems as a symptom of their urge to dominate. This same urge is therefore often present in our religious systems, where it is may not be limited to just the oppression of women.

For example, the Hindu religion promotes caste systems that favor the wealthy over the poor, whereas Judaism favors men born of Jewish racial origin, leaving it no reason to recruit "gentiles." In this regard, an element of self-interest for the sake of wielding power permeates most religious belief systems with many favoring men over women with no attempt to conceal such gender prejudice given that men can literally beat women into submission in the privacy of their homes, as has also been a long tradition. Nor does this kind of behavior have anything to do with spirituality — but only men's selfish Bio-Psychology.

In modern times, as our collective faith has slowly migrated toward the tenets of science, the mentally-oppressive influence of our ancient religions and their exclusively male priesthood is waning in terms of their credibility and power over our lives. Yet given men's controlling nature, someone must pick up the patriarchal mantle by creating yet another storybook narrative to make women feel as inferior as had the story of Eve's undermining of God and men having to suffer for it.

Enter the world of modern advertising. Today, no longer under the oppressive eye of an invisible man judging her every move from above, women are now faced with a new invisible critic of their social worth. This is the nameless, faceless "catch" — that as-yet-unknown man of healthy genes and finances who will condemn her to a life of childless, loveless longing lest she obey the sacred commandments of the beauty industry, starting with 1) Never leave home looking like yourself, and 2) Dedicate your life to learning how to please men.

If this sounds all-too-familiar, it should. And so, rather than having come "a long way, baby," as advertisers in the 1970's once had proudly proclaimed, today's woman is still being dragged, crying and kicking, into the clit-chopping hut of modern society in preparation for an oft unfulfilling future life of servitude to men.

Subsequently, just as we are removing the mental shackles of various oppressive religions, women are being indoctrinated into yet another cultish belief system by a mostly male-dominated beauty and "surgical enhancement" industry that proclaims a woman's only value to society is as an attractive receptacle for men's ejaculate.

And that's typically where this new narrative ends, with no mention of her venturing into outer space as a scientific explorer; no talk of her finding a cure for cancer; or being socially significant in any other way beyond her attractiveness to men and her housebound duties as a good wife and mother. She is a perpetual afterthought.

Moreover, to remain atop society's dominance hierarchy, men must keep finding new ways to keep women looking opposite to where true power resides. As already mentioned, one such demand pressures her to shave her pubic region to appear more like that of a prepubescent girl. And so, in provoking a woman to color her face, hair and nails, to wear unstable footwear, to undergo cosmetic surgery and various other diversions, men are able to keep women's attention off becoming more socially and politically empowered as they embark instead on a lifelong journey of fear in not being sexually attractive enough.

Although many women recognize when they're being conned in this way, there still remain those who allow men to sneak past them in the lineup for power by fighting with other women over male attention or cowering in shame from their own imperfect bodies. In this way, they can also be tricked into remaining last in line.

And at the most primitive reaches of female oppression, there await those men who want women to move back down into the dungeons of weak, ignorant dependence so they can be traded again like livestock for their father's or husband's selfish gain. To such men, this is their Heaven on earth, and to create it, they must make the lives of women a living hell.

Yet this also brings us face to face with one of life's greater ironies in that, if not for women, misogynists could not exist, given that all were born of mothers And this is a fact that every woman-hater is forced to choke on, lest he finally learns to love and respect his true creator.

CHAPTER 12
Asking for Directions

The Gender Wall that exists to keep women out of power is both real and relentless in its oppressive influence over their lives.

For instance, if you left home today without putting on makeup or fussing over what to wear, then you are most likely a typical man or a braver woman than most for rejecting the hype of a fear-based female beauty culture that taunts women throughout their lives. Moreover, with men having been mentally conditioned by that culture, we find among them many who will protest a woman's "radical" urge to present her true, natural self in public, whether through an unshaven body or by wearing clothes for comfort rather than for sexual display.

As a consequence, women in many western cultures are subjected to lifelong media and public pressures to put on physically constraining sexual enticement costumes and full facial camouflage, if only to avoid being shunned by men or harassed by their panicked peers for daring to step out of line to be more authentic.

To make this point even more obvious, consider how often you have seen a movie poster or fashion photo of a woman where one side of her top is suggestively sliding off her shoulder — then try to find even one example where a man is being presented in the same way. In fact, you won't find them any more than you will find porn videos where women are choking out men while having sex. It's a power dynamic that has men on top and women doing their best to stay beneath them.

Beyond social domination politics, what also keeps the Gender Wall in place are the vast sums of money being made by selling goods that are specific to each gender, be it makeup and high heels for women, or pickup trucks and cowboy outfits for men. In that regard, our minds have long been trained by commercial advertising as to what products we must buy based on our gender.

Gender-based product marketing can have a powerful influence on our spending because it often caters to our Bio-Psychological urge to procreate. As such, we can find countless products being sold for the sole purpose of sexual display, whether it's sexy clothing for women or expensive sports cars for men to flaunt their economic superiority.

Yet one aspect of procreation-based consumerism that retailers do not want us thinking about is why men buy diamond rings for women. Marketed as a symbol of a man's enduring love for a women, the act of placing that ring on her finger is actually a form of territorial marking to ward off potential rivals. In western cultures, this gives women a temporary lift in power over her suitor by threatening to put her naked body back on the open market if he fails to follow up that ring with a formal declaration of their union via a marriage ceremony.

Ironically, this costly territorial marking ritual was invented in 1938 by marketers for the de Beers mining company, who needed a premise to sell more diamonds to the public. Since then, it has worked so well that men are now duped into spending months of wages on a needless item that ultimately has no influence on the success of a marriage. In fact, a man's urge to mark a woman as his territory can destroy it.

But what the marketing of engagement rings ultimately proves is that the premise for selling a product can vasty differ from our reason for buying it. In the case of a diamond ring, it conceals a man's desire to possess a woman behind a media-generated romantic gesture. As a result, this not only proves that men's biological instincts are being exploited for profit by commercial interests but that their thoughts and social behaviors are also being shaped by those same interests.

...

While every culture is uniquely different from most others, what often remains similar from place to place are the interactions between men and women. As such, we can find men in any part of the world who feel hopelessly insecure about their ability to attract a woman. And this exposes another oppressive aspect of the Gender Wall wherein men are purposely exiled from being able to more fully express themselves so that they can be better exploited politically and for profit. This is done by promoting male stereotypes that can have men behaving more like a fictitious Hollywood movie character than someone who lives in the real world. In short, they must become an imposter to succeed.

We can better understand this problem by recognizing that nature places no restrictions upon men's behavior aside from wanting them to compete for dominance to prove their genetic suitability as a mate. In other words, for better or worse, men are born to be as they are.

In stark contrast, the rules of the Gender Wall seek to confine a man to a narrow range of stereotypical masculine behaviors that are meant to prove his dominance. At the same time, women are having their own authentic selves subverted by feminine stereotypes to limit them to a narrower, less natural and more subordinate range of behaviors.

Subsequently, this creates many social impediments for men beyond their existing struggle to win a woman's sexual favor. But even more significant is that men's masculinity training causes them to feel highly suspicious of womankind in general given that the Gender Wall seeks to control their behavior by separating them from all that is considered "soft" and thereby feminine. As a result, if a man believes himself to be as his patriarchal mentors insist, then he is also more likely to conform to their "hard" masculine stereotypes by abandoning his softness.

This has resulted in a familiar behavior wherein men try to prove their masculinity by denouncing all things feminine. Yet in doing so, they must also denounce all that they yearn for in a woman, including her inherently kinder, gentler disposition and nurturing ways. This is why we may hear some men ridiculing the better traits of their own innate humanity — traits that they began to surrender in childhood in order to become this illusory "real man" in the cult of masculinity.

This regimen of gender-based brainwashing has created some rather ironic paradoxes, such as men being confused about their love for what they claim to hate. For instance, we might hear a man claiming to love a woman's "pussy" for its soft, penetrable nature while denouncing men as "pussies" as though he hates them. Which is it then?

Given men's fear of being associated with the stereotypical traits of feminine softness and vulnerability, and adding to that his inborn urge to claim dominant status, we can begin to understand some of the peculiar behaviors exhibited by men on their side of the Gender Wall.

This chapter's title, for instance, alludes to one such behavior which has men refusing to ask other men for directions, even if his passengers are on the verge of heat stroke from being driven around in circles. This is because men are taught that a leader is all-knowing, which has them afraid of being humiliated as a failed navigator; a fear which has surely caused many a family to arrive late at their desired destination.

For men, there exists a long list of "off limit" behaviors. This includes wearing pink and flowery-printed shirts, or even crying if feeling sad. In the latter case, we often see a man trying to fake their way through a delicate moment of emotional release by grunting like an animal, lest his tears be seized upon as a sign of weakness. No, he'll never live down having wept like a little girl. Instead, he is better off to just lash out in anger to protect his *tough guy* image. Or maybe even shoot somebody.

...

While men's struggles to avoid being associated with femininity can be a source of comic relief, this culturally-induced fear can also lead to dangerous confrontations that threaten the peace of our societies.

Pressured by the so-called *cult of masculinity* to project a facade of rugged, unfeeling toughness, men must also force themselves to deny any sign of human frailty that could signal a loss of their masculinity. This sets them on a confusing treadmill of having to repress some of their softer, gentler traits for the sake of living a lie.

Let us then consider how this struggle to prove one's manhood can often rage dangerously out of control to hinder the cohesion of society and thereby also the emotional richness of men's lives.

Man Enough to be a Woman

Homosexual men have long suffered for heterosexual men's lingering fear of the feminine. This is because gay men represent a confusing hybrid identity that does not conform to a simple, two-tiered system for assigning power and status based on gender. Instead, the dominant male rulers of our world must deal with widespread confusion among their herds in struggling to decide on which side of the Gender Wall these defectors from the cult of masculinity belong.

As expected, the comfort-seekers of our world become distressed in the presence of such unscripted behavior as it injects chaos into their predictable lives of routine. And so, rather than create extra work for themselves by accommodating those who do not fit into their narrow world view, they have historically chosen to either kill homosexuals or torment them into pretending to be "normal" like them. We can then understand why so many gay men have pretended to prefer sex with women as a way to avoid persecution and even death.

Fortunately, the last few decades have seen changes coming to many cultures, including to their tolerance for homosexuality. Unfortunately, fundamentalist zealots have retaliated by trying to drag their societies back into the dark ages where their intolerance was better tolerated. Such was the case for Iran, a once moderate nation until it was overrun by religious fundamentalists in 1979. Seemingly overnight, women went from wearing stylish modern clothing to full body coverings. As for homosexuality, it became punishable by death.

However, as an alternative to death, gay men were offered the choice of having their penises removed as part of a government-sponsored attempt to turn gay men into straight women. In this way, its strict interpretation of gender could be protected from the threat of reality.

Iran's sadistic approach to curtailing social diversity was exposed in the 2008 film, Be Like Others, showing the struggles of gay men and lesbians to exist in a culture that makes no effort to hide its intolerance for female sexuality or men who dare to exhibit feminine traits.

But Iran's use of gender reassignment surgery to "correct" gay man creates some obvious conflicts for its male victims. For one, a gay man may not want to be a women, let alone lose his penis. Secondly, not all men who undergo such reassignment surgery are gay. Subsequently, as a government-approved *woman*, a transgender man may still seek out sex with women, thereby presenting religious fundamentalists with yet another dilemma in having created a lesbian.

While such fear-based demonstrations of hatred toward gay men are disturbing to those of reasonable mind, they are also not without their moments of comic relief. In one such instance, during his 2007 speech at Columbia University, one former Iranian president's claim that "We don't have homosexuals like in your country," was met with a round of laughter as deserving of any great comedian

Iran is not alone as a political regime claiming to be the solution while creating the problem. In shifting from a progressive leadership to a domination governing style, societies often become intolerant of those unable to abide by its latest list of public restrictions. As such, the historical intolerance of gay men explains why even heterosexual men have long feared to be seen acting like a woman in any way.

One irony in this intolerance of differences is that scientific research has shown that men and women share 22 pairs of chromosomes with a 23rd pair determining our gender — but not our sexual preferences. As such, men and women mostly share the same biological code, while a few percentage points of difference causes some men to treat women like an alien species to be conquered for exhibiting feminine traits. But as demonstrated by the IPSFA Sequence, our intolerance is largely a symptom of mental conditioning to keep us on our designated side of the Gender Wall — and within our assigned social caste.

Admittedly, gender prejudice and homophobia are not easy subjects to confront in societies that teach us to shun complex thinking or a diversity of belief. We can therefore understand why many men opt to become hyper-masculine as a defensive measure against becoming a target for gender-based social terrorism or murder by other men.

Knowing this, we can also better understand various male social behaviors that would otherwise remain a mystery if we relied only on what our governments, schools or media dared to reveal of the truth.

The Courage to Feel

As a general rule, the unofficial cult of masculinity permits men to only demonstrate strength and anger; any other form of self-expression is subject to intense scrutiny by one's peers in a patriarchal culture. For instance, if we look at movie marketing images, we can easily identify which are targeting male audiences based on a hero's defensive stance, angry facial expression or holding of a gun as a symbol of power.

Nature also begins her alpha male recruitment drive early in life, which fills the daytime fantasies of many boys with wishful images of having great power over others — thus the allure of superheroes and *action* films featuring male combat, as well as famous athletes in sport.

But not all boys aspire to become championship boxers or decorated war heroes, nor their equivalent as corporate raiders on a mission to dominate the market. Instead, they may want to use their creativity or imagination to prove themselves, as is the case with those who aspire to be "rock stars." Yet even in the art world, nature taints the creative process with an urge to stand out and dominate; to prove we are better than the rest. In short, the urge to compete seems inescapable.

This harkens back to the boastful lyrics of Bon Scott cited in chapter one, a form of musical male posturing that made him seem a superhero to many an adolescent male. Women in rock music are equally potent, as the Wilson sisters in Heart proved through their powerful writing and live performances. Yet our focus remains on the Bio-Psychology of men and the often toxic culture of male aggression that it promotes, even in the otherwise enjoyable domain of music-making. As such, we often find that many male music makers express themselves within the narrow confines of the masculine stereotypes of their culture.

Although long past their prime, some of the more legendary names of rock music's bygone glory days continue to stand out as examples of both excellence in their field and narcissistic male showboating.

In the rock genre for example, Gene Simmons, bassist/singer for the band KISS, seemed compelled to boast of his many sexual conquests of female fans as a symptom of a competitive urge to prove himself dominance to other men. Clearly, he was *in it* to win.

Likewise, Ted Nugent seemed obsessed with letting us know that he was always killing something, whereas rock's favorite MC, David Lee Roth, used early Van Halen videos to show off his martial arts kicking skills. In this way, no male fan could doubt that these were "real men" according to the masculinity myths of their time, nor that they were the kind of men who would be seen asking anyone for directions.

But this also created some notable ironies, as was the case with Rob Halford, lead singer for Judas Priest, who projected those same macho traits to an audience of male admirers who had no idea that he was also gay. This must surely have caused some moments of inner turmoil for him if encountering some dullard who might ask: *"So what do you think about these queers and what they're doing to our country?"*

Well, they're making great music, for one. And if they come out in public, as Rob Halford did, then they help to make life easier for those still struggling with their sexual identity in a world of shallow thinkers who want to deny them their right to exist.

...

As the member of an enthusiastic rock audience, listening to music can have us wanting to emote or move to the rhythm of a song. Yet even in this enjoyable context, a man's competitive Bio-Psychology and his exposure to patriarchal brainwashing can have him feeling much too intimidated to express himself naturally.

This is understandable, given that the Gender Wall that mentally divides men from women was build on myths about what it means to be a man. This scripted separation from reality has many unfortunate consequences, including that it keeps many men from exploring and expressing their inner selves. Subsequently, in adopting those traits of stoic apathy and competitive paranoia that so often define masculine programming, many men go through life feeling too inhibited to let others see them for the person they truly are.

A familiar example of this affliction is seen in the reluctance of many men to dance in public. This requires allowing our emotions to control our bodies in an unpredictable demonstration of our inner being that is bared for all to see. It is therefore no wonder why many men will choose instead to sit through a night of music rather than risk getting up on the dance floor to be judged for showing how they feel.

We generally don't intellectualize dancing in terms of its challenge to the male psyche, yet this melodrama is nonetheless unfolding for many men faced with the prospect of having to move their bodies to music as others watch their performance. And what many dread most is to be seen by other men as dancing "like a girl."

This reluctance to avoid emotional self-expression is also evident in how we are taught to dance. For instance, rather than have us dance alone to "let it all hang out," we are instead encouraged to dance as groups in a choreographed act of conformity. This has us following a series of predetermined steps that allows us to hide amidst a crowd of others all doing the same. And so, rather than dance our way to a life of mental freedom and self-expression, we are instead encouraged to remain within the box-like limitations of social conformity.

This trend toward conformity in dance was evident during medieval times in formal court dancing and also appears in country line dancing and disco where our every step is choreographed to save us having to decide for ourselves what our next move should be.

In this way, aside from facilitating social contact between genders, structured group dancing provided men a safe haven from judgment by allowing them to follow what everyone else was doing.

Ironically, even as people began to separate and dance alone in clubs, there was a continued emphasis on copying the latest dance craze for fear of self-expression. And so, by doing *the Charleston, the Twist,* or *the Boogaloo,* one could appear culturally ahead of their time while still safely hiding behind what others were doing to express themselves.

In making this connection between men and their common fear of dancing in a joyful, unencumbered way, we can then understand why it often takes great courage for a young man to approach a young women in a public setting to ask her to dance. After all, not only is he courting potential rejection as a mate, but he is also presenting himself to be judged for his physical performance. Will she see in his bodily motions a physical confidence that will translate to his love making?

Will he seem unsure of himself and thus make her unsure of his being a suitable partner? There is so much that can potentially be expressed through the silent language of dance that we can see why sitting it out at the sidelines is a popular path of less resistance for many men.

More than anything, genuine expressive dance requires freeing our minds. As such, in feeling too inhibited to lose control of himself, a young man's moment of opportunity to connect with the object of his desire may likely also pass. And sadly, the cult of masculinity promotes many such fears in men to resist becoming all that they can be.

…

Not surprisingly, women have an easier time expressing themselves on the dance floor because they have no fear of being seen to "act like a girl" as boys are typically raised to do. Instead, they can even dance as a couple without their sexual orientation needing to be questioned. On the other hand, in having been trained to posture for dominance, men must create the appearance of being entirely in control of themselves. Subsequently, a man's ability to spontaneously surrender himself in the context of dance or other emotive form of self-expression is difficult if his mind is fighting that impulse for fear of appearing out of control and thereby "not man enough" to his potential male onlookers.

And so, beyond the fear of rejection, a further major hurdle for many men to overcome is their unwillingness to joyfully express themselves as individuals rather than as a fearful reflection of male tribal culture and its rigid rules of conduct regarding masculinity.

It should also not surprise us that this same fear predicts the advent of mosh pit "dancing" wherein young men slam into one another with such aggression that no bystander would ever mistake their touching as an expression of feminine tenderness or homosexual intimacy.

But is a gentle man any less a man? No. But perhaps if his attitude proves to be contagious, he may incite other men to refuse to go to war. And that would not turn out so well for those plutocrats who make their fortunes from engaging in this most violent of money sports.

Smiling and Other Signs of Weakness

The typical male mindset is easiest understood from the perspective of the dominant and the dominated. As such, whether in making love or being raped, the act of penetration itself is symbolically interpreted as a relationship between the dominant and the submissive. Given that penetration is one of their greatest fears, this has some men going out of their way to develop excessive body mass to avoid appearing weak and vulnerable to other men. Moreover, the scene most remembered by audiences from the film *Deliverance* was when the least "fit" among a group of men was raped by his male abductors; an unexpected twist in the plot that no male movie goer of that era has ever forgotten.

This is why "pussy" became an insult among men in that a woman's vagina is a soft opening designed for penetration. Thus, to be labelled a "pussy" compares a man with female softness and submission rather than hard, dominant manhood. Of course, this is all just empty male posturing given that every man will become a pussy in the presence of a wild animal predator. In the meantime, if may help the weak to feel stronger by tormenting those even weaker than themselves.

The fears that men may experience in regard to women and the traits of womankind could fill books and still leave much unsaid. However, this exploration of the scripted male psyche will hopefully give readers food for thought as to how society can create impediments to men's freedoms of thought and self-expression by promoting unrealistic and baseless prejudices against the female gender.

And wherever those freedoms are being imprisoned in a dungeon of primal fear for the benefit of our patriarchal dominators, or to soothe the fears of comfort-seekers that everyone is on their designated side of the Gender Wall, there we will also find great sadness beneath the social facade of men forced to live under such an oppressive regime of mental restrictions.

Yet how we feel is not always something we want to reveal during any form of competition. And this leads to a final example of how men are trained to repress their gentler human traits by associating them with women and creating a fearful prejudice against them. As a result, there is a long list of what men may fear to be seen doing and sadly, one of them is smiling.

Smiling, as we know, is a simple human gesture to let others know that we have no hostile intentions. Yet in commercial advertising, we often see women presented with a friendly smile to suggest openness to contact, whereas men are often posed with a detached expression and defensive body stance as though expecting a challenge. In short, marketers typically present men as feeling opposite to women in their temperament: a hard versus soft exterior, and paranoid versus inviting.

Given advertising's reach, this may influence some men to adopt this cold mental attitude just as it influenced other negative behaviors in the past, such as smoking cigarettes or voting for corrupt politicians.

And so, while women are encouraged to smile, men are taught to signal suspicion as though on constant guard against loss. And unless you are a psychopath, you are also not allowed to smile during combat.

Here as well, gender-based cultural brainwashing takes on a rather cartoonish appearance as men are seen struggling to maintain a "game face" to not appear penetrable, even to women. Yet it should also make us wonder what kind of society we are hoping to create by forcing men to repress all higher forms of self-expression for fear of being defeated? Surely, that society will be one wherein men are neither honest with themselves and others, nor likely to be seen smiling.

And so, the obvious solution is to rewrite our cultural scripts; to do away with these bogus street theatrics that have men virtue signaling their adherence to some self-defeating male stereotype, lest they never evolve to become happier within their own skin.

After all, it is not the man who seeks to get in touch with the softer traits of his humanity that we need fear, but a detached psychopath compelled to eliminate us as part of an ancient male plot to win for the sake of winning itself.

Nor should we want to encounter his kind in asking for directions, for he may well be a man on a mission to prove himself.

PART THREE
The Aftermath & Fallout

CHAPTER 13
Man on a Mission

Sometimes terrible things happen in our world for which there seem to be no obvious answers. Yet wherever a human being is the cause of that tragedy, there is always an answer. Moreover, we can often narrow the cause down to a common motive and gender. And so, from benign activities such as gambling, to atrocities such as raping women, killing animals for sport or going to war — all are directly connected by the urging of men's Bio-Psychology and therefore need not be treated as an unknowable mystery. Plain as day: men are always looking for ways to prove themselves *a winner*.

As such, the influence of Bio-Psychology offers a viable motive for many of the most heinous crimes ever committed by men. While not the origin of psychopathic behavior, its nagging, subconscious urging to dominate others can take on a life of its own within the imagination of someone whose reasoning has been compromised by mental illness, even if the cause of that illness remains unknown to science.

In such cases, a man's relentless biological drive to "win" may find its ultimate expression in a gruesome act of conquest over a victim, with the death of that person serving as final proof of the assailant's victory. As such, those targeted often represent a symbolic "trophy kill" in the mind of a deranged hunter of human prey. Moreover, it gives their lives a sense of meaning and purpose in having to prove themselves to both themselves and their victim — like a man on a mission.

Let us then pursue this topic to understand what is happening and why, and how we might better mitigate these supremacy-based mental aberrations to better protect our societies in the future.

…

On that fateful day when beloved musician and ex-Beatles frontman John Lennon was killed, many felt the weight of the world upon their shoulders get even heavier. Here was a man who brought so much joy to many and helped to focus our attention on important social issues rather than just his talent. Sharing our planet with one so dedicated to uplifting the human spirit made it all the more tragic to hear of his sudden death at the hands of a man who pretended to be a devoted fan in order to gain his trust.

John Lennon's killer, or any murderous glory-seeker of his kind, will not be named herein, yet it was clearly his intention to be associated with the death of a famous celebrity. As proof of his glory-seeking ambitions, he had also created a list of potential victims based on their celebrity status, including talk show host Johnny Carson, ex-Beatle Paul McCartney, film actress, Elizabeth Taylor, and even US president, Ronald Reagan.

Clearly, all those on his list were well-known public figures. As such, we can deduce that he was a man on a mission to defeat someone of alpha status. In his twisted logic, this would allow him to claim victory in having dominated the dominant, thus elevating him in prominence — as happened in the aftermath via media coverage of his crime. And so, one could say that his mission was a successful one.

Knowing what we know of Bio-Psychology, his urge to compete for status was clearly the underlying cause of his quest to defeat someone of greater prominence, whereas his deluded mind invented the basis for such a conquest. In this way, he was not only able to express his inborn male compulsion to compete for status, but also to invent some twisted heroic plot within his mind to justify killing those of higher social standing than him.

Not surprisingly, military soldiers are trained to do the same, incited by their leaders to kill the alpha males of other nations in competing for global dominance. In short, this predatory way of thinking is not unique among men. In fact, it is all-too-common.

Further evidence of his glory-seeking urge came to light when it was discovered that John Lennon's killer had once planned to commit a highly public act of suicide to gain attention by jumping from the Statue of Liberty. And for his legal defense, he claimed to be working for God, which he felt would further elevate his status as someone in the employ of religion's highest ranking male leader.

Ironically, claiming to work for God is a common feature among the dangerously deluded because it infers having the highest possible rank aside from God himself. Such claims follow a familiar pattern wherein men with low self-esteem issues try to compensate for their feelings of insignificance by dominating others — including animals by way of hunting, torturing or killing them. Others may claim to be the target of a global conspiracy — which not only redirects blame for failure to others but also suggests they are important to those in power. All of this helps to explain how the life of John Lennon's killer and others of his kind can devolve into psychological mayhem.

As a former security guard, Lennon's killer could not have competed for glory against rock stars or presidents. As such, his chosen path to greatness was to kill his rivals for attention by stealing their spotlight and having it be directed at himself instead.

Ultimate proof of his desperate want for alpha status recognition came when he chose to remain at the crime scene for police and news reporters to show up to see his "trophy kill." In having planned out a high profile, attention-seeking public relations spectacle, he ensured himself the legacy of being remembered as the man who defeated John Lennon. And once in prison, many a music-loving inmate will surely have wanted to defeat him, as well.

...

The violent actions of John Lennon's killer bring to light a pattern of reckless social behavior that is often seen among men seeking alpha status recognition of any kind, regardless of the harm it may cause to themselves or others. And once we see what miserable lives that many had led, we can better understand why those of limited potential to "leave their mark" may opt instead to leave the bloodstain of a famous person on a New York sidewalk. In their ambitious minds, this is a better option than living a life of anonymous insignificance. And behind it all is an unconscious drive to prove one's genetic supremacy.

To be clear, the kind of people who behave in this way are mentally broken; hapless victims of their own damaged minds. To hate them is pointless as it solves nothing. However, by observing their behavior, we can better understand the competitive dynamics that often fuel such seemingly pointless crimes. After all, their crime scenes often reveal that the killer wanted to make a particular statement. Therefore, by our exploring the competitive mindset of these "men on a mission," we can potentially lessen the occurrence of such tragic events in the future.

This exploration would obviously have to begin by engaging in open and honest public discussions about men's inborn urge to dominate. In this way, we can immediately begin to lessen the threat to society from competitively-driven male violence by taking steps to control it before it either lands those men in prison, or us in the morgue.

Ultimately, this could also lead to further open discussions with any deranged captain of industry whose own near-psychotic mission to win alpha status has him destroying our natural world.

Catch Me If You Can

It is a fair observation to suggest that each of us is like an unfolding mystery, even to ourselves. As such we cannot ever know a person's life history, nor the kinds of physical and emotional trauma they may have endured as a child — or if they are suffering from an undiagnosed brain tumor that is causing them to act in some strangely chaotic or violent manner.

Yet a common factor among men who kill for the competitive thrill is a preoccupation with glorifying themselves as a supreme being. And not surprisingly, this is also the attitude that nature imposes upon the minds of men in forcing them to compete for alpha mating status. As such, many aspects of men's conquering and killing behavior make perfect sense from the perspective of this basic biological relationship.

What makes each man's behavior unpredictable is his relationship to sanity itself. Subsequently, what seems to happen in some men is that they lose control of their mental faculties while their procreative urge to prove their genetic dominance continues to rage within them. This would also explain why some men become killers in their sexual prime, thus linking their status-seeking activities to their procreative urges. As a result, some will go on to become a man on a mission to massacre, guided by a heroic conquest fantasy courtesy of an imagination that is running off the rails within a broken mind.

Among the many tragic examples of this psychotic man on a mission impulse is the one that took place during the Boston marathon. Here, the two young brothers responsible for killing and maiming innocent spectators chose to hide their competitive alpha male hostility behind a veil of supremacy-based religious beliefs to justify their murderous actions. As such, their attitude in planning this attack was informed by seeing themselves as morally superior to their victims. But here again, their actions had no basis in spiritual logic given that the God of most religions advises: "thou shalt not kill." Nor could they know if any of their victims belonged to their religion. In short, they were just stupid young men on a mission to feel special.

Equally twisted was their belief that God would reward them with 72 virgins for killing innocent people. Logically, what kind of God would reward deranged killers — let alone, what kind of virgin would offer herself to them? Instead, it sounds more like a wishful fantasy dispensed by old patriarchs too cowardly to fight their own battles for social dominance. But if such a heaven did exist where heartless killers were being celebrated, then why would any loving individual want to spend even a minute there, let alone an eternity?

And while religious scholars remain largely silent in addressing this paradox of men's murderous faith in God's love, the number of killings inspired by such psychotic reality distortions continue.

...

There are many examples of men of faith choosing murder as a tool for gaining status over others. For example, the "BTK killer" appeared from the outside as a devout Christian father on a mission to please his God. However, his true goal was to prove himself dominant, as evident by his taunting of police in letters boasting of his superior intellect for having eluded them. Engaged in his fantasy-driven plot of "killing for God", he destroyed not only the lives of his victims but also that of his family who shared a home with a man who was raping, torturing and killing people from their own community.

...

A similar case was that of "the Night Stalker," a mentally ill young man who took an opposite approach by claiming that Satan was his partner in crime. Here too, his wanting to be associated with the alpha male of Christianity's underworld exposed an obsessive need to be recognized as someone of ultimate rank and power. But despite having ambitions of a biblical proportion, he proved himself as ordinary as the rest of his tortured kind; a low level competitor who was desperate enough for attention that he was willing to kill for it.

...

Ironically, the public's fascination with notorious killers has also led to some unusual status-seeking behavior among women who hope to win the attention of such men.

To better understand their behavior, let us recall that nature directs women to choose an "alpha" male for mating purposes. Moreover, this is an unconscious drive independent of one's intellect. As a result, some women may seek an alpha male mate from among those criminals who the news media has turned into *celebrities* by keeping their names and faces in the public spotlight, which implies their social dominance.

As to why a woman would take this route to romance, we can only theorize that she has failed to succeed in maintaining relationships in the outside world and is seeking a partner of limited social mobility whose activities can be easily monitored for her emotional comfort.

Naturally, seeking a partner among men sentenced to lengthy prison sentences defies the prevailing logic of any society wherein women are taught to seek men of success and ambition. Yet other considerations may also be involved, such as having less female competition or feeling less pressure to keep the sexual interest of someone who may never see them naked in an intimate setting. Another potential factor is her own competitive vanity in seeking to be part of a "power couple" with a man who has risen to the highest ranks of celebrity killer status.

However, we must not blindly assume that all such connections are made in error. In fact, some have led to happy endings where a women has helped to free an innocent man falsely imprisoned due to equally criminal behavior of reckless prosecutors seeking to advance their own status by sending innocent people to languish in prison.

Nonetheless, most of us would agree that prison remains one of the least likely places for a woman to find her perfect match.

As a final example of how "crazy" psychopathic thinking can get, we have the case wherein famed actor and director, Jodie Foster, was being stalked by a man who hoped to win her hand in marriage by killing then-president, Ronald Reagan — a seemingly popular target among psychopaths looking for someone famous to conquer.

As for that love-struck would-be killer, his criminal actions mirrored those of any aspiring alpha male seeking to win the right to mate with the female of his choice by defeating the reigning alpha male. As such, we need not feign ignorance when such incidents occur; this is not a matter of mere "insanity" but also one of biological inclination in the life of any truly motivated social predator.

Hunting Humans

At the opposite end of the criminal justice spectrum we can find the enforcers of that justice; groups of uniformed men assigned to impose the laws of their government upon the citizenry. Yes, there are women among them, but this is more an equal rights accommodation, given that the kind of brutish thugs required to beat the protesting masses into submission are typically found among men.

Here, in the world of law enforcement, we also find men who are on a mission. But what kind of mission are they truly on? After all, what could motivate a man to seek a career in such an overtly dangerous and conflict-oriented profession?

To be fair, that answer is best sought on an individual basis by asking those involved. However, what cannot be denied is that being a police officer gives an otherwise ordinary person an extraordinary amount of *unqualified* power over the lives of others, including the right to shoot and kill them when necessary. Moreover, such power is within grasp of ordinary civilians.

And therein lies the problem: in opening a public portal for ordinary men to acquire the legal right to dominate others, we are forced into a kind of cognitive dissonance associated with police work. This involves our having been taught as children to see police officers as our valiant protectors; men bestowed with the honorable traits of honesty, bravery and good faith. As such, that is why it comes as a shock to see a police officer in his crime fighting uniform behave worse than any criminal.

Naturally, this invites confusion as to who among those who serve and protect the public is actually on the public's side? And if an officer is involved in illegal activity, he may even benefit from a professional *immunity* against justice when it is his word against that of the public. Moreover, we expect police officers to be honest, which can also taint a jury's better judgment in viewing the evidence against him. In other words, the criminal justice system is rigged to favor police officers.

Aside from offering greater immunity to criminal behavior, working as a police officer also fulfills nature's primary goal for men, which is to compete for dominance. Perhaps this is why certain kinds of men are attracted to this line of work, while others shun it. But the mere wearing of a uniform does not allow us to see into the mind of those who wear them, nor to what degree they are affected by this natural Bio-Psychological urge to prove their dominance, be it over men and women or even animals. In regard to the latter, the US Dept. of Justice has estimated that police officers shoot at least 10,000 pet dogs each year "in the line of duty," but Univ. of New Hampshire studies of police-initiated pet killings suggest a much higher number. This begs the question: how many dog killings are truly necessary, and how many are just a show of force to prove one's dominance to its owners?

Uniforms can make those men wearing them more anonymous, but what they cannot do is magically transform them into a superheroes and crime-fighters. After all, police officers come from the same kinds of neighborhoods that breed criminals, with some even joining with criminal intent. Once notable incident occurred in Miami, Florida, in the 1980's when street gangs infiltrated the its police department to enforce a new kind of justice.

Unfortunately, such breaches of integrity are rarely brought to light before many victims have been claimed. Nor would it be good for the public to realize that criminal gangs with police badges are ruling their streets while they pay for their criminal activities with taxes.

But this is not a revelation. After all, Al Capone, a once notorious gangster, ruled over his criminal empire with the assistance of corrupt police officers and officials in Chicago. In addition, the documentary, *The Seven Five*, recounts how officers from New York's 75th precinct were purged during the 1970's on charges ranging from murder and extortion to selling narcotics. In other words, they were engaged in the kind of behavior for which they were sending others to prison.

This begs the question: *who can be trusted to enforce the law?* Clearly, any system that allows criminals to masquerade as public defenders is a broken one. Subsequently, our first concern ought to be for fixing a police recruitment process that would invite criminals into its ranks to prey upon those they are otherwise hired to protect.

Our second concern should be for why a system meant to enforce justice defends its own criminal elements from having to face justice? In fact, we can argue that the punishment should be higher for those hypocrites who defile the values they expect everyone else to uphold.

Luckily, there is hope for a solution if we have the courage to police our own fears of systemic change and greater transparency.

...

On the basis of the information already revealed in this book, there are three conditions that threaten the integrity of any police department, all of which relate to men's status-seeking Bio-Psychological urges.

The first assumes that a genuine peacekeeper does not behave in a loud, boastful or aggressive way towards others. Instead, such behavior is more typical of sociopaths and psychopaths bent on showing their dominance over others. Taking this into account, if a psychopathic cop threatens a peaceful cop from his department, especially from a higher position of power, the peaceful one will often cower to protect his own interests, whether to avoid death and injury, a loss of income, or his chance to win a future promotion. As such, he becomes as any victim of a crime who is unable to help himself.

The outcome of his acquiescence is predictable. Just as with political dictators, we often find the most violently insane people in positions of authority because others failed to challenge them during their rise to power. Moreover, domination by force is a natural behavior in the wild, so it may not seem out of place in the lives of policemen whose fear of losing their jobs or positions of power are a major consideration in whether to challenge those of higher rank in the department.

The second problem relates to conditions surrounding social group loyalty. After all, police departments can be as cult-like as any religious order in defending their own against the outside world. As such, this *us versus them* attitude can cause officers to close ranks and aim their aggressions outward at those threatening their tribe, including those prosecutors hoping to serve justice to some rogue officer within their ranks. Naturally, this defeats the purpose of justice itself by turning it into a farce; a situation that would not concern the criminally-minded.

The third problem is the most significant from a Bio-Psychological perspective in that police departments do not hire quitters who easily give up a chase or run from a challenge. Instead, they intentionally hire men who want to compete to win — as is necessary when confronting violent armed criminals who may also stop at nothing to win.

But hiring excessively competitive men also invites trouble because they may look for opportunities to prove their dominance over others, including fellow officers and members of the public. At best, this may involve harassing innocent people on the street to feel a sense of power over them. At worst, such men will use their positions of power to gain an unfair advantage over those they could otherwise not compete fairly against on a level playing field.

Knowing this, we have a clearer line of sight about what happened in Minnesota, USA, when George Floyd, a towering black alpha male, was attacked by four much smaller police officers clearly not his equal in nature's natural selection process.

After using their legal powers to subdue him, one officer proceeded to then kill a physically superior human being under the intoxicating spell of his urge to defeat any rival to his dominance. After all, why else would he continue to sit on Mr. Floyd's neck artery even after he had stopped breathing? Surely not to enforce the rule of law.

Clearly, here was a criminally-minded man who snuck through the cracks of a flawed police recruitment system, then used his position of power to serve his glory-seeking ambitions. And to protect this killer cop from paying for his crime, his lawyers conjured an alternate reality wherein Mr. Floyd died from a drug-induced heart attack as four brave lawmen came to his aid. In this regard, the struggle of police to police themselves is often a struggle against reality itself, as when millions of people worldwide watched a man being publicly executed by a group of men whose true mission on that day could not be determined by the mere wearing of a police uniform.

Another way to interpret what is occurring in the minds of the more aggressive enforcers of the law in that perhaps they just enjoy the act of hunting humans for sport and felt compelled to join the police force to facilitate that goal. In many cases where no viable explanation can be found for an officer's excessive use of force or domination behavior, perhaps this one may prove to be most appropriate

...

As we leave the insular bubble world of law enforcement, we can find the same status-based domination behavior among men whose true intentions are hidden behind a similar veil of heroic posturing.

This would seem to be the case with the boy of seventeen who was cited earlier for having killed two men yet walked away free. While his name will not be mentioned, his story is much like that of the officer who killed George Floyd under the pretense of upholding the law. Yet in this case, he brought his rifle to a protest march in a nearby city under the premise of wanting to discourage violence and destruction.

Clearly, he himself failed to live up to that standard.

So what was his true mission? As it turns out, he had tried and failed to join the police force and obviously felt he had hero potential; all he needed was a chance to prove himself by killing a few *bad guys*.

Sadly, after making his trophy kill, rather than pay for his crime, he became a celebrity among those who may also have secretly yearned to turn their guns on those with whom they disagreed. Ironically, none of these advocates for gun violence, it would seem, wanted to shoot those violent protestors who stormed their nation's capitol to kill their vice president and other prominent politicians. Clearly, living out one's domination fantasies requires some level of self-control, lest we lose sight of society's true purpose as a protective sanctuary rather than a public shooting gallery for aspiring alpha males.

…

In another widely publicized killing in the USA, a homeless man was strangled to death on a subway by a former marine who claimed to also be acting on behalf of the greater good. But as someone trained to kill, he knew at which point a man would die from lack of blood or oxygen to the brain. Clearly, he was driven to overshoot that limit for reasons not justified by the victim's threat level as he acted out his frustration that no one cared that he was hungry. Ironically, the whole issue could have been easily settled by offering him a sandwich instead of using him as a convenient prop for alpha male showmanship.

Such opportunistic acts of violence are often carried out under an admirable premise to camouflage their true intent. As such, war is yet another example of this same impulse. Yet no matter how we choose to rationalize our domination of others, the outcome is always the same in that it requires someone to lose for the sake of our victory.

Taming the Savages

This "man on a mission" metaphor is widely applicable to many kinds of activity beyond killing to prove one's dominance. In fact, history offers us many examples wherein men who have set out on a journey of alpha conquest in various forms.

For example, our world's current configuration of nations and their governments is largely the result of white European men setting out to steal the land and resources of indigenous tribes. Ironically, they used the same alibi as many a deranged serial killer as they set out on these voyages of plunder by claiming to work for God as they raped, pillaged and slaughtered their way from one continent to the next and often left their hosts enslaved, starving or living in squalor.

Others on a mission to save the world on behalf of God included the Catholic Church missionaries who prepared the minds of indigenous tribes for their conquest by defeating their "savage" culture and values. As with police officers, we would hope that most men of religion are working for the greater good of society. Unfortunately, it was no one's God that led these native populations into cultural holding pens but a stampede of opportunistic white men who saw themselves as superior. Nor was this an isolated incident. Instead, the same program of mental conditioning was implemented in many cultures worldwide.

And naturally, thanks to the winning combination of God and guns, they succeeded in exercising their right to take as they wanted.

As for the missionaries, they practiced a kind of mental warfare that taught native people to fear an invisible sky God who would punish them for disobeying their white European overlords. Ultimately, using these conquest tactics, indigenous tribes were taught to disavow their traditions, spiritual practices, and to surrender much of their land.

This kind of bloodless mental warfare is now our primary means to conquer nations. Today, invading a country is more a mental coup that involves the Trojan Horse approach of disguising defeat as victory for the host culture. But upon closer inspection of that gift horse, we may not see any remarkable transformation in the quality of life but rather a river of wealth flowing back towards those making big promises.

...

And finally, the most common mission of conquest among men is the one that has them killing wild animals to prove their dominance over nature and those predators that threaten their existence.

Armed with guns and guides, they enter jungles and grasslands to kill lions, tigers, elephants and whatever animal can kill them with ease by natural design. In this way, they hope to "exorcise" their feelings of vulnerability within the true hierarchy of natural dominance wherein humans are nearest the bottom — naked, scared, and defenseless.

Recognizing their lowly status as more prey than predator, men lash out in defiance by killing animals far above their competitive class if they were to encounter those animals without having rifles and jeeps within easy reach.

The result is a global tragedy for all Earthly species as these men set out on a mission to claim for themselves a "trophy kill" in any form.

The greater part of this tragedy involves men measuring themselves by seeking to kill <u>the largest males</u> of a species in what is a reckless act of murderous stupidity. After all, if nature has designed a world where the largest and strongest are favored to mate, then killing the large and strong of a species guarantees that only the small and weak will remain to breed. How many hunters have given this outcome any thought in aiming their shiny new rifles at a big buck? Surely not enough.

Today, we proudly continue to invade the territories of other species to thoughtlessly weaken their gene pools in a selfish quest to prove our "winning" status, thereby ridding our world of its largest males, but then politely leaving its females and their young to go in peace.

In light of this, we can understand why a greedy, self-serving species such as ours, one dominated by its own skilled hunters, is unlikely to survive in the future lest we make some critical changes to our survival strategy. A respect for life itself would be a good start.

Then, although we cannot bring John Lennon back, perhaps we can at least save a few species currently targeted for extinction by jeeps full of blood-lusting men on a mission to prove themselves a winner.

CHAPTER 14
Faking It

Ivan Rebroff was a beloved Russian singer who captured the hearts of many an audience with his astonishing vocal range, lavish costumes and charismatic onstage presence. As a tireless performer, he recorded and toured relentlessly until his death in 2008. And all throughout his long career, he was known as a big-hearted Cossack who projected the celebrated traits of manhood through a larger-than-life stage persona. But what many didn't know was that Ivan was faking it.

In reality, what his adoring fans discovered only after his death was that Ivan was actually a German born Berliner named Hans. And even though no one can fake a spectacular singing voice such as his, it also came as a further shock that this Russian icon of rugged masculinity was secretly gay.

Fortunately, our social attitudes have evolved sufficiently over the decades that the sexual orientation of others should not interfere with our ability to admire their talent. But Hans rose to fame during a time of intolerance, thus requiring him to hide his sexual orientation from those clinging to a social order defined by strict gender stereotypes. Had they known, some might even have refused to buy his records and concert tickets in protest. And so Hans did as many do to protect their careers and status. But his pretending to be a Russian singer named *Ivan* was clearly an attempt to deceive the public into believing he was more than just a German singer of Russian folk songs.

Yet deception is a common aspect of the entertainment field, as the former fans of 1990's pop duo, Milli Vanilli, also found out. Here was another case of musical false identity wherein the industry had fans buying records they believed were sung by the band's two statuesque frontmen. But just as they were reaching the pinnacle of success, their lip-synced performance at the Grammy Awards triggered a backlash that exposed them as fakes for pretending to sing on songs that other more talented vocalists had recorded. Young and eager for fame, they chose to lie their way to the top because the potential rewards were so great. And for many attention seekers, that's an easy decision to make.

Never known for its brutal honesty, the entertainment industry has always thrived on illusions and trickery, which often begins by having us believe in the public image of its star performers. In this way, it has proven that if they can't fool all of the people all of the time, then at least they can fool enough of us to grow incredibly rich. And this holds true for any aspect of life where the promise of future rewards may require an adjustment to the accuracy of our truth-telling, or the image of ourselves that we present to the public.

...

A common method of faking our way to the top is to pretend that we hold the same values as others by reflecting them in our appearance or behavior. In other words, if we want to trick people into accepting us, then we merely have to present ourselves as a stereotype of what they value most in people or in society. And if we then talk loudly and with boastful authority, they might even make us their mayor.

As a typical example, in the southern USA, many men drive pickup trucks out of necessity and wear cowboy hats to guard against sunburn. Proud of their country, some also display their nation's flag on vehicles — perhaps as a bumper sticker. While those who truly live a rugged lifestyle are often sincere in presenting themselves this way, others may adopt their mannerisms and clothing styles as a stereotypical indicator of hard-living, patriotic manhood; a form of *virtue-signaling* to win the trust of those who are genuine. In reality, their social identity is just a store-bought illusion reinforced by cowboy folklore and TV ads that try to sell us pickup trucks and other masculine identity products.

As a result, we cannot always tell a real "cowboy" from someone who is faking it. Subsequently, whenever US politicians are campaigning in cattle country, we may also see them donning cowboy hats or driving a rented pickup truck in displaying their borrowed virtues to potential voters. And this seems to work well enough to fool some of the people some of the time, but luckily, it does not fool all of them.

Yet *faking it* obviously works well enough that it has even put many an imposter in charge of our nations. It is therefore no surprise why so many of us engage in the same kind of public theatre to trick others into hiring, admiring or even marrying us. And while faking it at this level is often relatively harmless, it can become a genuine threat to our nations when political impostors and predatory businessmen seek to control our government to guide us in a direction that best serves their own selfish interests.

For this reason, let us give some thought to this plague of human dishonesty so that we might better protect our world against the worst of these fraudsters on the frontlines of human fakery.

Are You For Real?

Lying is to politics what a steering wheel is to a car — with just a few well-executed turns, voters can be moved in almost any direction. And although lying is not a political act, its prevalence in politics represents a serious threat to voters who may no longer know who or what they are voting for, let alone who they can trust. And voter confusion, as we know, is the ally of every crooked politician. But lying to the public can sometimes also backfire in very humiliating ways.

Such was the case for Lindsay Graham, a Republican senator from South Carolina, USA, who fought to keep Donald Trump from being the presidential candidate for his party in 2016. Speaking candidly for a TV interview, he denounced Trump as: "a race-baiting, xenophobic, religious bigot…[who is] undercutting everything we stand for…" and then finished off by saying: "Tell Donald Trump to go to hell."

Graham's public denouncing of Trump was an admirable departure from the typical fare of politics where representatives must toe the line to avoid offending voters, especially on their own side of the aisle.

But what no one expected was that Graham would flip on his moral axis after Trump's election to become his staunchest supporter, despite having denounced him as an enemy of the people.

In regard to Mr. Trump, we may never understand why voters put a man with massive debts and a history of bankruptcies in charge of the world's largest economy. But what we do know with certainty is that Mr. Graham was faking it either before or after Trump was elected.

Like the entertainment industry, politics is a profession known for its dishonesty. As such, Senator Graham's public shaming was a matter of bad luck in having his honest opinion posted on the internet for all to see. But this is not about him or the broken US political system. Instead, such incidents prove that all political systems are threatened by those who treat governing as a contest for personal gain or glory. If this were not the case, Graham would have been expected to maintain his original opinion about Trump rather than become his advocate.

As expected, conspiracy theories were offered as to what Trump had on Graham to break his resolve. But like most US politicians, he was probably terrified of being lynched by Trump supporters like those who stormed the nation's capitol, attacked Senator Nancy Pelosi's husband in their home, or plotted to abduct Michigan's female liberal governor. Yet no matter Graham's reasoning, we can assume his main goal was to stay in power, which he did by turning the steering wheel of his moral convictions in a direction that best ensured not having to turn his keys over in the next election. Unfortunately, this also caused his political integrity to swerve into the ditch. And whatever good he may still hope to do for his country, this one episode of public deceit may well overshadow all of his future contributions as a leader.

But what about the voting public? While his political career escaped the wrath of Trump supporters, did a downgrading of Graham's values actually serve the greater good? Might his continued public resistance to Trump's presidency have created a healthy counterbalance in those troubling times that ensued? Sadly, we will never know that answer.

On the other hand, his deceptive behavior did serve the greater good by reminding us that political fakery inhibits social progress. After all, how do we know if a politician is lying if they keep changing their values for each audience they hope to seduce? Consider, for instance, that politicians may offer speeches of hope and sweeping change to the needy while dispensing messages of selfish entitlement to the monied classes. As such, do we ever really know whose side any politician is on besides their own? *WikiLeaks* documents suggest that we don't.

But perhaps most troubling about political deception is that many voters seem not to even care that their leaders are lying, as long as it's being done for their side to win. However, as many soon realize, there is only one side in politics and the voting public is not on it.

To be fair, there are some genuinely competent and honest people in positions of political power, yet they are too few in number. However, the examples of political fakery cited here are not meant to condemn any one individual any more than studying weather patterns is meant to condemn the weather. Instead, they are offered as empirical data in support of the assertion that where at least one politician has been caught lying, there may be more.

...

During the process of becoming an adult, it becomes apparent to all of us that our world is full of dubious characters. This is especially true in the world of politics where the promise of ultimate power seems worth the risk for any ambitious social climber to lie their way to the summit. As such, many of us are duped into voting for dishonest politicians. And since no democratic nation is a *direct* democracy that would allow us to vote for social initiatives rather than these charismatic con artists, we often pay a high price for putting our collective trust in only one person to decide our future fate.

Based on the alpha male template of the wild, this "all for me — none for you" governing style has caused many problems for ordinary citizens throughout our history. Yet they are seemingly never enough for inspire our leaders to change their systems to better protect us from their selfish ambitions. Instead, it appears that their systems have been purposely designed to protect our leaders from the rest of us.

As a result, our mental journey from hope to disappointment is often a short one as we soon discover that the promising new politician that we voted in is as selfish as the one we voted out. And if particularly dishonest, they will serve their own interests rather than deliver on the promises they made to us. In the meantime, they may try to distract us from our demands by engaging in mock battles against imaginary foes as our bridges, schools and incomes collapse from chronic neglect.

This purposeful wasting of time may result from a politician's fear of losing their job for making an unpopular decision. As such, they may prefer to grandstand rather than legislate; appearing to look busy while actually doing nothing for constituents. This popular form of "faking it" even has some politicians acting as full-time disinformation agents to tarnish the reputation of opposing party members. And where there are calls for decency or morality, we can be sure that the loudest of those making accusations are the most guilty. A quick glance would give us a long list of names of politicians who are wasting our time and money by "projecting" their own shadowy defects upon an opponent, a psychological ploy identified by Carl Jung decades ago. As such, they are better at finding their own faults when they appear in others.

Cumulatively, this lax attitude toward governing has turned politics into a kind of farcical theatrical performance wherein our promising future is just a prop used to trick voters into surrendering our money and power to the self-serving actors onstage. And once they take off their costumes at the end of each performance, we as the audience are left a little weaker and poorer for having paid the price of admission.

Seen in this light, it is little wonder why many people refuse to vote, given that they expect nothing but disappointment in exercising their only show of power in a democracy. — a single, largely useless vote.

And so, whether it is a local politician heading out on the campaign trail in his rented cowboy boots or a larcenous legislator accusing his rivals of corruption, the end result is that our societies cannot make it by faking it when fakery is the main reason for most of our problems.

What we need instead of lying politicians pretending to be who we want them to be are genuine leaders who are what we need them to be. As such, our best defense as citizens is to create a more trustworthy system of governing that protects our collective interests against those of any impostor on a selfish quest for power. Only then can we hope to win future elections that are truly by and for the people. Luckily, the last chapter introduces such an open and honest way forward.

Looking the Other Way

The prevalence of political fakery has left many of us feeling frustrated as to the future fate of our societies. This is made worse by watching gullible people being duped into voting for unscrupulous villains who prey upon their trust. But are they really all that gullible — or are they perhaps also just faking it?

This brings up another interesting topic to ponder whenever we feel anger or pity for those being misled. Instead, what we may find upon closer inspection is that voters use politics as a venue for proving their own dominance, just as many political leaders do.

Like racism, politics is also a form of social competition wherein one need not be a winner to act like one. All it takes is to believe that we are on the winning side — that ours is the political party that's best.

We can confirm this notion whenever voters come to the defense of a politician who is caught lying, cheating or otherwise proving to be a poor leadership candidate. Ordinarily, we would expect those voters to admit they made a mistake by putting their trust in the wrong person, then remedy it by voting for a better qualified candidate, regardless of their party affiliation. But instead, it seems that many voters remain undeterred in wanting to elect even the most unsuitable of candidates as long as they're not working for the opposing side. As such, honesty or facts often have little bearing on the outcome of elections, whereas voter denial plays a far more significant role. In short, winning in the field of politics often depends on which side is better at faking it.

This begs the obvious question: what kind of society are we hoping to create by voting for the wrong leaders? After all, life is challenging enough in knowing who to trust. But if someone is a proven liar, then why support them in their rise to power? It makes no sense.

Any thoughtful person who cares about their future will feel greatly disturbed in witnessing this mental mutiny against reality by their fellow citizens. It almost seems as though some people vote for the worst candidate just to lash out at *the system* — a form of protest that often leaves their future in worse hands as dozens of glory-seeking sociopaths come out of the woodwork to announce their candidacy. As for making actual progress, that's not why they are running.

...

A useful way to understand what is happening in the minds of many voters is to think of them as sports fans watching their favorite team play. As such, it doesn't really matter who is playing against them or how many infractions their team incurs in trying to win because they feel a sense of team loyalty that often transcends reason itself.

This is a further expression of our human need to belong to a group — much like our tribal ancestors did. Through such group affiliations, we feel a sense of identity and purpose in life. In other words, forming tribes and uniting against a common enemy are a natural part of our human behavior — which is why it is a global phenomenon expressed most often through politics, religion, class warfare and sport.

In addition, sports fans often live vicariously through their favorite teams and players. Likewise, if a political candidate wins, those who had supported him also feel like winners. And if their candidate loses, they also feel a sense of loss in being forced to wait for another election season to start. As such, many people make the best of this opportunity to celebrate and elevate themselves by living out their lives through their favorite players on the political field.

In support of this metaphor, our government may also treat us like spectators to a sporting event wherein they alone plot the path of our nation's future. Forced to sit on the sidelines of the political process, we watch from afar as that future unfolds. Nor are we involved in making any decisions beyond selecting a team to cheer for while they choose the strategies that promise to lead us to victory.

In other words, we can yell all we want from the sidelines, but no one is obligated to listen to our ideas, regardless of their merit.

As further proof of our political insignificance, the media also treats elections more like a spectacle; a battle for the championship between political gladiators rather than an important function in determining our future and that of our nation. In place of facts and details, we are offered the equivalent of a half-time show scheduled to repeat on an endless cycle, like any other form of sports entertainment.

The net result is a world wherein petty insults among political rivals capture our attention far more than the need to fill the potholes on our roads or the cracks in our weak environmental laws. And maybe that's why many leaders also take part in this drama — to avoid leading.

Yet the strongest evidence that politics is being used as a venue for underperforming status-seekers are the millions of men sitting at their computers each day to belittle those on the opposing team. Borrowing from a lexicon of peer-approved putdowns that include "Libtard" and "Snowflake," one may get the impression that this has less to do with politics than underdogs posturing for dominance.

And beneath it all, this pretense of supremacy is supported by the same time-honored principle that has long been tearing us apart in our homes and everywhere else — ***if I believe it, then it must be right.***

Given this competitive gaming perspective on politics, we can then understand why those denouncing others as "Sheeple" are then forced to look the other way if one of their own political players breaks a rule that leaves the entire team open to defeat in the next election.

From this perspective, establishing social group dominance appears to be what inspires many to vote. Beyond that, it a night on the town to see our favorite political heavyweight punch out his opponent.

The Endless War for Peace

Beyond the entertainment spectacle that politics offers to voters, it also represents a gateway to power for aspiring male glory-seekers. As such, to grow his personal empire, a newly-seated ruler must keep those below him from rising up to challenge his dominance.

Here as well, his ambition to lead is just a natural extension of the same unconscious Bio-Psychological urge that drives male animals in the wild to fight for dominant mating status. In other words, this kind of behavior is to be expected among men in any group setting, whether a small town community or a nation. Once we view our political power struggles from this perspective, their solution becomes more clear.

Subsequently, we must expect that beneath the actions of almost any male ruler is a want for power over others. What keeps most of us from challenging his rule, beyond police brutality and military might, is our own lack of obsession with acquiring power or an unwillingness to live a life of faking it — as most political leaders are forced to do.

In that regard, the kind of fakery most prevalent among leaders is the attempt to disguise their grasping for power as a form of service to the public. Yet the most destructive form of fakery is when a ruler seeks to engage us in a war to grow his personal empire. In doing so, he must defeat a foreign leader and those defending him by making us believe that going to war on his behalf is in our own best interests.

In democratic nations, leaders must deny such selfish ambitions in public, whereas fascist dictatorships have no need for such modesty. Subsequently, if an elected leader wants to send the teenaged sons of voting mothers to fight in his war for dominance, he must disguise his intentions by having us believe we are fighting for "freedom" or some other euphemism for chivalrous goodwill. In this way, leaders are able to distract us from talking about what role their own personal lust for power is playing in creating these armed military conflicts.

Given that our tribal leaders have engaged in wars for dominance since the dawning of human history, most nations now have weapons manufacturing facilities to cater to their war-making needs. Like a hardware store for selling the tools of mass murder, here one can buy anything from nuclear missiles and fighter jets to bullets and body bags, as long as the public can be tricked into paying for it all. And like the automobile and fashion industries, they also have trade shows with loud music and booming voices to sell us their latest kill ware.

Salesmanship in the weapons industry is critical. After all, just as women are being sold fashions by exciting them about the prospect of winning a man's attention — or losing it to another women — so are the men leading our countries being sold weapons by exciting them about their prospects of gaining future power or losing it to some rival nation. And like any commercial enterprise, the arms industry has its salespeople hustling to sell its latest generation of mass-murdering solutions to the craftsmen of war in any nation willing to buy.

And so, even when we die by the thousands, war is the best of times for those who make weapons; a time of celebration as governments spend billions to ensure that good prevails over evil, or however they choose to pitch death and total destruction to us. And if things don't turn out as planned, a future war can always solve the problem. In the meantime, those upon whom our tax money rains like a tropical storm don't want these good times to end — nor their stock prices to fall. As such, peace is the enemy of those who prosper from war. After all, one cannot sell guns to those who refuse to shoot them.

Ultimately, making war is rarely the choice of the people but rather something forced upon them by their rulers and industrial profiteers. Yet it is always the people who must pay the price in these glorified acts of mass murder with their awesome array of costly killing toys.

In Iraq, for example, it was reported that 500,000 innocent civilians were killed for getting in the way of the USA's hostile takeover of that nation. Moreover, their homes, plumbing and electrical systems were also destroyed despite being mere spectators in a war between two rival males and their oil industries. Instead, their deaths were but "the cost of doing business" to those on a never-ending quest for more.

Thirty years on, the USA's invasion of Iraq was a costly genocide that brought no improvement to anyone's quality of life — including that of the two disgraced leaders and the soldiers who fought there. On the other hand, it created a decades long revenue stream for the industries that catered to that war, just as the armed conflicts of today continue to create new revenue streams for them.

For this reason, whenever the USA, Israel or Russia fires a missile, we can be sure that whoever sold it to them is also making a killing.

...

Ultimately, war has never led any society to greater freedom or peace because its sole purpose is to transfer power from one man to another. As such, our forced subjugation under any system of social control does not change the urge of leaders to grow or abuse their power. Nor will any man seeking ultimate power want to end the selling of weapons or the making of war, lest we find some alternative means to negotiate the sharing of land and power upon this planet.

Yet there are exceptions. After having fought in many wars, one of the more qualified voices to rally against the war-for-profit addiction of our nations was former **US Marine Corps Major General, Smedley Darlington Butler**, who wrote the book, *War is a Racket*.

As a double Medal of Honor recipient, his years of military service proved to him that making war was a business strategy to keep a few wealthy men profiting from genocide. Such profiteering also offers an incentive to keep human warfare continuing in perpetuity as a means to enrich everyone from bomb makers and money lenders to the stock brokers selling shares as war industry stocks start to surge.

In this light, we also cannot ignore the profits made by industrialists in Germany during World War II as they outfitted soldiers for combat, or supplied concentration camps with everything from barbed wire and prison uniforms to shower heads and canisters of gas. Clearly, even on the losing side, the killing business was booming.

And so we are presented with a dilemma: shall we continue to pay for these costly killing sprees to avoid bankrupting the war-catering industries of our nation? Or might the threat of peace force them to look elsewhere for new money-making opportunities?

But having tasted ultimate killing power, we also cannot expect our leaders to go back to street level fisticuffs for their competitive thrills.

The ability to bomb one's rivals into submission is simply too tempting for those to whom winning by any means is all that matters.

And yet, the claiming of dominance at gun point has always been an act of fakery of the most transparent kind. After all, it is the demand of nature that a legitimate male contender engage in direct combat to prove his dominance, whereas anything less is cheating. Yet those on a quest for glory in politics are not often known for their scruples but rather a willingness to cheat their way to the top.

And so it is that we arrive again and again at the same violent end, as young men lay dead while our governments spend vast amounts of taxpayer money on something that does not add to the quality of life of those on either side of a conflict.. Nor can any amount of political propaganda obscure the collateral damage being done to our humanity as we leave our need for caring and community in a pile of smoldering rubble, along with our intellectuals and peacemakers.

And to obscure our selfish intent in making war, we also treat it as an entertaining form of competitive sport wherein we sit as spectators on the sidelines watching history repeat itself under the command of men driven to prove their genetic dominance through genocide.

On that note, let us quote famed musician and social critic for the creative thinking-class, Frank Zappa, who once opined that "politics is the entertainment division of the military-industrial complex."

Unfortunately, we are often too busy fighting our way to the summit of economic success to consider such offerings of wisdom by the wise. For that reason, little has improved since Frank offered us this quote beyond the technical ability of leaders to kill us with even greater ease. In fact, many of us are now so immersed in a virtual world of handheld phones that we give little thought to the real one that surrounds us.

But we should be paying attention because if we happen to look up one day to see a UFO hovering overhead, like those that *Steve Barone* films daily from his home in Nevada, USA, then we may encounter the most flagrant form of political fakery wherein those who profit from the making of war and weaponry try to convince us that what we saw was just a figment of our imagination — no such technology exists.

And once we are convinced that our eyes no longer see what they see nor our ears hear what they hear, then these men can return to working in peace to integrate UFO propulsion systems into their secret arsenal of world-dominating war machines. And if we one day happen to look up and see a fleet of those machines hovering overhead, it will already be too late to do anything about it; our world will thereafter remain in the guiding hands of its best killers.

And this leads us to our final thought on the matter of fakery, which is that UFOs are real — it is people who often prove to be fake.

CHAPTER 15
Fighting for Attention

Sigmund Freud was a neurologist widely recognized as the founder of modern psychoanalysis — which contends that problematic human behavior can be treated by a discourse between a troubled patient and an experienced analyst of such behavior. And although he may have ventured down many a theoretical path, including the promotion of cocaine to treat depression, his lifetime of work in the field has often been dismissively stereotyped as being "all about sex."

In recognition of this common habit of generalizing to simplify the complex, let us retrace some of the logical steps in our understanding of Bio-Psychology to avoid making the same assertions that it is also just "all about sex."

As you will recall, we began with an explanation as to why males compete for dominance in general — which is admittedly *all about sex*. Yet this is actually due to nature's purposeful agenda of having only the very best candidates of any species in terms of size, strength, mobility, etc., to pass their genes on to future generations for the greater good of that species. And so, from an inherently selfish act based on personal pleasure-seeking (the orgasm) comes an altruistic, shared reward, thus proving once again nature's genius as the guardian of life.

However, even if a man doesn't have what it takes to be a winner in the contest for genetic dominance, he nonetheless feels the same urge to compete and engage in sex with females. And here we begin to see the origin of many social problems as nature inwardly compels all men to compete for social status, regardless of their suitability for combat.

This urge to win is part of our Bio-Psychology, which also controls various other behaviors to ensure our survival and ability to reproduce for years to come — by seeking pleasure through sex, naturally.

As such, men's perpetual drive to compete for dominance is a critical factor in understanding our individual and collective behavior within the context of society, including the rise and fall of social cultures and also their purposeful structuring, both economically and politically.

Although remaining competitively violent as a species, we now tend to live within "monetary ecosystems" defined by the trading of *symbolic* energy. Herein we no longer judge dominance by physical signs of a man's genetic supremacy but by the symbolic power he has amassed in monetary form. Subsequently, this redefined contest for judging alpha status among men has long undermined nature's own system to ensure our species' long-term biological health as we become more and more focussed on the health of our bank accounts instead.

...

Nature's long-term life strategies aside, most of us now live in highly complex, money-driven societies while our primitive animal biology continues to incite us to compete for dominance. This ongoing drive for alpha status also explains why we find ourselves as part of various classes within the dominance hierarchy of any society, whose levels are determined by one's supremacy as an economic competitor. Here, our topmost male combatants are favored above all others, receiving the best treatment that a surplus of symbolic power can buy, including unlimited access to a wide variety of physically attractive females and luxury hotel suites to accommodate a life of discreet polygamy.

Given that this urge to compete for status is meant to affect all men, we can then also understand why these battles for dominance occur at every level of the social pyramid relative to one's economic means. In other words, if a young man in a poor neighborhood wants to compete for the attention of the pretty girl next door, he must still prove himself a dominant suitor over the other men clamoring for her sexual favor.

And this forces him to find some way to stand out from that crowd of ambitious male suitors by appearing superior to all of them.

Admittedly, these are not groundbreaking insights to anyone with a rudimentary understanding of human behavior. Yet by retracing our ancient biological footsteps into modern times, we can get a clearer understanding of how we arrived at this current juncture. Moreover, it forces us to acknowledge an obvious connection between alpha male posturing and the more troublesome and socially destructive behaviors exhibited by men in their efforts to stand out and win attention — for the purpose of having sex with females of one's choosing, of course.

Although these battles for social attention take many forms, they have only two motives, namely to gain female sexual favor or to present ourselves as someone "special" in keeping with nature's demand to seek a position of alpha dominance. This is why societies are full of boastful men aspiring to greater power through which to dominate others.

This desire to stand out has inspired many kinds of predictable social behavior, including merchants selling us lifestyle products or strategies to assist our quest for attention. Subsequently, we give vast amounts of money to people who promise us a winning advantage — even if only a fake one, such as buying a counterfeit gold watch to appear wealthy.

Long trained by TV ads and movies, we can choose from a long list of status-based products or services to display our dominance, whether by driving a luxury sports car to some exclusive country club, or dining in various restaurants that are too expensive for the poor to afford.

Moreover, we also employ mentors to help us attain a higher status within society by drawing more attention to ourselves. They include university professors or just about anyone laying claim to a formula for our attaining future success, be it monetary, sexual or otherwise.

Ironically, what is ultimately being sold is the *the promise of joy* by associating it with our rise in power. This is a familiar ploy from TV advertising and explains why the models and actors in commercials are always smiling — to trick us into believing they're happy. The message of materialist advertising is clear: all we need to be happy is whatever is being sold. And if we don't succeed at buying our happiness on the first attempt, then we must simply keep on buying until we do.

Whether such promises of future unbridled joy ever come to fruition is something we must each discover for ourselves. In the meantime, we can expect that every merchant of hope will take our money because that's how we prove a person's value to society in a money-ecosystem — we pay them. Yet no matter what level of success we may ultimately attain, our journey must always begin with the seeking of attention. As such, if we hope to ever make a grand entrance into the winner's circle, we must first gain the attention of those who own the circle.

…

Suppressing our disruptive human urge to stand out are those who feel a sense of competitive envy and fear in being left behind, or who want to keep the peace, whether for altruistic or just selfish reasons. Yet the seeking of attention is a natural and necessary phenomenon, as evident by the squeaking of newborn puppies crying for their mother's milk or loving touch. Moreover, our need for attention never ends due to its link to our survival and reproduction. Subsequently, we are each forced to make sufficient noise within society to ensure that our many needs are being met, whatever we interpret them to be.

Complications arise, however, in having to seek attention within a monetary ecosystem. Here, our cries for more must also reach the ears of employers who can pay us to work for them. And once we can afford to survive, we are free to spend our remaining money however we wish — which often finds us investing it in ways to gain more attention.

While such behavior may be obvious to many, it can help us to retrace our own mental footsteps just in case we leave anything behind in our haste to get ahead, including our happiness. In fact, many of us have no actual plan to secure our future emotional well-being. Instead, we may simply hope that our happiness will result from having regular sex and a steady income.

In reality, a genuine quest for joy requires shifting our attention inward to identify what makes us feel truly happy. Unless we embark on such an inner journey, we may find ourselves lost at sea in terms of our sense of fulfillment; unsure of where to steer the drifting ship of our aimless life. Nor can money save us in this spiritual predicament.

Continuing with this shipping analogy, our life can begin to founder in following our unconscious competitive urges and the advice of those equally out of touch with their own inner being. As a result, we may find ourselves acting like a person we no longer recognize. Worse still, we may start to act like an automated machine on an endless quest for attention for lack of a genuine goal in life. As such, we may live in a kind of lifelong trance, answering nature's unconscious call to compete for attention without any kind of meaningful destination in sight.

Imagine, for example, the plight of those famous for being the child of someone rich and famous rather than their own unique gifts. Once accustomed to getting public attention, their primary goal may be to stay in the spotlight while using their narcissism as a protective shield to ward off the unsettling feeling of being an impostor.

Here again, I invite anyone interested in exploring these deeper life issues to read my book, *Clearing a Path to Joy*, which is full of practical advice on navigating this shared human quest. In the meantime, let's see what society has prepared for its top-ranking attention seekers.

The American Dream

The United States is often referred to as "the greatest country in the world" by those who live there. However, as with most proud patriots, it is unlikely that they have undertaken a survey to compare the quality of life in other countries. Instead, such boastful claims reflect more an attitude of supremacy in a nation wherein competition has become its primary focus, often to the detriment of various other priorities.

In promoting itself as "the best," the USA also attracts the attention of less fortunate people from other nations who one day hope to live the "American Dream" as a proud citizen of that country.

But what is *the American Dream* really about? After all, the people of other countries also live in houses or apartments; sleep in beds; wear clean clothes; eat cooked food, and may even enjoy sex far more due to a less conflicted attitude about morality and pleasure. In addition, they may have "free" healthcare and less violence. So what's the attraction?

In reality, the USA is a nation deeply divided along economic and ideological lines, with many political leaders fighting to ensure that the *American Dream* remains inaccessible to all but the wealthy by making life ever more costly for the poor. As such, this hopeful dream is more an illusion than a real opportunity for a happier life. As George Carlin, the beloved comedian and social satirist once said, "…they call it the American Dream because you have to be asleep to believe in it." And although at least one poor migrant field worker went on to become a famous astronaut, the odds of winning here are like playing the lottery. As such, reality quickly dispels any notion that life is somehow easier for those living in the USA. This is obviously not the case, otherwise the entire country would be populated by successful, happy people.

As for the dream itself, what we find upon closer inspection is that it has less to do with achieving a comfortable life than "making it big" as a rich or famous seeker of attention. In that regard, the USA truly excels by offering a vast marketplace for acquiring unlimited personal wealth, power and news media exposure. In other words, it offers more opportunities for winners to take it all than nations more focussed on serving the greater good. As such, those who reach the pinnacle of power often have no ideological qualms with the USA's "every man for himself" attitude once they have claimed a lion's share for themselves.

And wherever winners are being declared, we find many more losers being cast aside with nothing to show for their efforts. As such, in any closed monetary ecosystem where we are forced to work for greedy men who demand ever more from us as proof of their dominance, we also find the American Dream turning into a nightmare for those who are struggling to survive the selfish attitude of others.

…

Given our common quest for attention to serve our various needs, it is inevitable that we will encounter those who succeed by promising us greater success. Beyond the various attention-seeking accessories that retailers sell to help us stand out in a crowd, we are also offered what appear to be time-honored and legitimate paths to attaining the kind of status and public recognition that our Bio-Psychology craves.

But let us step back momentarily to make two critical observations about human society and the economy of our nations.

First, if we all drove Ferraris and wore Rolex watches, they would be so common as to make them ordinary and unappealing. Naturally, this would be a disaster for those who buy them to win attention and those who sell them to make their fortunes. Subsequently, showy items such as these are purposely priced out of reach to all but the most wealthy to maintain their elevated status as consumer products.

Secondly, the people who seem to make the most money are those who promise to help everyone else make more money. In other words, our want for more enriches those who promise us more. Some notable examples include Charles Ponzi and cryptocurrency merchants.

Others promising to enrich us are the brokers and consultants of the famed *Wall Street* who likewise make their fortunes by offering to help us make ours. And just as our hope of winning the lottery can keep us buying tickets despite decades of losing, so does the hope of striking it rich keep us buying stocks to enrich investment firms.

Let us then return our focus back to this book's theme, which is the competition among men for dominance and how this urge to win is causing all of us to lose. Subsequently, in a highly competitive culture such as the United States, those getting rich from selling promises also don't want to refund anyone's money — be it a politician raising funds from hopeful voters or a stock broker selling mortgage derivatives to American dreamers. We can therefore expect the economic system to be rigged in ways that protect its big winners from losing. This leads to a form of systemic corruption wherein our leaders endorse lying as a business model while punishing whistleblowers for telling the truth.

This was confirmed in a 2019 documentary, *Inside Lehman Brothers*, which recounts how top executives and brokers lost their jobs for their questioning of fraudulent practices by the company or reporting them to largely disinterested government regulators. And with everyone in power looking out only for themselves, no one was looking out for the ordinary citizens who would ultimately be left to live in tents. After all, what use are they to anyone on a quest for power?

It is undeniable that nations must create more losers than winners to protect its privileged few. And if everyone around us drove a Ferrari or wore a Rolex watch, then some other symbolic standard would need to be invented by which men could measure their dominance.

Yet the citizens of most countries, including the USA, rarely know to what extent the dice are loaded against them because we tend to glorify our winners while hiding our losers in the shadows. A quick glance at tabloid media confirms this suspicion — no one cares about the man who ran a second place finish, which also reflects nature's own apathy for the struggles of the underdog. As such, a typical American Dream success story features the accomplishments of a wealthy man of business, but not those around him who have sacrificed their own dreams or family life cohesion to help that man succeed.

But what of the winners? Are men such as Donald Trump happily living the American Dream in commanding their excesses of wealth and female attention? Or is their obsessive want for more leaving them to feel perpetually unfulfilled?

We could ask the same of any past or present economic dominator, be it Mark Zuckerberg, Jeff Bezos, Howard Hughes or the man who inspired the film *Citizen Kane*, William Randolph Hearst — has their own journey felt like the fulfilling of a dream or has it become a kind of living nightmare along the way? Do they feel compelled to keep moving forward based on an inspired vision or just a fear of losing their own privileged status? Few seem interested in talking about this darker aspect of the American Dream — at least while there's still money to be made from selling it to the have-nots and hopeful. But if they were honest with us, we might hear many top combatants in the *Global War for Status* admit to being unhappy and feeling doomed to keep on searching for a meaning to their lives like the rest of us.

Here again, if the media ignores this topic, it leaves those of the hopeful class to assume that the mere possession of wealth can make us happy, a false belief further reinforced by lottery commercials filled with jubilant, jackpot-winning faces celebrating money as the answer.

But money is far from the answer. As a community-oriented species that depends on close contact and a need to trust our surroundings, we are then forced to live in cultures that attack those conditions upon which we rely to feel safe to protect the rights of its privileged few on their greedy quests for glory. Surely, living in fear for our future and in distrust of our leaders is not a life which anyone dreams about.

As demonstrated by the USA, a nation's obsessive focus on winning threatens the very conditions required to maintain a thriving society, including the sharing of resources and a concern for those not getting their share of attention. And if life in modern human societies remains a perpetual battleground for selfish gain, there will be ill consequences for all of us, including increased social isolation and emotional poverty for its rich and famous; a fact alluded to by the word "Rosebud," which gave the film, *Citizen Kane*, its greater social relevance by reminding us to not leave anything behind that can later leave us wanting.

Swiss Accuracy for the Win

The same selfish jostling for power at the upper tiers of the economic pyramid occurs below as men compete for dominance with equal zeal against those within their social class.

As stated earlier, nature plays no favorites, allowing anyone to enter her competition for alpha male glory. And although the purpose of all such male competition is to prove one's genetic supremacy, those at the top of our monetary ecosystems have rigged this contest by putting an admission price on entering. As such, the more money one earns, the more likely one is to attract a receptive mate over someone poor yet perhaps better qualified physically. Whether we favor this reordering of the natural order or not, these are the new rules of our mating game. And unless a woman is independently wealthy, she is likely to succumb to the boastful strutting of various peacocks of inferior plumage who flash at her instead their various indicators of symbolic wealth.

Men's exile from these upper tier contests for social dominance has created a lower income marketplace for selling competitive advantages to those hoping to win attention at their level of society. Here, one can also purchase income-relative goods and services to help one stand out among the competition, from higher priced cars to clothing. As to why many of us play this competitive game of show and tell, it is our hope that we will ultimately win our happiness through playing it; a belief that drives many a man or woman in their daily pursuit of success.

And here is yet another opportunity to mention Sigmund Freud and specifically, his nephew, Edward Bernays, who was hired by American marketers to teach them how to trick consumers into buying more in their pursuit of happiness. Bernays' claim to fame was conning women into becoming nicotine addicts by marketing cigarettes as "torches of freedom" at a time when women were fighting for more independence. How anyone can equate addiction with freedom remains a mystery, yet it proved the effectiveness of moving us as large herds of consumers to thoughtlessly spend our money on foolish things.

Through their social studies, marketers learned to manipulate people into buying products not for their practical sense but for their value as items of competitive display. Furthermore, they realized that we may deny our selfish motives in buying such items due to the stigma of appearing morally corrupt or overly desperate for attention.

For example, a common dilemma among men who wanted to buy expensive watches to boast of their income was shame. Yet marketers anticipated their reluctance to be judged a vain poser by offering them a clever alibi. That is why advertising for luxury watches no longer implies a man's desire to show off his wealth but his want for a zen-like serenity that can only come from owning a quality timepiece claiming "Swiss" accuracy. That such accuracy is not much greater than a discount store wristwatch while costing more than what most people earn in a year only proves that what we are truly paying for is access to greater attention. And yet, whether we are rich or poor, we all recognize the status symbols of our society and why people seek to possess them.

...

Knowing that marketing psychologists are long sought to manipulate us into buying more, we can better appreciate their attempts to lure us into a needy state of mind by way of their television commercials. This experience can be both entertaining and revolting as we uncover the various tricks being used to incite us into paying for various goods and services. Many such selling tricks are explained in my book, *Clearing a Path to Joy*, wherein entire chapters are dedicated to the psychology of selling and the mental manipulation of the masses.

To better understand how this works, let's use the classic example of selling a costly sports car. Here, a loud, booming, masculine voice can be heard proudly boasting of that car being a "LEADER" in its class that "leaves the competition BEHIND." Here, marketers associate the desire for alpha status among men with their products. As such, if an advertiser uses the term *leader*, he is not referring to the car but the driver of that car and his own leadership status in owning that car. This selling approach works because the actual product being sold is status and success rather than just an expensive mode of transportation.

On a related note, this quest for attention may also hinder some men from buying electric cars whose noiseless engines do not command the same kind of auditory attention as a gas-powered vehicle.

Conversely, the prohibitive price tag of such a car will ensure that its driver draws the attention of men and women alike alerted to his being able to afford such an expensive vehicle. In this way, the driver may also find himself attracting various kinds of selfish opportunists hoping to use him as their own vehicle to greater attention and personal gain.

In this light, there is always a downside to fighting for attention as we make ourselves a target for others to either use us as a stepping stone in pursuing their own ambitions, or a rival to be defeated.

In this regard, we can understand some of the pressures that those atop society's economic pyramid must withstand in clinging to their seats of power until eventually defeated by a better man, or their own advancing age. It also offers us a clear view of that struggle when those men hold a place of prominence within the media's daily focus.

Rebranding Failure

Victory is never assured and we all must learn by making mistakes. As such, those who claim to never make mistakes must be prepared for a lifetime of humiliation and disaster.

Unfortunately, in a world run by male attention seekers vying for dominance, the contest rules state that a man must present himself as an infallible image of human perfection so as not to be mistaken for a loser. And this invites a world of trouble not only for vain leaders but also those being lead by men whose fear of losing has them pretending to be far more qualified to lead than they truly are.

Such behavior is familiar to all of us in having watched any man as he struggles against the reality of his failure by putting on a brave face or worse — by blaming someone else.

In reaching for a widely familiar and recent example of such tactics, we find then-president Donald Trump's reacting rather unfavorably to losing the 2020 US presidential election by declaring that the voting machines had been rigged for him to lose. In showing his defiance to the prospect of loss, he also refused to congratulate the winner of that election, Joe Biden, to avoid conceding defeat in public. He then spent the next two years sending his lawyers without any solid evidence of such tampering to make his case. Naturally, he lost there, too.

Since that time, much has come to light about Donald Trump's own behavior as a man of business, including that he cheats both on taxes and in playing golf. And rather telling of his mindset, he made the very same prediction during his first bid to become president by putting the blame on the system in the event that he lost. Like all narcissists, he must constantly blame others to protect his delusion of perfection. As such, by denying reality itself, he offers a prime example of just how far some men will go to present themselves as undefeatable winners.

Admittedly, it is a rare person who does not offer excuses for failing, even if that failure doesn't involve losing a presidential race. As such, we can understand why many of us deny our wrongdoing or pretend that nothing is wrong with our lives to postpone the inevitable pain of admitting our failures. In fact, denial is so fundamental a human trait that even children use it to avoid punishment or humility. As such, we can understand why adults continue using it as a life strategy once the cost of failure rises significantly. But whether it actually improves our lives is highly doubtful.

...

As we come to the end of our exploration of attention-seeking, one of the more entertaining denials of reality occurred during Elon Musk's recent launching of his SpaceX company's rocket, which is part of a new space tourism industry for people with money to burn.

Having earned much attention for his accumulation of wealth from other successful business ventures, Musk's test launch in April 2023 was to be an attention-seeking event to put his company in a dominant position in this new space race between rival billionaires, including Jeff Bezos, the founder of the Amazon online empire.

With all eyes on his rocket and reputation for succeeding via a live internet broadcast, the launch was expected to put Musk's company on firm footing for future flights. However, shortly after it left the ground, the rocket exploded in mid air, thereby threatening to create a public relations crisis by undermining confidence in the company's ambitions to create a viable space tourism industry.

As NASA knows all too well, technical failures are common in the early stages of any space program. In addition, failures of any kind also teach us to do better in our next attempt. However, for reasons we will interpret through the lens of male competitive Bio-Psychology and its demand for dominance posturing, the company's public reaction to its failed rocket launch took a rather unexpected comical turn.

It began with the use of distancing language when the announcer referred to the event as a "rapid unscheduled disassembly," despite its having had the uncanny appearance of a rocket blowing up in midair. Another indicator of defensive posturing came after the ground crew made an audible groan as the rocket exploded, but then immediately erupted with happy applause as though the operation had succeeded. It was almost as if someone among that group had cued them all to act this way — an event that only a whistleblower could confirm.

While everyone was clapping and cheering, a commentator then come on the air saying: "There as you saw, as we promised, an exciting end to the Starship inaugural integrated test flight!"

This was clearly an attempt to put a positive spin on a this negative outcome. But we cannot transform a loss into a win by simply stepping into the winner's circle and demanding a trophy. As such, this unusual and seemingly counterfeit response by company employees may have been far more disappointing to viewers than the failed flight itself.

Great challenges require great risks and we cannot condemn those who have invested their hearts and ingenuity toward succeeding. But the fact that the fear of losing caused this near *cult-like* reframing of reality may have undermined for some their trust in the company. After all, what failure might next be reframed as a success? And so, an honest, humble response would likely have served everyone better.

Again, this has nothing to do with Elon Musk or the work being done by his company and others like it. It is merely presented here to show us the kind of theatrics we can expect in a global war for status wherein winning means everything and failure is not an option.

And so, when loss seems imminent, we can expect most competitors to minimize their failure by pretending not to be disappointed, or even to blame others for it — as is the choice response of many a loser.

And if a leader continues to fail while everyone is watching, then he may become so desperate to divert our attention from his inadequacy that he may even start a war against imaginary foes to distract us from our many troubles at home.

CHAPTER 16
This Means War

Diplomacy is the fine art of concealing our true intentions from others for the sake of appearances. And whereas an armed robber has no such restrictions on revealing his own, the making of war, on the other hand, requires a more tactful approach wherein the robber must shoot the person, steal their money, and then try to convince bystanders that this was all being done for the benefit of the victim.

In reality, the making of war means saying no to all the best that we can bring to the table of our civilized humanity. It is a tragic regression to a primitive state of mind wherein our only goal is to defeat whoever stands in the way of our selfish ambitions. And leading that charge is the instinctual instigator of all such competition, our Bio-Psychology.

The theme of war has been addressed throughout this book, but let us now consider finding a possible cure for its offensive presence in our lives from within our savage origins. As earlier stated, war is often sold to us in an attractive mental packaging to obscure the fact that it is the same old genocidal impulse that has been shadowing our species since its dawning. And no matter what the recruitment posters might claim, there is no honor in killing the so-called "enemy"—it has always been a selfish endeavor that sets one group of humans against another to ultimately prove nothing of value about the winners' way of life, or that any of those involved in that conflict are genetically superior. However, it does make a lot of money for the people in the weapons industry.

As in the past, many men make a career of organized killing, which requires a certain detachment from the valuing of life if one is expected to use all necessary means to defeat one's enemy. At present, nuclear weapons offer the most convenient killing solution by allowing us to destroy entire continents full of "enemies" without leaving our chairs. And given that men are constantly urged to buy better weapons from arms retailers, this also creates a surplus of weaponry among leaders who either believe they can use war to increase their hold on power, or who live in fear of losing it to armed foreign invaders.

Aside from defying nature's law for authentic competition, our new militarized methods for proving our dominance also contaminate our gene pool and that of many other species due to our careless handling of nuclear radiation and deadly chemicals, including nerve gas leaking from canisters dumped into our oceans once our military forces had no further use for this outdated killing technology. As a result, they pose a threat not only to fishermen dragging them up in nets, as happened on the US east coast, but also to sea life and those consuming it.

Ultimately, militarized warfare has turned our human competitions for genetic dominance into a farce now that our bodies have all been contaminated by various industrial poisons and the diseases attributed to them. In short, everyone's blood and organs are compromised.

Subsequently, what our world desperately needs is a cleansing peace. Yet this is all but impossible given our habit of allowing psychopathic men to lead our nations, many of whom favor militarized mass murder as a means to gain new power or cling to what they have. As such, any demand for peace will likely be met by brute force.

Further to this dilemma, as highlighted in chapter four, we must be smart enough to know when we're being stupid. Likewise, anyone who is mentally deranged has no objective point of reference with which to compare their state of mind beyond their own insanity. As such, they see the sane as having lost their minds. This lack of mental objectivity affects all of us to some degree yet is most prevalent among leaders whose competitive narcissism always has them seeing themselves as always in the right while acting with a sense of entitlement upon their selfish impulses without regard for the suffering of others. In addition, the male gender of our species was not born to raise or protect young but to compete against other men for our right to mate. As such, our calls for peace to career warmongers is an exercise in futility given that men such as these are typically natural born killers.

But perhaps the most important consideration, as also stated earlier, is a glory-seeking psychopath's willingness to kill, which gives them a natural mental advantage in conquering those of peaceful mind. We can see this dynamic at play even today in how easily aggressive men can push their way into power among those too timid to resist. And once seated, their mental derangement will set the standard for how all of us are to treat one another, as occurred both in Germany under Adolf Hitler's reign, and in the United States after Donald Trump rose to power. The latter example is a reminder that we have not yet come along as far as we might have hoped in our social evolution. Insiders even spoke of Trump inquiring about limited nuclear strikes to deal with resistance from foreign nations — as though incinerating people and irradiating their lands was as simple a decision to make as the choosing of the right tie for a political rally.

...

Clearly, war is a pointless activity for anyone but the kind of men who want to dominate our world or sell weapons. As for ordinary people, it represents a violent abomination that leaves our lives shattered and our homes destroyed. And yet, as global citizens, we have yet to formally address the true cause of our war-making behavior. As such, we have no solutions in place beyond engaging in a paradoxical *war for peace*.

Meanwhile, we remain in the vice-like grip of our instinctual fear of losing, which makes it a challenge to discuss peace when we lack a basic trust in others. In the meantime, we must continue to reproduce, which requires answering nature's call to compete to prove our genetic superiority, which we do through various venues, including organized sport, financial gamesmanship and militarized mass murder.

There is no denying that the impulse to fight is an inherent part of men's natural design. Moreover, that impulse is intensified by greed, and calls to masculine patriotism by our culture, which are then further agitated if the person competing suffers from mental illness. As such, there seems no end to the armed conflicts that have littered our human landscape since the first group of men raped and plundered their way through a nearby village without regard for its inhabitants. Today, we live in a false state of peace in having been conquered by military and police force and laws that demand our submission. As such, many of us also live in a state of agitation wherein we feel that our lives could be better, yet our leaders won't allow it. Hence, war always beckons.

Fortunately, there are many clever people among us who can show us a way out of our collective decline based on what they have learned about life and the art of living. One of them is Jane Goodall, a world renowned authority on primate behavior. In studying chimpanzees, an animal that shares 98.8% of the same genes as humans, she found that they also engage in many similar social practices — including the use of organized warfare.

But unlike we humans, chimpanzees have no governments through which to enforce moral codes or legal justices to curb their natural behavior, nor do they have media for dispensing political propaganda or calling its most violently ambitious males to war. Instead, they seem to know instinctively when it's time to kill.

Whenever that urge strikes, the alpha males of the troupe set out to conquer a neighboring group of chimpanzees. But instead of attacking all of their able-bodied challengers at once as human soldiers often do, they instead target a single dominant male and commence to beat him to death with rocks, sticks and their bare hands. Once he is dead, this invading army of male apes will return home to rest until they once again feel the urge to kill. Thereafter, they may return multiple times to that neighboring troupe until most or all of its alpha males are dead. In this way, they also achieve a kind of counterfeit peace by leaving no adult males alive to challenge them.

As to why these marauding gangs of male chimpanzees want to kill one another, it is for the same reason that males of most species engage in combat — to win access to females by conquering the males who are guarding them for their own selfish convenience.

Subsequently, when we humans engage in similar behavior, we are acting upon the same instinctive impulse to spread our genetic seed by conquering the territory of rival males. However, we also face a greater challenge than chimpanzees by having political and religious systems that demand a moral basis for our violent behavior. And so we offer them one by pretending to engage in an honorable shedding of blood for the freedom or salvation of those we seek to conquer.

Does this mean that all men are inherently violent beasts? No, that would be a ridiculous assertion because we have so much proof to the contrary. However, what it does suggest is that the natural urge of men to compete for dominance may trigger in some a desire to exploit or even kill other people as the result of a character inclination toward pathological selfishness, or an untreated mental illness.

A further indicator of this mental skew is that ordinary citizens do not want to go to war. Instead, it is glory-seeking leaders who exploit our natural instinct to compete in ways that have us proudly killing one another in this variation of the divide and conquer strategy. Such men are the true instigators of humankind's endless suffering and our bloody demise through war. As such, the primary goal in bringing peace to our world must be to rid ourselves of those kinds of leaders who want to engage in wars. Neither humankind nor nature has any practical use for them given their predictably destructive results.

But lest we forget, many of these men are legitimate sociopaths and psychopaths; people who are masterful manipulators in overpowering their human prey; people practiced in becoming the kind of person we desire them to be in covertly preparing to strike against us. And the more we see ourselves in their public image, the more we feel comfort in knowing that someone of similar mind and values is now leading us toward the promised land of fulfilling our mutual interests.

And then comes the inevitable shock — we are being tricked!

Masterful Madness

Thanks to Jane Goodall and others who have dedicated their lives to the study of wild animal behavior, we now have a valid explanation as to why our leaders might prefer to spend our taxes on weapons rather than to improve society. And as our schools, healthcare programs and social services struggle for lack of adequate funding, it seems that there is always enough money in the budget to fund another killing spree to fulfill the biological mandate of our glorious alpha males — or at least buy them some updated weapons in planning for the future.

Given the destructive influence of male domination upon society, we would expect it to be a topic of serious daily discussion in the media. Instead, it is presented to us more as a form of entertainment through stories of swashbuckling billionaires and champion athletes who help affirm our social priority of competing for economic dominance.

We may even disguise our urge to dominate as part of our spiritual journey by suggesting that *God* wants us to rule the world by killing off those who are "evil" and unruly. Yet the ugly truth is that we are acting like typical animals, which would not be such a problem it not for our easy access to guns, fighter jets and nuclear weapons.

As such, now is the time to reconsider the quality of our leadership and how it affects our chances as global citizens to achieve a genuine and consensual worldwide state of peace in the future.

Yet always standing in our way is the masterful madness of men who know how to manipulate us in groups and see killing not as a problem but as a convenient solution to all of their problems.

Here, the specter of sociopathy and psychopathy enters into play in that such people feel no remorse in acting as they do for lack of a basic concern for others, or because their desire to win has overshadowed it. Returning to the murder of musician, John Lennon, his killer raised a gun at him not thinking about what affect his death would have upon his wife and children. Instead, the only consequence to which he gave any thought was getting his name in every newspaper as the victor over a celebrated dominant male within society. But luckily, he did not have political aspirations to lead us with his psychotic ideology.

But what about a man like Adolf Hitler, what concerns did he show for anything but his own glory-seeking ambitions as he prepared the youth of Germany for their slaughter in an ill-fated attempt to claim ownership of our world?

There were many indicators of his unsuitability as a leader, starting with his book, Mein Kampf, a confession of his darkest urges that later were renounced to create a more agreeable public facade. As for family values, proof of his sociopathic tendencies was seen in his disregard for long-time girlfriend, Eva Braun, who he agreed to marry only because he planned to kill himself the next day. He also poisoned his loyal dog during this time to test the efficacy of his cyanide capsules — fearing he would be tricked into remaining alive to face justice. In short, Hitler could not have been mistaken for someone who was concerned for the well-being of others. And yet, he was portrayed by Nazi propagandists as the bearer of a new standard to *make Germany great again*. What no one realized was that his standard was based on a deranged mind, as is a common dilemma among mental cults whose glory-seeking leaders have also abandoned reality in pursuit of a self-serving delusion.

What would help us most, beyond crazed politicians having to wear identifying bracelets, is to understand how we are being conned into surrendering our power to people undeserving of a leadership role. This topic was considered earlier in presenting the IPSFA Sequence, which offers a means to make it easier to identify the psychological mechanisms involved in manipulating the minds of the masses.

Furthermore, desperation is the perfect political lubricant, as proven by the fact that Hitler came into power at a time of economic hardship when people were willing to try anything to escape their misery. This also made it easier for people to ignore signs that Hitler was not an ideal candidate for leadership because they were too distracted by their suffering and fear of losing Hitler's offer to make them great again.

As such, Hitler's first job was to conquer the citizenry, which he did by lying about his intentions and also killing his detractors. Hence, we find a familiar mental ploy to which the German people fell victim:

- (I) **IDENTITY:** The big, bright and glorious future ahead of us.
- (P) **PROMISE:** To be in a better situation than our present one.
- (S) **SCRIPT:** Elect whoever promises us that future; put him in charge of everything and relinquish our power to him.
- (F) **FEAR:** A future like our present, and traitorous non-believers.
- (A) **APATHY:** Putting too much trust in what we cannot see.

As for inspiring men to kill, Hitler needed only to trigger their urge to win or fear of losing, not unlike the way a woman can trigger a man's sexual interest by exposing her cleavage — it's in men's nature. This he did by convincing Germans that they were part of a "master race" of racially superior humans entitled to rule the world, with Hitler as their leader. In other words, he did as many religious cults do by having its members believe themselves superior to those outside the cult; a tactic made effective by our inborn competitive lust for status.

- (I) **IDENTITY:** The Master Race.
- (P) **PROMISE:** To be a dominant force within the world.
- (S) **SCRIPT:** Engage in a global war for status against all rivals.
- (F) **FEAR:** Losing our winning status and its promise of power.
- (A) **APATHY:** Ignoring that our own genetics are low in quality.

Such mental trickery requires a degree of denial among those being tricked, as evident by Hitler's own lack of pure "Aryan" genetics over which he obsessed in his speeches. It was also not to be spoken of that he was actually Austrian, not German. In short, he was an impostor.

Initially, positive signs of remedial action distracted everyone, while money flowed into massive building projects and the recruiting of boys into the new Hitler youth training program. And then came the big surprise: World War II and an end to a promised future of peaceful prosperity, replaced by a time of misery greater than before. It was the tragic end to Hitler's mental seduction of the hopeful masses, made all the more tragic by his privately denouncing the German people for having failed him. Like a true narcissist, he never took the blame.

The tragedy of our modern times is that we have not learned enough from our violent history to stop repeating it. And so we still find men ready to go to war, whether against a foreign enemy or even people within their own country for having political or ideological differences. And all it takes to rally them into an army of conquest-minded killers is to appeal to every man's inborn selfish impulse to dominate and then make him afraid of losing his status and right to succeed. This explains Hitler's use of the *master race* theme and outside agitators as the enemy, a formula echoed by religious cults declaring themselves "chosen" by God in a non-specific war against *evil*. In this way, any deranged person is able to summon the collective might of the masses to destroy those so-called "enemies" who refuse to surrender to their will.

Today, there is little difference between Hitler rallying the German people and any modern politician rallying voters into a violent frenzy by triggering their fear of threats to their status, including immigrants, taxes, homosexuals, or women who demand equal treatment. Donald Trump, for instance, tries to frighten people into voting for him.

...

Given our connection to the warring behavior of male chimpanzees, we now have a premise for why ambitious men form their own groups and why countless men join such groups to use its strength in numbers to elevate their own status. This gives us a clear, concise explanation for why our human societies have long been plagued by warring tribes of men intent on using political, economic, military and mental warfare in an effort to dominate others.

Yet we must not forget that their competitive behavior is meant to serve a simple agenda, namely to promote the most genetically healthy combatants to the top of the mating hierarchy. And while this occurs with great success among animals in the wild, we cannot claim the same rate of success in our human societies wherein guns and money are largely responsible for determining our alpha males.

Clearly, it was nature's intent to automate the selection of the best sperm donors through direct combat — even if that battle is symbolic, as is the case with male rattlesnakes "wrestling" for dominance or male birds competing to build the most impressive nests. But now that our own species sends armed soldiers to conquer the rivals of our leaders, we have clearly lost sight of the role of male combat from nature's own perspective. And where one would assume that the urge to dominate would elevate only our best in that hierarchy, we now find ourselves led by men often too old to maintain a viable erection, let alone genetically fit for reproduction. And if they suffer from some undiagnosed mental illness, they may lead entire nations to adopt the symptoms of their malfunctioning minds as the new standard for our social behavior.

Today, we have many such deranged men in seats of political power who insist that everyone adopt their deluded way of thinking. And this attracts others facing similar mental challenges to their negotiation of reality, thus forming ill-informed political movements whose ideas are clearly not designed to elevate our species. And yet, their willingness to opt for violence can easily have them prevailing over us.

The War for Profit

At this point we may wonder how such information can be applied to our everyday life. The answer is "cognitive housecleaning" in that we can begin to unmask the selfish motives behind many a group's quest for power in knowing what we know about male group behavior.

Selfish motives are often hidden behind a veil of moral posturing to make the group's destructive behavior appear to be righteous or even praiseworthy, as is a common feature in war and police brutality.

Serial killers may also use "moral veiling" to justify their violent acts by reframing them as a retaliation against an *amoral* society; an ironic stance for the immoral. Yet on all sides of male conflict is a desire to win, even if a gun is needed to ensure having the last word.

This creates a convenient segue into the serious topic of gun violence introduced in chapter four and its influence upon public safety in the United States; a nation where many groups of men use moral veiling to hide their urge to compete for dominance, including those who advocate for their right to carry guns in public places.

Gun control is a complicated issue because there are several reasons why this conflict exists, all of which are hidden from view to keep their selfish nature from being exposed. However, let us expose them now.

The number one reason why so many men defend gun ownership is to gain power over more dominant men. As such, it also boosts their feeling of masculinity to have the means to face any man who could otherwise force them into submission.

Men's fear of losing their masculinity is not an acknowledged aspect of the pro-gun argument, yet we know that men associate submission with femininity and may even equate peacemaking and anti-violence with being "liberal"— a form of veiled insult in the cult of masculinity often used to condemn anything associated with emotions, weakness, a maternalistic tolerance of others, or gender ambiguity. This would explain the stronger support for gun ownership among patriarchal groups of right wing conservative men wherein manhood is often seen as a political issue and matter of personal pride.

This premise might seem laughable until we realize that some men may even refuse to recycle because they see caring for the environment as a womanly trait; an argument made in the 2011 article: *Cool dudes: the denial of climate change among conservative white males in the United States*. Subsequently, we face far more challenges to saving our planet than developing more recycling programs — we must also find a way to overcome men's knee-jerk fear of the feminine.

Gun safety legislation shares a similar impasse in that many men equate holding a gun with alpha male dominance; the ability to subdue those against whom they otherwise could not compete. What they are hoping to protect is their personal territory and access to females in their midst. In short, the same concerns as any alpha male lion.

Using our acquired knowledge of male Bio-Psychology and men's forming of groups to amass power, we can understand why conflicts among men are rarely settled, including those concerning gun control. The truth is that men are looking for a premise to fight and compete and the selling of guns is but one contest among many like it. It could just as easily be a fight over the right to sell rainbow colored chewing gum — it really doesn't matter as long as there is a reason for men to compete in their lifelong quest to prove themselves dominant.

Here again, the proof is found in sports teams wherein men literally fight over nothing but the public's perception of their alpha status and the money they can earn to prove their superiority. In short, it is a way to monetize men's natural impulse to engage in tribal warfare.

We can then transpose this knowledge onto any conflict fueled by a desire for social status and/or wealth, including men's seeking to make a fortune from selling guns to other men who are afraid of losing.

Here too, the sellers of guns want to protect their economic alpha status by defending their profits from gun sales. To win this conflict, they have merged with groups of male gun owners seeking to protect their sense of masculine identity or feeling of power by defending their right to buy guns. In essence, this is a battle over the holding of two kinds of symbolic power over one's social rivals — both economic and existential. While this may sound complicated in theory, it is simple in practice in that men on a quest for status are defending two ways to attain it — whether by aiming a gun at any threat to their existence, or by profiting from the selling of those guns being aimed.

In addition, this contest is taking place in the United States, a nation defined by its competitive struggles for dominance, whether through military, economic or ideological warfare. As such, men are expected to compete as an expression of their culture, thus putting any quest for peace or compromise at an immediate disadvantage.

Bringing corporate greed and men's fear of losing into this debate, we now have a viable explanation for this ongoing war against peace by wealthy gun manufacturers and men who buy guns to either prove their masculinity or achieve a false sense of alpha dominance. This in turn influences their selfish approach to gun control legislation.

During the Trump presidency, for instance, we saw how groups of men felt emboldened to strut in public with legally purchased combat style rifles. This was a purposeful flexing of group power to intimidate liberals into surrendering their right to protest police violence or their nation's sudden embracing of fascism. And yet, they did not defend their nation as Trump supporters fought to keep then-vice-president Mike Pence from ensuring a peaceful transfer of power after the 2019 election — as was his constitutional duty. As such, this new brand of patriotism appears to be rather one-sided and opportunistic.

Joining these groups of gun sellers and gun owners is another group that gives them their power; a cluster of career politicians who vote to fend off legislation aimed at public safety and sanity itself. In return, they attain a higher economic status from legal bribes by gun lobbyists hoping to keep assault rifles in the hands of eager male shoppers. Such bribes are a matter of public record, making it impossible to deny this connection between gun legislation and political payola. The problem is in trying to make their selfish ambitions appear to serve the greater good. As such, what they needed was a moral veil — a curtain of righteousness behind which to hide both men's greed for money and their existential fears of being dominated by bigger, stronger men.

Enter the United States Constitution — the legal document upon which the USA was founded. A "Second Amendment" was then later added to allow men to own single shot rifles to offset the threat of a rogue government using its military forces against them — not that they stand a chance against its modern fighter jets and drones.

Subsequently, to divert attention away from gun violence, gun sellers and their customers invented a "straw man" argument that is based on patriotism wherein those who deny them their constitutional right to own a gun are seen as treasonous. In other words, anyone limiting their right to buy a military assault rifle is an enemy of the state.

In reality, this righteous-sounding diversion is meant to avoid the real argument — having to choose between an anti-government gun fanatic's right to hoard rifles versus protecting the lives of ordinary citizens, including school children yet to be killed by a trophy hunting social outcast with easy access to a wide selection of weapons.

Daily news reports bear witness to this assertion. For instance, at the time of this book's writing, five people were shot in a Bronx subway station because a man with the gun did not want to lose the argument he had entered into with a group of strangers. Without his gun, he would likely have gone home to sulk over his wounded pride. Instead, as the winner of that fight, he'll be awarded a lifetime of prison work.

The same day in Kansas City, twenty one people were shot during a Super Bowl celebration, including eight children. The suspects are also in custody, but as with all gun violence, justice arrives much too late.

...

The topic of mass shootings brings up a rather strange dichotomy in that Canada, the USA's northern neighbor, also allows ownership of guns, yet has a far lower incidence of gun violence.

Beyond enforcing stricter gun laws, Canada also does not promote a war-like atmosphere of social competition to encourage hostility between its citizens. After all, guns make it far too easy to be on our worst behavior when our fear of losing is triggered. Competitive fear also makes it too easy to shoot first and ask questions later — as police officers can attest when existential fear or competitive pride take over one's decision-making in any street-level contest for dominance.

This fear of losing is also a prominent feature in the argument for gun ownership. In fact, many US gun owners fear losing to their own government — a distrust widely used to market guns by promoting an *end of times* mindset wherein we revert to a *survival of the fittest* state of uncivil society. Is this the hope of survivalists — to start over again in a nation where *real men* reign and armed might makes right?

What we don't know is how many gun manufacturers plant agitators inside survivalist groups to drive up gun sales by presenting their own government as a looming threat. Regardless, surely we can all agree that we must do far better to keep guns out of the hands of troubled teenagers with a grudge against society, and toddlers who accidentally shoot their own siblings with guns purchased to protect the family.

There are many fundamental concessions to sanity that can be made as long as we don't panic in our fear of losing, or treat this like a war between rival troupes of male chimpanzees set upon killing each other.

And whenever politicians try to scare us into surrendering common sense with claims that "they" are coming for us, ask them for names and proof instead of wild-eyed storytelling. Chances are, they can't.

Predicting the future

Predicting the future is a responsibility best left to fortune tellers and campaigning politicians. But if we were to make a prediction based on our current trajectory, we might see a world resembling a prison colony wherein our future overlords have eliminated the threat of other men challenging their hold on power over a lucrative empire of global trade and banking systems.

Logically speaking, global domination is the ultimate *end game* for any ambitious tyrant because that is nature's own end game — to have one male prevail over all others. And given the tendency of men to act like warring chimpanzees and the continuous development of ever more lethal and decisive weapons, we all have good reason to fear the worst from the kind of men who seek ultimate power over others.

In any case, even if we manage to defend our freedom from the tyranny of others, we may still destroy ourselves by treating our planet like a dumpster for industrial waste.

Luckily, there are many kind and caring people among us who have no qualms about sharing resources and power to ensure that we can all thrive in peace on a healthy planet. Their presence offers a reason to hope for more than a dismal future as long as we each have an equal say in our direction as a species. Failing that, we can march in protest and find other ways to flex our strength in numbers.

But regardless of how well things may go in the future, it is certain that men will always feel the urge to compete for dominance as is the demand of nature. For this reason, there will always be clashes among men, whether at a local pub or in the halls of government. And where any ambitious man sits second in command, his desire for status will often see him plotting his own rise to power. This is typical behavior among men and there is little we can do about it beyond learning how to manage it better in the future and to not invite the most ambitious of armed killers or insane men to become our leaders.

Ideally, our world ought to be working together as one unified front defined not by race, religion, culture or gender, but by our identity as a unique species representing our planet; global citizens working toward a common greater good on behalf of the many rather than a privileged few reaping great benefits at the cost of everyone else.

But men's Bio-Psychology inherently rejects unification of this kind due to nature's pressuring them to stand out as a winner. To feed this selfish impulse requires a narcissistic seeking of constant attention and presenting one's self as being above others, including one's leaders. For this reason, we will find men assuming the role of a charismatic cult leader over a group of followers, controlling their minds and spending by exploiting their instinctual need for strength in numbers while also setting them against the rest of the world by playing a fear-based game of divide and conquer to keep them loyal and obedient.

A modern example of this involves *Alex Jones*, a now-waning right wing radio personality whose rapid-fire delivery of conspiracy theories laced with overblown theatrics creates an exciting alternate reality for his followers to enter wherein they can also validate their private fears of being persecuted by untold enemies known collectively as "they."

To explain what is happening, let us create a few conspiracy theories of our own. The first is that Alex Jones is tricking gullible people out of their time and money by keeping them in a constant state of fearful agitation to which they react by buying products to make themselves feel better, including gold and various doomsday survival products. In regard to his economic dominance, it was revealed by Jones' lawyers in a legal proceeding against him that, aside from "playing a character" in the media, he has also made as much as $800,000 USD in a single day from scaring listeners into buying products touted as life-savers in an impending apocalyptic future that has yet to arrive. If this sounds familiar, it should, because it is a theme borrowed from the Christian bible's own promise of salvation at the end of the world.

In making these claims, Jones's legal team also created a paradoxical problem for itself in that if they are lying about Jones faking it, then they be perjuring themselves. And yet, Jones himself later contradicted their statements by saying that he is "100% real."

And perhaps Jones may even believe that he is real in having no other point of reference beyond his own tainted state of mind. As such, a second conspiracy theory is that Alex Jones is mentally ill, a claim he himself made in a court deposition, saying that he suffers from a form of psychosis that has him believing that *everything is rigged* — that all events are carefully orchestrated by a host of various unseen entities with names such as *the Illuminati, Globalists* or the far less-fashionable of late *Freemasons*. Either way, "they" are always to blame.

Whether any of this is true or not, one thing is certain: Jones knows how to make money from gaining people's attention with his rapid fire storytelling and antics. But he also knows how to lose it as well.

Case in point, among the fear-based conspiracy theories that Jones has forwarded to peddle his wares is that the US government is about to start herding its citizens into concentration camps to exterminate them; a process that must obviously begin by taking everyone's beloved guns away to leave them weak, vulnerable and easy to conquer.

In drumming up his audience's fear of losing their guns, Jones also created a false narrative regarding a tragic mass shooting of children known as *the Sandy Hook incident*. Rather than accepting that this was the work of a deranged gun owner, Jones claimed instead that it was a "false flag" operation staged by his [globalist/illuminati] government to hasten taking away people's guns. As a consequence, many followers began to terrorize the grieving parents of those dead children, accusing them of being "crisis actors" working on behalf of the government.

In other words, they were drawn into a psychotic drama that is more aligned with people who suffer from paranoid schizophrenia.

Fortunately, none of this is about Alex Jones or his waning media empire, but about us recognizing that anyone of questionable motives can seize control of our minds and actions — if they can make us feel afraid of *losing* or promise us *victory* in the end. And rather than bring progress and peace into our lives, they will usually offer us a portal to hateful division through which to feed their own hunger for status.

The result is a world wherein it is nearly impossible to convince the followers of any cult and its charismatic leader that their adopted way of thinking is not going to save our world but only make it worse.

For this reason, it is not so much our governments but their people who are at war over the conquering of the human mind. And that war is raging worldwide with neither a winner, nor any sign of surrender in sight. After all, when it comes to belief — we are all right.

But whatever the source of people's negative programming, we can counteract it by taking back our minds from those seeking to distract us from reality or exploit our attention for profit. We could start this process of mental detoxification by imagining that one day we may be able to return to this planet after our current life has ended. Perhaps 100 or more years into the future.

While this is purely a hypothetical event being offered as a mental exercise, it is a perspective actually shared by religions that incorporate the idea of reincarnation or resurrection of the spirit into their belief systems — a transferring of the *me* within us to a whole new body.

If such a renewal were possible, what kind of world would you hope to find awaiting your own return? And what is it that you can do now to better ensure that your vision for the future becomes a reality?

Once you have envisioned that world, simply proceed to create it for yourself — don't wait for others, especially our leaders who may be too distracted in tending to their own concerns. You must fulfill your own dreams. Otherwise, you will remain a spectator

Thereafter, who knows: perhaps if you could actually return, you will have a legitimate reason to celebrate those seeds you had sewn when it mattered most — right now.

And if planting them in some war-torn country, you may also find landmines carelessly left by men as a relic of our psychotic human past. Please remove them so that your children, pets and the unsuspecting wildlife of our planet need not worry about making their own trusting steps forward in creating for themselves a more joyful future life.

And if you see something amiss that threatens the greater good of the many, then loudly and proudly blow the whistle on it, otherwise it may succeed in undermining all the great work being done by you and others to make this world a better place.

Here's to an enlightened future that we need not fear.

PART FIVE
Working Towards Solutions

CHAPTER 17
Woman Rise

Politics was never meant to be treated as a joke, the way it is today. At one time, it was the means by which a tribal society could ensure that its mutual interests were being met and that the man with the biggest fists didn't steal food from the mouths of babies. It was raw, informal and likely quarrelsome as well, but the smaller size of our early tribes surely made overseeing them far more personal and manageable.

Today, however, all of that has changed, as the governing of society has become yet another venue for ambitious men to compete for alpha male dominance. As such, it is also no coincidence that most nations are ruled by a single male based on the same Bio-Psychological urge that pushes the dominant males of other group-based species to seek a top position. And this arrangement sets up the punchline for the joke that so many of our political systems have become in that a man's urge to dominate is not motivated by his desire to help others; a disparity borne out by any selfish male politician who has ever pretended to be serving the greater good while actually serving only himself.

As such, we can expect the majority of ambitious male leaders to do little for our society upon achieving their true goal, which is to win the highest seat of political power — not to help others rise. And this also creates a further comical aspect of politics wherein they are forced to lie to win elections, and once in office, to conceal their apathy or gross incompetence. Yes, it's all a big joke — but it's never been funny

While this bleak prognosis does not apply to all male leaders, the political and social history of our world proves that such accusations are neither unfair nor inaccurate. Moreover, it becomes apparent from watching men govern that many are not psychologically equipped to take on so important a role — whereas women are born for it.

But before we explore the basis for such an argument, let us reorient ourselves as to the main topic of this book, which pertains to the study of "Bio-Psychology" and how, under its relentless, lifelong influence, men's socially disruptive and violently competitive behavior has long been pushing life itself to the brink of extinction.

As such, the purpose of this section of the book is to present ideas and potential solutions to these male-borne social problems before it is too late to solve them. And this invariably brings us to yet another aspect of our Bio-Psychology that we must address, which is women's natural inclination to nurture and protect life and thereby successfully govern the lives of their growing children. If this is not a clear example of true leadership in action, then what is? Men going to war?

...

Admittedly, the mere possession of female genitalia does not guarantee that a women will be a loving mother to a child any more than having a penis qualifies a man for leadership. However, no one can argue that a woman is far more essential to the life of a child than a man. To start, her responsibility does not end at the point of orgasm. And regardless of our stance on gender equality, nature has clearly given women every emotional and physical advantage in raising a child to maturity, as demonstrated by men's lack of viable nipples.

By entrusting women with the earliest care of our species, nature has also ensured that newborns are kept warm and well-attended at birth and can suckle on the nutrients flowing from their mother's body to ensure their comfortable existence into the immediate future. Nor are women special in this regard as the same tender treatment awaits all mammal offspring born in the wild. This is how nature succeeds.

And while this rudimentary lesson in biology may seem redundant, it should not be so easily dismissed because in the process of preparing human females for motherhood, nature has also bestowed them with the most critical of social attributes, which is a willingness to care for and share with other human beings without feeling a sense of loss or need for repayment. Instead, like all mothers, she does this purely as an intuitive expression of her gender's inherent Bio-Psychology.

Amazingly, if we then look to the writings of most world religions, we find celebrated therein not the ability of a revered spiritual master to kill the most men with his bare hands but to care for and show them kindness — actions attributed to God in religion and to women in context of their maternal instincts in raising a child. In short, woman are very much *God-like* in their maternal behavior.

And yet, despite this obvious association between women's natural inclinations and the higher aims of spiritual wisdom, we instead put men in charge of governing and leading us to enlightenment, thereby turning both institutions into venues for male competitive hostility and ceaseless combat. As such, we should not be surprised by the often mediocre results attained in both venues.

From this perspective, we can then look back upon our history with regret in having enlisted so many deranged madmen to guide us into the future, whether Adolf Hitler or any modern version of the worst that humankind has to offer — of which there is a great selection

Today, we continue in that long, naive tradition of pretending that a hateful authoritarian dictator or greedy sociopath will better serve our society than putting a woman in charge — at least this is what the majority of men — and too many women — have come to believe.

Granted, there are valid reasons for our biased thinking in favor of patriarchal domination. Primarily, we are a highly vulnerable species that instinctively seeks protection against the dangers of the wild. This often has us cowering behind the most brutish and war-like of men. For that reason, we can also expect little more from them than to loot our societies and create an oppression style of governing to assist them in that regard. In return, they will fight off our "enemies" so that they can continue with their parasitical feeding upon our lives. It's not an ideal arrangement, but it beats being shot as "an enemy of the state."

As to why we choose such self-serving men to be our leaders, this is largely due to an aspect of our herding instinct wherein we believe that a man who appears "powerful" — loud, aggressive and warlike — is better equipped to protect us than a soft-spoken pacifist. And yet, in almost every case, that loud aggressor becomes a greater threat to our society than any foreign invader. Moreover, their vision for our future is often tainted by a hyper-competitive male psyche with little concern for the plight of others. And while a society based on personal gain may be appealing to selfish glory-seekers hoping to take everything for themselves, it often leads to the ignoring of the basic needs of women and children — such as having a society that does not openly promote competitive hostility, as is the fallout of economic and class warfare.

A further negative outcome of putting selfish men in charge of our societies is that their government policies come to reflect a competitive values system rather than one based on nurturing inclusivity — which is a tendency associated more with the psychology of women. In fact, we often hear men openly ridiculing those aspects of society that tend to nurture its needy as they bluff their way through life proclaiming their own rugged independence. As such, this attitude has given rise to societies that are in a constant state of conflict due to governing systems, industries and business practices designed to accommodate the rise of individual men battling for power rather than for tending to the needs of the many. As a result, protecting others within society is often treated more as an afterthought — or none of "our business."

One common symptom of promoting selfishness as a social priority is seen among institutions or businesses without a social mandate beyond enriching their owners, even if this has a negative impact upon society — as does the selling addictive products, including cigarettes and opiates. This also sees some charities taking our money under false pretenses to enrich their overseers. Meanwhile, to ensure their future hold on power, organized groups of men will attempt to privatize or monetize every aspect of society without concern for how it will affect others, including women raising children in a world that undervalues their existence. The problem, it seems, is that there is no profit to be made from raising children, nor in offering free services to the mothers raising them. One can even suggest that protecting society becomes an impediment to any man seeking great wealth, which is why they are often seen to engage in breaking laws, bribing politicians, or trying to deregulate their industries to allow for even more collateral damage.

All of this goes a long way toward explaining the shadow of apathy that has long swept across our world as a direct reflection of men not being of the gender upon which nature calls to nurture others. For that reason, we can also still find greedy businessmen plotting to sell cancer causing cigarettes to kids or putting industrial poisons into our water, while others dump anything from plastic fishing gear to crude oil and radioactive waste into our oceans as a matter of convenience. And with each report of a train derailment, a leaking oil pipeline, or a breached mining containment pond, the focus of many of those men involved is less on preventing such events in the future than on trying to avoid the loss of their money in the present.

We should also remind ourselves once again that the great majority of all human hazards have not been created by women, but by a male gender with an enduring history of profiteering from the devaluation of life in every form. And this kind of myopic thinking has now led to this precarious moment in time wherein we are teetering on the edge of our own future non-existence.

Subsequently, as nature provokes the most hyper-competitive male glory-seekers among us to do whatever it takes to enter the top ten list of the world's richest men, the rest of us must find some way to protect ourselves and our natural world from the kind of men who appear to have no inclination whatsoever to protect anyone or anything but their own selfish path to future glory.

And so we are faced with a fateful decision: do to continue to move in the same misguided direction that has allowed countless greedy male psychopaths to treat our planet as their private business empire and shooting range — or do we finally put a woman in charge?

Defeating Female Ambition

It stands to reason that women have long been kept out of positions of political and social power largely due to the fact that men are larger physically and can therefore dominate them. But men cannot use the same "might makes right" logic to rule over women as they have always used to beat their male rivals into submission. Instead, they needed a convenient alibi to make themselves appear more as heroes even when they were acting like selfish villains.

As such, while a closed fist remains the ultimate rule of law in many a patriarchal household, men have also had to create a premise for why women must remain beneath them in every sense of the word.

The first of these, as related in an earlier chapter, was the use of God as a tool to deflect blame for why men treated women as lesser beings in the struggle for social power. By accusing women for humankind's original sin and downfall from grace, men were able to downgrade the female gender ever since this religious myth became widely circulated thousands of years ago. The authority of God created a built-in excuse for why men should then be able to do as they pleased to keep women at the lowest ranks within the dominance hierarchy of society.

While God could initially be blamed for men's prejudice against the female gender, their misogyny became even more transparent as laws were written to prevent women from voting or earning money. And while some women protested, most resigned themselves to a life of ill treatment at the hands of men competing to rule over society.

In addition to laws, various customs and traditions helped to create a Gender Wall of prejudice against women — a kind of invisible mental barrier that continues to impede the ambitions of women in all parts of our world today. In teaching women to stay on their side of the wall, they must also be subjected to a regimen of mental conditioning that has them accepting their position as the less-than-equal gender so as not to interfere in men's competition for social dominance. Today, this is evident even in product advertising, which has women focussed on a narrow list of ambitions that center mostly on pleasing men to earn themselves a cheerful life of looking after a household.

While there is no shame in a woman's choosing to be a housewife instead of a high level player in the world of politics or finance, what matters is that she has the right to choose her own path, which is the reason women have been fighting for equal rights and why many men have been fighting against them since that struggle began.

In addition, the regimen of mental conditioning to which men are subjected, in conjunction with their innate competitive urges, has far too many of them judging a woman's worth not by her intelligence or other socially-redeemable trait but by her physical anatomy as a vessel for sexual release. And while social attitudes in this regard are shifting, the stereotyping of women as inferior beings from countless centuries of institutionalized prejudice has kept everyone's expectations low in terms of a woman's leadership potential. This is evident by how women have only recently been *allowed by men* to become doctors, lawyers and legislators in comparison to how long men have held a monopoly over these institutions.

Even today, our prejudices against women reveal themselves every time we assume that our appointment with a "doctor" is with a man rather than a woman. In short, we are still not used to seeing women in a leadership role, whereas a nurse is still assumed to be female.

It is also worth mentioning again that no female president has ever been elected in the USA, although fate has made it possible for current vice president, Kamala Harris, to become the first black female to lead that nation if she is elected in 2024. Beyond the obvious racial barrier, as a woman, she also faces the resistance of many male voters who do not want a woman leading them. In short, if she loses, it will not be for lack of competence but rather for lack of a penis.

One byproduct of keeping women so narrowly focussed on life as a domestic servant is the "empty nest syndrome" wherein she comes to realize that neither she nor society has planned for a future for women beyond being a housebound breeder. This feeling of disorientation may not affect professional women so much, but it remains a common form of female mid-life crisis due to society's failure to envision a future for women beyond that of serving a husband or children.

The most important lesson to be learned from all of this is that there are reasons why women are not in charge of our societies today, and it has nothing whatsoever to do with their level of competence. Instead, it has everything to do with interference by men.

This brings to light an *elephant in the room* of human civilization, one whose looming presence is not being addressed. This has to do with patriarchy not existing as a natural governing state in the wild. Instead, we may find a single male acting as a protector for a group of females and their young. His own interests are served by guarding his sexual access to those females, which is the only motive he needs in seeking such a position of power over them. As such, there is no reason for him to control every aspect of a females life to serve his own interests; he simply has to keep other males away. And this appears to be true for all group-based alpha males in the wild, from gorillas to lions.

In stark contrast, human males seek to restrict women's behavior using complex political and religious belief systems that also promote the assumption that men are natural born leaders. In other words, they seek to equate physical *dominance* with competence, and their use of *might* with knowing what is right; a logic for which no kind of rational argument can be made. After all, a male gorilla could easily kill our nation's top leaders, but that still does not qualify him to lead us. And yet, men have used a similar logic to dominate women and our society because thinking otherwise would not serve their quests for status.

In the meantime, women are prevented from encroaching upon the so-called "traditional" territory of men in politics, business and religion by promoting prejudicial beliefs suggesting that she is not competent enough to take on a critical leadership role — perhaps she will start a nuclear war during a bout of PMS, or become "hysterical" if she does not get her way with the United Nations. We've all heard this kind of dismissive banter from woman haters; it's nothing new.

Putting such silliness aside, there may be some rational trade-offs to consider. For instance, how can a woman oversee a military war effort while also keeping her own sons alive? Instead, she may choose a path leading to peace for the sake of all mothers and their children.

In a world wherein women are raised to anticipate the same levels of success as men, a further trade-off will be her availability. If pregnant or tending to children, she cannot make herself as readily available to the worlds of politics or business as a man. Furthermore, upon giving birth, she is obligated to raise her child for many years, as is a common need for female primates in preparing their young for their own future independence. Yes, she could hire strangers to raise them, but this risks the loss of a maternal bond upon which the offspring of mammalian species rely. And so, in committing to her role as a caring mother, she also limits her options for achieving greater independence socially and financially. And in turn, men have taken advantage of her needs.

Such observations are not revelatory, given that women have long been aware of these restrictions upon their time and lifestyles since the first human pregnancy was witnessed. However, they do establish a foundation for better understanding the challenges women face in having to navigate societies that have been purposely designed by men to keep women from succeeding without their help.

As such, being a mother forces women to take far more about their personal circumstances into consideration than men are required to do. In fact, nature places few burdens or restrictions upon men beyond the discouraging of battles with larger males. However, forcing them to raise a child is not one of them. And this is generally true for all males in the wild, most of whom have no further contact with a female after insemination. This may also help to explain why so many men seem instinctively driven not to pursue a deeper connection with their own children, which has left many mothers to raise or nurture them alone — and often while also having her rights to succeed restricted by those very same men as they rule over her society.

As such, controlling her birthrate it is critical matter for any woman who wishes to succeed in a male-dominated world. Such control must give her the right to avoid unwanted pregnancies, but also to terminate a pregnancy that she cannot justify — including those resulting from incest or rape. Yet here is where the women of many cultures are faced with yet another barrier to their success, which is the moral outrage of men who claim to be opposed to abortions on moral grounds, even as they engage in wars that kill children as collateral damage in the name of industrial profits and the amassing of political power.

Here, we return to the notion that men don't want women to see them as selfish villains. And so, to avoid this accusation, they defer blame to a masculine God who then insists that women not kill their unborn children. But while such an appeal to God's authority seems a convincing argument, we need only refer to Exodus 11:4–6 in the Old Testament wherein God cold-bloodedly kills the first born children of Egypt to win an argument with a stubborn rival. And so, rather than punish that lone heretic directly, God instead chooses to kill countless innocent children to make a more convincing show of his own physical dominance over all challengers. In short, if we are to consider this part of ancient scripture a historical fact, as many do, then clearly God is depicted as a mass murderer of children. As such, how could he then be morally opposed to aborting fetuses if he has no qualms in killing an innocent child once born?

Realistically, the only way that such behavior makes any sense is by our refusing to think about it. And that's what many people choose to do when encountering conflicting beliefs — they refuse to think about them. This is one reason why people advise us not to talk about politics or religion as it forces people to think about things over which they have already made up their minds, for better or worse.

But once we look deeper, ancient religious scripture reveals that God is often engaged in murderous or cruel behavior, not the least of which is sending people to burn in Hell for all eternity. In other words, God seems to have issues relating to violence and anger that make him a questionable authority on creating a peaceful, loving society. And if such stories do represent "the truth," then there is certainly a dark layer of psychosis beneath that truth which must not be ignored.

Moreover, once we see how quickly those morally-outraged men of religion abandon the unborn upon their entry into this world, it brings into question their true intentions in wanting women not to terminate their pregnancies. Are they truly concerned with the welfare of unborn children, or are they just trying to keep women from having any kind of freedom over their lives and bodies? In other words, is this not just another facet of men's attempts to defeat female ambition?

As feminists have long suspected, the latter is the likely explanation; that the criminalization of abortion is simply a patriarchal ploy to keep women powerless and dependent upon men. Moreover, by keeping her at home, she cannot interfere in men's competition to rule our societies by their own selfish, war-centric value systems, which protect neither pregnant women nor their unborn children. It truly is that obvious if we dare to look beneath this pretentious political veneer of hyperbole and altruistic grandstanding. Here, what we will find is an unending path from our primitive past into an equally primitive future paved by men's age-old desire to claim ownership of those fertile females over which most male animals compete in the wild.

The Assumption of Male Entitlement

If women didn't already face enough male-sponsored obstacles on the road to social equality, the most impenetrable of all seems to be men's attitude about women in general.

Given that organized religion has seemingly been with us from the start, it represents part of an enduring Gender Wall of prejudice that seeks to keep women from gaining any kind of power over men, even by controlling their sexuality. Beyond men's physical advantage, their exclusive overseeing of religious texts has greatly influenced our views on women worldwide while satisfying their lust for dominance and status by having someone to rule over in context of a marriage. As such, the most stubborn obstacle a woman is likely to encounter to her future progress within society is a man who feels entitled to dominate her rather than see her as his equal.

Today, we still find men being mentally conditioned by their culture to either treat women as sexual trophies to be won, or a form of human livestock to be bought and sold for personal gain. Luckily, such archaic attitudes are beginning to change wherever young women are able to speak openly and freely about the social disadvantages they encounter in societies that have been rigged to favor men since the dawning of human civilization. Yet many people still believe in those biased truths offered by patriarchal religious storytelling, including their prejudicial judgments against womankind, which leaves modern day women still having to fight against blind faith rather than proven facts.

Whether we believe such things or not, what seems clear is that no "loving" God would instruct men to treat a woman as a lesser being — or to exploit her as his personal slave. Instead, such behavior is more a reflection of a Bio-Psychological values system that has men seeking to dominate others. And so, we can suspect that men added various amendments to religious texts, thus transforming a spiritual manifesto into an instruction manual on social and female oppression. Nor could women have stopped them, as even today they are being shut out from engaging in the politics of their religion.

...

The patriarchal leaders of many nations and their religious institutions continue to promote prejudicial treatment toward women. Yet it is far more tragic for a woman to accept being designated as a lesser human being within these male-centric social caste systems.

Fortunately, we can use the IPSFA Sequence to *deconstruct* a typical "traditional" female gender identity script. For example:

(I) **IDENTITY:** Woman (One who is born to serve a husband).
(P) **PROMISE:** A life of joy in serving one's husband and children.
(S) **SCRIPT:** Attract a husband; serve and obey him; multiply.
(F) **FEAR:** To be rejected and remain single as a "failed" woman.
(A) **APATHY:** Having to endure a tragic life of servitude to a man who may prove to be a thankless, selfish abuser.

While this is a simplified version of a much more extensive identity script, it nonetheless defines the essence of a woman's role as decreed by men under the influence of their selfishly-guided wishful thinking.

What we must remember is that belief exists only within the mind and that it manifests from there into the physical world. As such, if women were to rewrite the traditional gender scripts of their culture, beginning instead with: (I) **IDENTITY:** Woman (One who is born to lead), then human social reality as we know it would also look a lot different.

Thankfully, with the specter of witch burnings behind us, modern attitudes towards women are changing as a consequence of our desire for greater peace and social justice. Yet the struggle for independence is far from over for women, especially in repressive cultures wherein she continues to be taunted, tortured and killed for defying patriarchal authority. And even in the western world it is too early to celebrate the gains of the female gender while women continue to be subjected to unflattering stereotypes designed to keep them "in their place."

The signs of women accepting a lower status includes mothers in the USA of the 1950's who advised their daughters not to disagree with a boy on their first date — lest he feel too intimidated to ask her out a second time. Even during the more recent 1990's, before the printing press was replaced by computer screens, magazines for boys featured a wide array of topics designed to encourage mental exploration and personal growth, whereas girls were limited to magazines that taught them how to look sexy for men while playing on their fears of rejection to sell beauty products that promised to make them more attractive.

As such, despite a growing trend toward female independence, we still find female "influencers" on social media offering photos of their breasts and buttocks in a ritualized affirmation of their belief that male attention is the only thing of value to women. And sadly, they revel in this shallow ambition, one inherited from the likes of Bettie Page and Marilyn Monroe, to compete for male attention by becoming the most almost-naked woman in public.

Watching a narcissistic women feed on male sexual attention, what we see is someone who is putting the needs of men above her own. In this way, she diminishes her value as a human being in a world that has taught her to parade half-naked in public while apologizing for having opinions about improving society or ambitions beyond marriage. As such, after centuries of top-down male oppression, it is common for women to approach life like an insecure child under the watchful eye of a disapproving father figure — be it her husband, or some unseen masculine God judging her every step from on high.

The result is an endemic feeling of low self-esteem among too many women who feel resigned to never be able to rise higher to fulfill their personal goals because men won't allow it. Instead, they may be living life as one who is morally defeated — a great loss for the rest of us who will never know her true life potential or its ensuing rewards.

In stark contrast, society raises men to adopt an entirely opposite attitude wherein even the most incompetent man still believes himself superior to women and thus entitled to have more than her; not unlike racists who feel deserving of more for simply being born of a particular color. And given all that their delusion of entitlement bestows upon them in terms of unfair advantages, we can then understand why so many men resist giving up their "traditional" patriarchal privileges, which have always allowed them to control everything, including the lives of women.

The War Against Sharing

Given men's ongoing struggles to keep women out of power, we must assume that they have a lot to lose by giving up their leadership posts. But what has them feeling so threatened about women taking control of our societies? What is the worst that could happen if mothers all throughout the world decided to manage society more like a family than a cut-throat business that seeks to eliminate costs and cut corners at every turn in the name of profit?

The answer is a simple one that also explains why most sons prefer their mothers to their fathers. It has to do with the simple fact that mother's show a greater willingness to share their resources with their offspring to ensure their future survival. On the other hand, most of the animal fathers in the wild have no such obligation, which is why nature did not equip them mentally for sharing or caring to the same degree as the female gender. As such, there is often a great disparity in how a mother engages with her children as opposed to a father. In fact, many fathers rule over a household with an attitude of entitlement that also has them competing against their sons for status by using fists or vicious insults to keep them "down."

Beyond a mother's willingness to share, she ensures greater peace in the home by insisting that her children share resources so that each has an equal chance to survive. In the wild, there may be some competition when feeding, but in general there is equal concern for the well-being of each member of a matriarchal family, including the injured.

In observing a mother's behavior, she displays the exact opposite of the male ethos of competing for dominance, which is meant to leave others behind for the sake of one man's victory over all others. In other words, introducing a more maternal values system would prevent men from competing for dominance in the selfish, apathetic way to which they have long been accustomed.

In such a world, we all would matter equally and that does not bode well for those who believe they should matter most. Yes, there is the question of how nature will adjust to a peaceful environment wherein men no longer kill one another to prove their genetic worth. But it's a better option than letting those with the most nuclear weapons decide how our world should ultimately be run.

Through the maternal eyes of a female leader, she may see the needs of others and feel compelled to help ease their suffering — rather than build a wall to keep them out. In doing so, she also helps to rise up in status without fear of being surpassed by those she helps — a behavior also common to the spiritual prophets glorified in the religions of men.

As a result, women often behave more like "socialists," whereas men often behave more like fascist dictators. This also causes issues within homes wherein a husband assumes that his strong-armed tactics for managing family life are superior, even as they are destroying the love and trust within that family. And often, all he has to back his position is his physical dominance over his wife and children, who then find it difficult to communicate their views to a man yelling insults or beating them to ensure his victory during any family quarrel or debate.

...

In light of these observations about the differences between men's and women's social behavior, we can then understand why men don't want women to become political leaders as it would change the rules of a worldwide game of male domination that has allowed them to take as they want, whether by physical, economic or military force. In essence, the male gender of our species is engaged in a global war on sharing in their selfish quest for more.

And this comes as no surprise once we consider how many of our male leaders have been running our world without concern for anyone else's well-being. In fact, their rise to power often depends on showing total apathy towards the suffering of others, as the tragic history of our male-sponsored economic and military warfare can attest. In addition, animals and the natural environment also become their victims.

And so there we have it — right before our eyes and as plain as day for all to see — our world needs women to claim their rightful place as the rulers of our societies before men have destroyed everything in a selfish display of their dominant alpha male stupidity.

In short, it's time for women to rise and shine. Look to anywhere that women have gathered, be it in hospitals, schools or animal rescue organizations — chances are that they have united for the greater good of others and not to make devious preparations for a future war.

Clichés are a common feature of social life and although we can talk as much as we like about learning from our past history, unless we actual start to make some fundamental changes to our systems based on the wisdom inherent to women, it is all just empty rhetoric.

Today, at a time in our history that may well represent the eleventh hour of our survival as a species, it is time to truly learn from our past mistakes and the lessons that life has been teaching us all along: let the minds of women finally show us the way to our future.

The inner compass of women represents our best chance at survival, whereas extinction surely awaits us in remaining on our present course.

CHAPTER 18
Speaking Truth to Power

Scientology is an organization that claims to be saving our world from itself. Unfortunately, like many faith-based institutions, its willingness to save even its own members has come under scrutiny. That is, unless they happen to be someone rich and/or famous.

Case in point, in 2023, a B-list actor and long-time Scientologist was finally sent to prison for having raped two of his fellow members many years earlier. Evidently, whatever world-saving wisdom had been imparted to him, his predatory urge to dominate women was a force too powerful to overcome. But rather than turn this man over to police at the time of the attacks, church leaders did as many institutions do by turning instead against the victims to protect their own lucrative empire against the fallout of negative publicity.

Unfortunately, that decision also held back justice for nearly twenty years while putting in doubt the organization's ability to keep rapists and other predatory types out of its ranks.

Various lessons can be learned from the plight of the rape victims, including that their religious institution would not save them in trying to save itself. Yet for our purposes, it highlights the risks of speaking truth to power. Namely, of trying to get people in positions of power to do what is right when doing so threatens their hold on power and their ability to profit from it. For this reason, the dominant will often choose to do what is wrong to save themselves; a self-serving behavior that continues to hold back justice and social progress in our world to this day. And so, instead of serving the greater good of humanity, our group leader may insist that we suffer in silence rather than speak out. As such, rather than helping us in our time of need, we are instead left abandoned and betrayed by those we have come to trust.

Such abandonment is typical among institutions that fear for their continued hold on power, a fact that formerly faithful church member, John Wojnowski, came to realize after being sexually exploited as a boy by a Catholic priest. Decades later, despite his demand for atonement, church leaders remained silent and dismissive. The predatory priest, however, was later promoted to a higher position in Rome.

Others betrayed by monolithic institutions include Julian Assange and Edward Snowden, who both sounded the alarm about abuses of power within various governments — heroic revelations for which they were instead treated like treasonous villains.

For this reason, top-down domination is often experienced as a zero sum game that has us losing in a direct confrontation with those in power— as was evident in Nazi Germany or the former Apartheid government of South Africa. More importantly, institutions survive because their followers often want to believe in convenient lies rather than question the beliefs upon which their lives are based. In short, for many people it is easier to live in denial than face the truth. As such avoidance behavior also benefits most the deceivers of our world.

...

The fear of retribution is a realistic one, given that we are a social and highly interdependent species. As such, we have a tendency to avoid conflicts out of a desire to fit in or be accepted. Naturally, this helps to protect the criminally-minded among us from having to face justice if we are too afraid to openly accuse them of their wrongdoing — which is the message being sent by persecuting both Assange and Snowden.

More tragic still is that truth tellers are often purposely ignored by the powerful so as not to disrupt the daily operations of their various lucrative empires and institutions. After all, we all have our interests to protect, whether our future pensions, job promotions, yearly bonuses or other incentives, while for those on top, the loss of status and power matters most. As such, a common attitude is to let others "take the hit" for speaking out or challenging the system. And for that, we all lose.

If we then blend this self-preserving disregard for others with men's inborn Bio-Psychological quest for status, we can begin to understand why various kinds of human tragedies continue to unfold around us.

One such tragedy was documented in *Deliver Us From Evil*, a 2006 film highlighting the choice of Roger Mahony, a Catholic Bishop, to remain silent about the sins of a confessed pedophile priest under his watch, to avoid a scandal that would disrupt his own future plans to become Archbishop of Los Angeles. Ironically, in having chosen to protect his rise to power over the lives of children, he also proved that his faith had not the power to defeat his own inner demons.

In confronting any large institution, we are best to keep in mind that its predominantly male leaders are also driven by the same selfish urge to dominate and fear of losing as what has other men taking up arms and building fortresses. Moreover, thanks to support from their loyal followers, institutions often have the financial resources to weather any legal storm, whereas their victims typically have neither the economic nor emotional means to endure a long, drawn-out legal battle. As such, bribes often work wonders to silence a victim's demand for justice. In that regard, the greater its wealth, the more the institution can afford to engage in *injustices*. This is "the price of doing business" and often proves a far cheaper route to success than doing what is right

Yet even in a world full of sociopathic predators wherein the greater majority of their victims prefer to hide from adversity, there are people working to improve the quality of life for all the living. And so, rather than let our hope for a better future curl up and die from neglect, we must instead help to pry it from the greedy clutches of those who are currently holding our world hostage.

When presenting men with this challenge, a great many of them will respond as nature has programmed them to do, by opting for violence in response to any leader who is reluctant to change his ways for the better. But as the recent wars in Israel and Ukraine have once again proven, gunfire and airstrikes are not the solution to all our problems because they always leave a trail of dead women and children behind while allowing violent psychopaths to decide our future.

Ultimately, the quest for absolute power over others is not the way to a more peaceful and democratic society, just as a battle between two male lions is not meant to end in a mutual sharing of resources. As such, we must decide what kind of world we want to live in and then plan accordingly. And once we know what we want, we must do all that we can to ensure that nothing gets in our way, including the lies of those trying to obstruct our path forward.

The greater majority of politicians has proven that lying is not the way to progress. Instead, it acts as an impediment or diversion from where we need to go. As such, we must do our best to always seek and speak the truth, both for our own sake and that of anyone to whom we wish to communicate our intentions. But when speaking our truth to those in power, we may often be met by lies, veiled threats and outright deadly force to keep us living a life of passive conformity wherein our exploitation is made easier by keeping us dumb and docile.

And herein lies the catch. Whether or not we believe that we are human spirits on an inspired journey toward our conscious evolution, we can still honor the gift of life itself by not treating it as disposable. Once we begin to see the value in valuing life itself, our own may take a sudden turn for the better, whereas maintaining an attitude that none of this ultimately matters will change nothing. If so, then the epitome of our human life experience will also remain a quest for more yachts, hookers and blow. In short, a journey toward spiritual stagnation.

For those who would dare to take the bolder approach, knowing the truth and speaking it is our path forward. And if we remain loyal to that destiny, then perhaps one day we will qualify for our introduction to the rest of the universe as the peaceful and democratic species we truly aspire to be rather than merely pretend to be.

So what kind of truths can we expect to encounter on our journey to greater wisdom? Luckily, this book has given us some options as to where we might begin looking.

The Ugly Truths About War

The winners of any war are not those fighting in it. Instead, the naive, over-confident boys of working class parents are sent overseas to keep shooting until they or the boys on the others side suffer the most bullet wounds, whereupon the leaders of the winning side can then begin to loot the resources of the losers. This is what victory looks like.

Moreover, once those young soldiers return, their innocence defiled by the first kill, and their minds and bodies often irreparably damaged, they can expect to find that nothing has changed for the better back home. The same wealthy men who sent them off to war are still in power, while they have little more to show for their efforts beyond scar tissue, nightmares and a military pension, if they live to collect it. And after each war, we as a society lament the futility of war until the next generation of boys can be duped into risking their lives for the sole enrichment of the sociopaths who organize these mass killing sprees.

War is inevitable when men are in charge of society because they are wired by nature to fight for dominance — which is also symbolized by such male inventions as monarchy, business monopolies and nuclear stockpiling. As such, let us also be reminded that women must take a far more peaceful approach to negotiating for power out of a need to protect their young. And so, we have a simple choice to make: let men continue to keep us on the warpath, or allow womankind to put us on a path toward greater peace as a result of their wiser inclinations.

In the past, the ugly truths of war were easier to suppress when our government leaders controlled all outgoing information. But now with the internet and video technology being so widely available, ordinary citizens have easy access to testimonials and documentaries from men who fought to defend their countries only to realize they were being played like pawns in the power-hoarding games of various male world dominators. They know best of all that the people making money from bullets and body bags are not praying for peace back home. Nor are the sons of well-placed politicians expected to drop out of their classes at ivy league schools to risk losing their lives and future, unlike the lesser educated and more expendable children of poverty.

This introduces yet another ugly truth about war that the filmmaker, Michael Moore, shared in his documentaries, in that young men don't necessarily join the military out of a sense of duty to their country but because they lack employment opportunities. This exposes a further ugly truth, in that a teenaged boy who has never held a steady job long enough to know what sacrifices his government will make for him as a result of his paying taxes is being somewhat premature in declaring his undying patriotic love for a country that may only be exploiting him for reasons of political gain.

After all, one should also not make payments on an untested car, lest it leave us stranded alone in the dark, far from home.

Moreover, all soldiers are patriots, including the Nazi soldiers who filled roadside ditches with the bullet-riddled bodies of women and children. They were also proud to be serving their country. And that is another ugly truth: killing for your leaders makes you a patriot.

But with their hormone-driven Bio-Psychology making them eager to prove themselves, young men are often as anxious for battle as any male bear or lion. For this reason, such things will never change, which is why we must be far better prepared to offer young men a legitimate path leading to personal growth rather than a crematorium.

Yet this exposes a further ugly truth in that the military leaders who send young boys off to die already know they are hot-wired to compete due to their awakening sexual chemistry. They also know that their brains are not yet fully-developed, giving them a limited window of opportunity to exploit boys between the ages of 18 to 25 as armies of impulse-driven glory-seekers before they grow too wise to risk their lives for someone's angry God or a government claiming its superiority by way of its military might rather than its quality of life.

…

Given that war is government-sanctioned murder, we should not be surprised that warfare also attracts psychopaths seeking a cover story to unleash their homicidal tendencies upon others. Among its many graduates are serial killer, Jeffrey Dahmer, who joined the US Military, then went on to cannibalizing his lovers. Another was David Russell

Williams, a Royal Canadian Air Force Colonel who spent his time off raping, torturing and killing women while meeting with government officials during the day to discuss national security.

And then there was a UK newspaper image published in 1952 that showed a British Royal Marine proudly holding a human head in each hand like two prize-winning bass caught at a nearby lake. And yet, if we saw him walking on the streets of London carrying severed heads, it would be seen as evidence of psychopathy, which it is. Moreover, we would likely not feel safe living next door to such a proud destroyer of human life upon his return from war, let alone talking with him.

Given such disturbing truths, it is safe to say that the values of war are incompatible with those of maintaining a peaceful society. Instead, they are compatible only with men dominating other men through the sacrificing of society itself. Moreover, turning the act of mass murder into an honorable profession is clearly a lifestyle that only men could have invented in that it lacks every positive, life-affirming touch of womanhood. Instead, it is based on a lust-driven urge to dominate that may see mere boys setting fire to family homes, raping daughters and slaughtering entire villages full of innocent civilians only to cry for their mothers as they're being carried out of battle on a stretcher. And if they live, they will be rewarded with a medal.

This is the hypocritical balancing act in which many governments are engaged in trying to make mass murder seem normal and socially rewarding in context of war, yet morally reprehensible and illegal if we indulge in it for personal gain. And this may also explain the cognitive dissonance felt by many soldiers upon returning home in realizing that there is no pride in being a killer, unless one is a psychopath.

The Truthless Society

As was earlier stated, being honest carries with it the risk of losing. For example, if we robbed a bank and then confessed our crime to a nearby police officer to clear our conscience, we would not only lose our bag of stolen money, but also years of life to prison. As such, robbers must wear masks to avoid being recognized for who they truly are.

Yet robbers are not the only ones needing to wear masks, but anyone having something to lose for speaking the truth. For example, Donald Trump is a man famous for wearing masks to make deals or political speeches. Yet in one notable 2016 TV debate, he stated "the system is rigged" and then unmasked himself long enough to confess taking full advantage of that fact — to which the US justice system responded by convicting him of various tax-related felonies after he left office.

Lone glory-seekers like Trump are not the only ones wearing masks. In fact, they can be worn by entire races and cultures to conceal their guilt while engaging in crimes against other races and cultures, or even nature itself. Among such "group masks" is the one worn by men to hide their gender-based history of crimes against humanity, our planet, and womankind. After all, it was not invading armies of women who stole North America from its original tenants through murder and the decimation of wild buffalo to starve out their "Indian" competitors. It was also not women who brought various animal species, including the beaver, to the brink of extinction in order to get rich from selling their fur pelts overseas. Nor was it women who started World War II or exploded over 2000 atom bombs into our atmosphere to test their future killing power. That was all done by men, and men alone.

And so, as men continue to make their promises about the glorious future that awaits us under their assumed superior political leadership, we simply have to look to their past behavior to predict the future. Or, we can look to present-day Israel, the Ukraine or anywhere that men are still hoping to solve problems by severing heads.

And yet, if we accuse those men of performing poorly, they either deny it or blame their mistakes on some competing group of men. In short, anyone but themselves. Subsequently, this mask of faultlessness will rarely ever come off because it is biologically embedded in men's need to appear dominant. As such, we should also not expect them to confess to anything that makes them look weak or inferior, especially if they are holding positions of power over others.

Naturally, this is a problem if that man is truly weak or inferior as a leader and thereby compromising our collective ability to prosper or even just to survive. In yet another Trump-related example, rather than admit defeat for being judged an inferior leader, he instead blamed his loss in the 2020 election on voting machines. And yet, had he won, he would have declared them to be operating flawlessly.

Moreover, as voters we often wear masks to hide the fact that we are supporting men who are not true leaders by any standard of excellence. Instead, they may be seasoned performers pretending to be leaders to win a position of undeserved power. And once they fail as leaders, we may continue to support them so the opposing side will not believe their own leadership candidates to be better.

In that regard, at least Joe Biden, the sitting US president in 2024, showed the courage to face that truth in his reelection bid when it became clear he was no longer the leader that voters needed him to be. On the other hand, despite years of exhibiting mental aberrations that put his leadership merit into doubt, Donald Trump continues to grasp for a second presidential term. Yet anyone speaking truth to the power of his voting fan base must pay the price, which would explain why many Republican politicians must wear a "pro-Trump" mask when in public to hide their true feelings about the man.

But whether we like him or not, Donald Trump has played a critical role in the conscious evolution of our world by proving beyond a doubt that many of us choose to live in a self-deluded bubble world wherein truth is not absolute but only relative to the bubble itself. In that world, Trump won the 2020 election because he can't possibly be a loser. After all, this is what he told his followers to believe. And so they did.

And on it goes, wherever people live inside mental bubbles designed to protect their beliefs from erosion by the outside world. We see this in political systems and religions, and also among various businesses that pretend to serve the greater good of society by denying those facts that prove otherwise. And with power and government behind them, our truths and the truth-tellers of this world stand little chance to be heard among those to whom winning is all that matters.

Welcome to Generica

As stated throughout this book and supported by numerous examples, it is clear that our world has a lot of problems to solve, the majority of which are caused by power hungry men leading us in the direction of their own selfish fulfillment. Luckily, here again, the IPSFA Sequence offers us a tool to both decipher those problems and allow us to create a structured means to globally improve our human condition.

Currently, our greatest problem politically appears like this:

- (I) **IDENTITY**: Citizen (a person without any political power.)
- (P) **PROMISE**: To be led to future prosperity by one man.
- (S) **SCRIPT**: Follow that one man for the next 4-8 years.
- (F) **FEAR**: Poverty, foreigners, troublemakers, perverts, etc.
- (A) **APATHY**: Tax cuts for the rich; cuts to social services spending to offset those tax cuts; deregulation of public safety laws.

This is a familiar form of citizen identity; a thoughtless, automated script for social management that is repeated throughout our human history as though we have no other options. And as long as men with guns are working to protect the interests of our leaders over our own, we will have no other options, nor even a chance to discuss them.

Luckily, the IPSFA Sequence is as flexible as DNA in its potential uses. Not only can we use it to create new forms of social identity for men and women, but also for businesses, politicians and entire nations.

In recognition of the mentally-adventurous creators among us, let us then challenge ourselves to invent an entirely new nation and form of government, complete with brand new laws and ways of thinking.

Given that it ought to be widely applicable, let's call it "Generica" and make it a country so great that everyone will want to live in it. Let us then further imagine turning that way of life into a franchise that can be shared worldwide by the people of every continent.

While only a simulation, the outcome of this mental exercise can be as real as we choose to make it. So take some time to think about why your own version of "Generica" will be a truly great nation to live in.

(I) **IDENTITY**: Generica (The greatest country YOU can imagine.)
(P) **PROMISE**: To live in the greatest country ever by unanimous consent, due to its outstanding social values.
(S) **SCRIPT**: ==> [THIS IS WHERE YOU GET INVENTIVE]
(F) **FEAR**: To live in the worst country by unanimous consent due to its incredibly low social values.
(A) **APATHY**: Generican values ensure that no apathy exists for anything democratically decreed as socially important.

The SCRIPT aspect of our Generican national identity is where you use your imagination to list the characteristics of an ideal homeland. For instance, what happens there? What do people do to survive? Do they compete for power and status, or help one another by cooperating more? Is all social activity directed towards personal gain, or do people use prosperity to elevate the quality of life for everyone? Are there rules and regulations to keep people honest, or can we do as we want without any consequences, be it killing, polluting or cheating others?

Clearly, such questions were pondered by the founders of all nations as they invented their own bubble world of laws, beliefs and activities. Yet their primary concern was likely more for themselves — to invent a nation to favor their own enrichment. And that is the premise under which much of our world continues to operate as the moneyed classes shape our laws and future lives to favor themselves, often at the cost of causing a state of lifelong fear and economic misery for everyone else.

As such, we can see how important — and difficult — it becomes to design a nation not created in the image of our own selfishness but as a means to serve the greater good of all — even those in foreign lands. For this reason, all things must be carefully considered to ensure that the system works for everyone and not just a privileged few plutocrats, or for men to the exclusion of women. Instead, Generica must serve all people rather than all people being in the service of one.

Some obvious goals are a universal healthcare system and a greater concern for individuality and creative self-expression — which is the foundation for inventing anything new in this world.

Ultimately, aside from those few wild-eyed men who want to live in a dog-eat-dog netherworld ruled by guns and sheer stupidity, what we may discover is that the majority of us want to live in a kinder, gentler world. And this would naturally require nations to create responsible adults who know how to raise responsible children. In doing so, what should we be teaching those children to make them more responsible?

In a nation of responsible adults, learning how to shoot a gun is far less important than learning how to build and maintain a community. To do so, we must also be willing to nurture the kind of freethinking that will allow us to design such a nation. In short, we cannot have freedom in our ideas about governing without freedom of mind.

...

As we conclude this chapter with you effectively having to redesign the entire world based on a single, realistic template, consider a quote by Noam Chomsky from his book, *Understanding Power:*

> *"The whole educational and professional training system is a very elaborate filter, which just weeds out people who are too independent, and who think for themselves, and don't know how to be submissive, and so on — because they're dysfunctional to the institutions."*

So what will it be, fellow Generican? How shall we proceed in going forward from here? Should we invent a school system that allows us to identify and appreciate freethinkers rather than teaching everyone to thoughtlessly obey authority like a glazed-over cultist at a pep rally?

What great new ways of thinking might a genuine freethinker have to offer us — and what benefits might we have already lost by filtering such people out by way of our traditional learning systems?

Surely there are many intelligent, creative voices out there with great ideas waiting to be heard. Let us create a world that gives everyone the right and a platform to speak openly and freely. And above all, let us not fear to speak the truth, for in Generica, we have nothing to lose that cannot be returned by the kindness and caring of others.

CHAPTER 19
In Defense of Men

Being a man is never easy. Almost from the time we learn to walk, we feel the relentless pressure to prove ourselves without understanding why we are driven to act this way. The answer, of course, is to appease nature so that we might one day prove ourselves a top contender for inseminating the choice females of society. Basic animal psychology.

How this urge affects us depends upon the character, temperament and psychological health of the individual. For some, it may cause an inexplicable drive to engage in combative sports, whereas others may reach for a position of higher authority as a police officer or a politician with ambitions to lead a nation. Ultimately, all men find some way to satisfy this instinctual urge to win, whether as lawyers battling to win in the courtrooms of our world, as entertainers touring to win a bigger audience, or as teenaged boys shooting their way to victory in some hostile, computer-generated world of simulated gun violence.

It doesn't really matter how we do it, as long as we're constantly trying to prove ourselves *the better man* by competing.

Making life even more demanding for men is that this pressure to perform never ends. Instead, nature has designed us to keep competing throughout our lives, as evident by those cantankerous old billionaires who refuse to relinquish control of their powerful business empires. This lifelong urge to keep winning is also the cause of most human conflicts in society, including those that may one day lead to a global nuclear war wherein no man will be left to claim the spoils of victory.

Fortunately, most forms of male competition involve bluffing and are therefore only for show, including our hoarding of nuclear weapons to intimidate rival nations. Other times, men may not even realize that they are being competitive.

For example, if you are sitting at the dinner table having to listen to your father or any man angrily denounce the members of another race, religion or political ideology, just realize that such banter is not always conscious or entirely his fault. Instead, he is engaged in a kind of mental combat ritual to declare himself a winner over a conveniently absent foe. And given that nature expects him to always be proving himself, his self-congratulatory rants may be a daily nuisance any time a captive audience has gathered for whom he can perform his one man power play. He may also refuse to stop indulging in these combative monologues if he uses them to counteract feelings of low self-esteem, in which case they represent a form of self-help mental therapy.

This exposes one of men's dirtiest little secrets wherein we may seek to purposely diminish others to feel better about ourselves.

Referring again to one of our more entertaining political villains of this era: it seems that Donald Trump also needs to constantly deflate the self-worth of others to inflate his own. Not surprisingly, his brand of political theatre attracts the downtrodden who may enjoy watching someone else get picked on for a change. However, turning hate into a form of entertainment has undermined US politics to where the goal of gloating seems to overshadow that of making social progress.

To be fair, bullies such as Donald Trump have often been bullied themselves. In fact, many men are victims of status-based abuse by fathers who judged them only for their value as a competitive game piece in their own quests for status. As a result, many male children are subjected to *conditional* praise in meeting a father's selfish demands, or used as a convenient punching bag when he was seeking an easy target to prove his dominance. Subsequently, whether praised as winners or vilified as losers, these sons often grow up never having been respected for making their own decisions or being their own men — some may not even be given their own distinct names. In addition, as they grow up, they may go through life never feeling satisfied or good enough for the simple reason that it is not themselves whom they aim to please, but the ghost of a demanding father who still haunts their minds.

Subsequently, men are not only victims of nature's constant demand to prove themselves, but also of other men's selfish demands in seeking to increase their own feelings of dominance or social status over them.

A further level of competitive assault is triggered by the discerning behavior of women, whose concerns for the future include the genetic health and economic security of their children. As such, all available men are subjected to a list of expectations that includes aspects of their lives over which they have no control, including their physical features or having been born on that side of the tracks where the most common kind of opportunity that knocks on their doors is petty crime.

Subsequently, a poor, unattractive man who was bullied by his father and exploited by greedy employers has every reason to feel insecure, lest he be graced with a healthy dose of self-esteem. And if not, he may go on to become the kind of man who tries to make up for his losses by defeating those even weaker or lower in status than himself.

...

Thankfully, not all men are created equal. As such, while nature has condemned many a man to a lifetime of anti-social depravity, others have proven themselves to be a valuable asset to their societies. Such men are beyond the reach of those shallow stereotypes promoted by patriarchal cultures or the schoolyard bully version of masculinity that encourages men to destroy our ecosystems to protect corporate profits or drop bombs to keep the war industry alive. Instead, they walk their own paths in life, seemingly immune to that plague of petty concerns for status that has most men frantically scrambling to salvage their deflated manhood.

Yet for men of a kinder disposition, there is no escaping the reign of self-indulgent tyrants and psychopaths who will do whatever it takes to take it all. And that is also why most human societies are constantly whimpering like a man on the ground gasping to catch his breath after being gut punched and kicked in the crotch by a gloating brute who thinks nothing of behaving this way in seeing no value in anyone's life — perhaps even his own beyond satiating its primal urges.

Getting back up can often seem impossible. And yet, we must, not only because nature demands it to ensure our survival, but also because there is so much untapped joy potential awaiting to be released in our world if we could only summon the courage to free it from within or escape those pathological male dominators now holding it hostage.

In that regard, the leaders of many patriarchal world governments and religious cults purposely deprive us of our rights and freedoms to maintain their power over us; sexual and mental freedom are common examples. But to stand any chance to survive as a harmonious network of global citizens, we must dismantle these primitive, instinct-driven domination and exploitation systems and begin anew in terms of how we want to structure and govern our human societies. It cannot be a "winner takes all" approach as such thinking has always worked against everyone's advantage — including that of the winner.

Moreover, a list of infamous winners from our past yields a lineup of psychopaths and sociopaths normally found in maximum security prisons. Yet by having us adopt their twisted world view, they were able to create cultures wherein behaviors normally associated with mental derangement became normalized for engaging in politics, religion and business. And as this happens, common sense and sanity will often be vilified as abnormal while our freedom to be ourselves is revoked.

For this reason, a recalibration of values and a rebalancing of power are required on a global scale, not only between men and women, but also between citizens and leaders. By taking action, we will be able to create genuine sustainable societies to replace the plutocratic cultures of resource looting and political gamesmanship that have long been steering our world towards ruin.

Moreover, this recalibration is needed in defense of men who have the potential to succeed, yet are being denied that opportunity by men who do not want others rising up to challenge their winning status.

The Spectator Society

In support of this shift in power, men and women must understand how they are being manipulated in the systems of their dominators; genuine conspiracies that keep us fighting for our rights and freedoms against a minority best served by our having none at all. Having given much attention to these topics, it will nonetheless be helpful to revisit some of the essential themes from the past chapters.

Given that this book concerns itself with the male competition for power, let us restate that *Patriarchy* defines the domination of society by men. As a social control system, it promotes stereotypes that keep women out of power while emboldening men to feel entitled to rule over them and also one another.

This has led to the creation of a Gender Wall that is maintained by having young men and women adopt various exaggerated social traits to make them appear opposite in every regard — big *hard* men in blue versus *soft* little women in pink. And whereas men are taught to wear sensible shoes in any race to the top, women are tricked into wobbling on high heels as a form of self-sabotage — or to constantly look in the mirror rather than ahead toward new opportunities for advancement.

But there is more to orchestrated social domination than this power divide between genders. For a better overview of how human control systems are typically structured, let us use the metaphor of USA style "football," a game played mostly with the hands. As such, it also shares a similar ironic mislabeling with democracy; which is a hands-off style of governing that requires letting others choose on our behalf.

As for the game itself, football is an event that fills large stadiums with cheering fans to watch a violent struggle between one tribe of large, aggressive male gladiators trying to carry an oblong ball through an opposing tribe of large, aggressive gladiators to prove they are the better tribe. As a result, many see football as a metaphor for life. But little do they know how much the game actually reveals.

For instance, when one tribe of men has proven it can escort the ball across enemy lines, they will then engage in a final act of humiliation against the defeated side by inserting the ball into an opening; a kind of symbolic vagina fiercely guarded against all intruders. As such, the scoring of a "goal" in sport signifies a kind of team ejaculation in a symbolic game of male sexual conquest, whereupon some men may get highly emotional while others triumphantly pump their fists in pride. And if we look to other sports including soccer, basketball or even golf, we find a similar theme wherein men are trying to insert an object into a hole as part of a subconscious desire to conquer and penetrate. As such, many sports could simply be renamed "Sperm Ball."

These "fighting off other men to get to the hole" contests represent a symbolic externalization of our internal Bio-Psychological impulses; a kind of staged play of nature's covert influence upon our lives. As such, any form of competition, be it tennis, poker or even just a hot dog eating contest is an outward expression of our impulse to compete for dominant mating status. And if such activities were eliminated from our inventory of human behaviors, it would leave many glory-seeking men with little to do beyond eating and sleeping, especially dictators and greedy businessmen who spend their entire lives acting out these biologically-motivated conquest dramas as a choice of career. This also suggests is that if a man is more self-aware, he can choose to engage in entirely different activities that may also prove to be more beneficial to society and thus far more personally fulfilling for him.

Our externalizing of nature's procreation drama is evident in other aspects of sport as well, including our choosing of strong and healthy athletes to comply with nature's own demand that only the best fight for dominant status. As spectators, we then live out our own conquest fantasies through such powerful men. Yet there is even more that the symbolism of American style football can reveal about the top-down ruling of society, including what is expected of our behavior.

Most notably, the majority of people are spectators sitting idly at the sidelines as they watch other men engage in rewarding challenges to win public attention and power. Moreover, we must pay to watch them win such privileges. In this way, society has prepared a place for those men who either do not wish to challenge themselves, or who do not qualify to play the game based on its strict rules of engagement.

Also noteworthy is that everyone's attention is on those alpha males; they are all that matters — beyond the team owners who exploit both the spectators and athletes from behind the scenes for personal gain and/or glory. And if we look back to our high school days, we see that little has changed in that athletes still command more attention than intellectuals as a direct reflection of nature's own preference for a good old-fashioned brawl between the biggest brutes among us.

This also explains the media's obsession with those men competing for glory, be they wealthy entrepreneurs, rich and famous celebrities, or high-paid athletes. Beyond natural disasters, little else seems to matter to society aside from those who are winning or competing to win; an obsession reinforced by commercial ads for casinos and lottery tickets, as well as costly material goods sold for competitive display, including yachts the size of small islands and cars costing more than a house.

In this environment, even music is reduced to a fight for ticket sales and the *number one* position in the charts. In this way, society teaches us that winning matters more than anything — perhaps even living in a peaceful society where everyone gets along. After all, if we want to promote greed, then we cannot expect to have peace.

Historically, it is mostly men who are exposed to the competitive hostility of other men, whereas under patriarchal rule, women are kept in the background and often treated as an afterthought.

Ironically, this aspect of top-down patriarchal gender values is also on display in USA football in the form of sexually attractive female "cheerleaders" who stand on the sidelines without any input as to how the game is played. In fact, their only role is to constantly lift their legs high enough to reveal the prize for which all men are expected to fight, including those salivating enviously from the stands.

And here we learn the most valuable lesson about the top-down structuring of society in that no man on the field or in management wants those competitively-aroused male spectators to come rushing off the stands to compete against them, least of all the owners filling their pockets with all the money being spend on tickets, t-shirts and hot dogs by a captive audience of passive male consumers.

And therein we also find a counterpart in the process of governing in that those in charge of our political systems also do not want us to come rushing down off the stands to interfere in their glory-seeking power games. Instead, they want us to mind our own business and stay out of their way, lest we demand more for ourselves.

Choosing Sides

As we can see, USA style football offers a useful metaphor for how the domination game is played in many venues beyond the stadium.

For example, we can see opposing teams of politicians who also treat governing like a sport in their quests for personal glory, while women have long been kept on the sidelines as men played their power games. And behind the scenes, out of public view, we find the orchestrators of much of what happens on the field and in the stands; the owners of the game — dynastic cabals of plutocrats and financial grifters with a long history of playing our world like a game for their own amusement.

As such, while many nations boast of being a democracy, they offer voters no political decision-making power. Instead, we are expected to also sit idly in the stands to cheer for our favorite team while dutifully paying taxes to keep this lucrative political enterprise in play.

Excluding voters from exercising genuine political power requires us to believe that we have no right to such power. This is something that monarchy and fascism have both done effectively. Yet today's aspiring politicians must put a better face on their selfish ambitions by at least pretending to be in the game for our sake. And in some cases, this may even be true. But for the most part, it's dirty business as usual, which is why we now need to clean up our political systems worldwide.

Yet to prevent this from happening, we have long been kept divided into opposing "teams" of social identity groups and encouraged instead to compete against one another despite our sharing a common enemy in those who exploit us, whether at the ballot box or the cash register.

As a result, we lose our focus in fighting the good fight against those who cause our collective misery by battling against each other instead.

For this reason, many political leaders do not even have to make good on campaign promises as long as they keep us fighting over petty issues — "straw man" arguments that keep us looking away from the problem or its actual cause. As such, genuine leadership is not required but only a ring master to regress voters to a reflexive state of primal anger, thus proving their claim that we, as citizens, cannot be trusted with power.

In this regard, we exist in a kind of social coliseum wherein we are the game being played by deceitful men who always seem to win.

...

Human societies are interdependent and cooperative out of necessity, whereas male domination is isolationist and adversarial by nature. In other words, they are mutually incompatible. Here again, we can only imagine how different our human societies might be today had women been in charge of guiding them as opposed to men on a glory-seeking mission to conquer. We might also speculate what kind of world would welcome us today had the kinder, gentler men of society prevailed rather than been imprisoned or assassinated as "enemies of the state" — a convenient, thoughtless moniker assigned to those who refuse to submit to their authoritarian demands.

Yet even peacemakers are challenged to keep their own peace when growing up in cultures that have them choosing sides, whether against women, or other men based on various real or imagined differences.

In addition to these cultural divide and conquer strategies that have us choosing sides in support of our favorite political party or religion, men are also divided and conquered from within by training them to abandon their own true identities and the better part of themselves.

To help explain this, let us first consider that great thinkers are not manufactured on a factory assembly line but born of unique traits that society can only nurture. Mediocrity, on the other hand, is the essence of an assembly line process that grooms a nation's children for a future of obedient servitude by eliminating all traces of their individuality for the purpose of making them uniformly predictable in their behavior.

As any experienced dictator knows, it is easier to control a nation full of citizens if they all think the same thoughts and share the same goals while clinging to a false hope that they will one day be invited to break bread at their master's table. This is why traditional school systems are designed to churn out graduates of a predictable consistency with low expectations of holding public power; people who want steady jobs to pay for mortgages and retirement plans; people who treat their dreams as a frivolous mental artifact to be discarded with youth.

And traditionally, boys have been expected to become the frontline soldiers in the global wars for status of the rich and greedy.

As anonymous combatants expected to follow orders, the training of adversarial male behavior often intensifies in high school. Here, many a boy has been put in a lineup on one side of the gym to face another lineup of boys on the other. Each side is then instructed to throw a ball as hard as they can at the boys on the opposing side, without regard for any damage it may do to their faces or genitals. The point was not to ask questions but to follow orders by attacking others for merely being on the opposing side. And since everyone is watching, we do as we're told to avoid being labelled "an enemy of the state" of manhood.

For those unfamiliar with this violent game, it has been aptly given the name "murder ball"— an ironic ode to killing for those pretending to cherish peace. Yet the quest for peace is betrayed at every turn in our training as men, even in our language. Consider, for example, that the term "killing it" conveys excellence or that "destroying" an opponent is the goal of debate. As such, the highest aspirations of patriarchal male culture remains in plain view — to kill and destroy.

But thankfully, times are changing and young people now realize that their dysfunctional ancestors had all been socially-engineered for a slave-like existence that many now reject as a path to their future.

Yet their more open-minded approach to gauging human potential is being met by a backlash from a patriarchal establishment whose comfortable control of our world is threatened by any change in our attitude toward their outdated social domination systems. But are we truly losing anything by leaving them behind? What awaits us beyond more of the same if we keep plodding along and doing as we're told by those who control the reigns of our society?

The Tag-Along Society

The USA style football analogy is useful in helping us to understand how human control systems work, even at a recreational level. It is also useful today as fundamentalist conservative forces are scrambling to herd humanity back into its designated holding pens on either side of the Gender Wall so the boys can resume dominating the girls while all obey the patriarchs in power. In short, they want us to keep playing *follow the leader* to protect their various social and political rackets. This is no secret to anyone in politics, as proven when former US President, Bill Clinton stated during his DNC speech in August, 2024: "These people want to dominate the system, politically, economically and socially." The problem being that we as citizens have every right to fear for our freedom, yet no right to protect it from corrupt leaders.

Luckily, nature and reality both oppose the wishful thinking of the more desperate defenders of the socially indefensible as they struggle to push their proverbial square peg interpretation of life back into the round hole to keep pretending that it's a perfect fit. This also applies to forcing men and women into prefabricated social roles that have them becoming caricatures of what others expect rather than what for which they have been designed by nature. After all, every conscious being requires the freedom to grow and explore its world, for without it, we cannot fully exist, whether as a wild animal trapped in a city zoo, or a citizen trapped in one of many suppressive political systems.

To demonstrate the negative affect that closed-minded stereotypical thinking can have on greater humanity, let us imagine that legendary Queen frontman and singer, Freddie Mercury, had been born in Iran after its occupation by religious fundamentalists. Here, he would have faced execution as a homosexual rather than being provided the means to develop a stellar musical talent and onstage charisma that ultimately transformed him into a beloved cultural icon worldwide.

Would our world have been a better place had he been executed for his sexual attraction to men? Or, if instead of walking onstage at Live Aid, he had walked past the stadium to a nearby bomb factory to assist his country's leaders in some future assault upon a weaker nation?

The same question applies to all of us: might our world have already been a better place had we refused to walk a default path of predictable consistency as trained to do? Might we have already risen to greater heights as a species had we not taken the assembly line approach to our conscious and social development and chosen instead personal power over handing the reigns of our lives over to our political leaders?

After all, there is no freedom without the freedom to choose, nor the ability to reject what others choose for us — for their sake.

And what is it that others will choose for us? As we may know, often from bitter experience, everyone expects something from us, whether to believe as they believe or do as they do so that they can achieve their goals — even if it defeats ours. Selfishness of this kind is inherent to all living systems due to nature's own urging and if we are unprotected from our right to choose, then we live as slaves, not free citizens.

Currently in our tag-along societies, we are expected to awaken each day at a certain time to keep our system running so that those in power can stay in power. For instance, in a monarchy, a king expects everyone to protect his hold on power, not to challenge it. And our government systems were surely designed with the same expectation, which is why our democracies are not genuine democracies but cheap imitations of the real thing made of a lesser quality for easier mass consumption.

But we are not supposed to think about such things. Instead, we are kept distracted on a path of conspicuous consumption wherein we are also offered mere cheap substitutes for the happiness or contentment we seek. And as we work year after year to enshrine ourselves in some costly strata of symbolic substitutes for happiness and meaning, we are also left with little time to tamper with the system that maintains our state of spiritual malnutrition — this material treadmill of hope.

In the meantime, the sinister intentions of society's worst human predators seems unstoppable. In fact, their degenerate visions for our collective downfall stand a better chance of being implemented in our current "pay for play" political casinos than do any safeguards against them. And this has to do with the imbalance of power that exists in all societies wherein its citizens have no say in matters that concern the future of their nations or their own. Even in those nations that claim to uphold democratic principles, critical decisions are largely made by a privileged few political leaders, the more corrupt of whom may also provide custom-tailored legislation for those who can afford it.

And although we can publicly protest the damage others have done once it's too late, we are never invited to the negotiating table to help guide our societies toward a more rewarding future for all. This leaves us stuck in our current economic models of selfish predation by the economically-dominant alpha males of society, men who use wealth as a sword to cut down the rest of us. And while they may try to hide their crimes against society and nature behind cheerful ad campaigns, we cannot unsee the damage being done, nor deny that those causing the most destruction are making the least effort to restrain themselves or to clean up their growing mess.

Here again, we have a chance to celebrate the efforts of someone like Boyan Slat, a young man who chose not to join the popular march toward mediocrity. As an outstanding example of a modern-day male hero, his daring actions and willingness to risk his future security beg the question: *why did it take a teenager to initiate cleaning up the plastic pollution from our oceans while wealthy industrialists ignored the problem?*

The answer is simple: Boyan was probably not thinking of profit or personal glory in initiating *The Ocean Cleanup* project. Instead, he had the fate of our oceans and its animal inhabitants in mind, which is why he represents the kind of man we can trust to pave the way toward a future wherein a higher social standard is met rather than that forced upon us by self-serving industrialists and corrupt career politicians.

This highlights an ongoing problem for all humankind in that, even though we have made some notable progress toward improving our world in various ways, the best we can expect in terms of exercising our political power in any pseudo-democratic human work colony is to cast a single vote for a politician who may turn out to have no desire to protect us from the greed of others if it serves his own interests. And since we are trapped within consumerism-based monetary ecosystems, we may witness people actively engaged in destroying our world in the name of profit without having any means to stop them, nor any form of recourse beyond sending an angry letter to a local politician. And naturally, leaving our future in the hands of competitive men whose intentions are dubious at best will not lead us to the kind of sustainable societies we must create to survive our inherently selfish attitudes.

In reality, we cannot expect even the most dedicated of politicians to have enough time to consider the needs of those watching from the stands, especially when engaged in heated battles against rivals who seek to ruin their political careers. At best, our list of concerns will wind up in a long queue to eventually be read by an intern.

In the meantime, the legacy of the greedy often lingers, whether in the form of a devastating oil spill in the Gulf of Mexico, or the misery we inherit under the tyranny of men such as Adolf Hitler, whose quest for power left millions sitting in the bombed out rubble with no place to sleep or food to eat; a far cry from the future promised to them. And yet, even today there are young men proudly marching with swastikas and other Nazi symbolism to celebrate a vision for our world that was drafted within the mind of a psychotic mass murderer.

And everywhere we find such groups of men pushing for an agenda that drives us farther apart while failing to address a basic truth in that we cannot survive unless we learn to survive together.

Yet such is the fallout of "tag along" societies wherein we are induced to behave like cultish followers of those pretending to have our best interests in mind — while their actions prove otherwise.

And so, we stand at a critical juncture in our human history wherein we are forced to consider how to save ourselves from the competitive greed and lies of other men before we run out of time — or options.

Luckily, there is a way forward never considered by any glory-seeker on a selfish path. And while it may be a difficult solution to implement globally, it is also the only realistic means for allowing our species and natural world to survive as more than just the basis for quarterly stock reports to wealthy transnational investors.

And so, in defense of all of us now living under the selfish tyranny of others, I dedicate this next and final chapter to you.

CHAPTER 20
Citizen Based Social Planning

Given men's inborn competitive nature and our entrapment as citizens within economically interdependent nation states, it is with certainty that more RMS Titanic-style enterprises will see us going down with the ship while their deckhands echo those infamous last words of the hopelessly selfish — "Every man for himself."

The global financial crisis of 2008, for example, left many sinking into the abyss of men's predatory greed, while Russia's Vladimir Putin and a constantly deployed US military remind us that some political leaders just aren't happy unless they're conquering someone else.

All in all, it appears we have learned little from our past about living peacefully, while book titles such as *The Art of War* will always attract more male readers than *Clearing a Path to Joy* will. Ultimately, nature always wins, and for nature to win, it must keep men fighting.

As such, beyond our mistakes of the past, what is also certain to keep repeating is our collective victimhood as disempowered citizens of any nation under the tyranny of men. In fact, even the most celebrated of modern democracies is not truly democratic in that it does not ask us to participate in the process of making decisions. As such, it is little more than a veiled dictatorship wherein one man or group of men still make all decisions on our behalf. For this reason, we must also be able to trust them and hope they don't prove to be social predators or vain narcissists simply wasting our time to gain public attention.

And yet, even the most promising leaders can fail to make good on their promises. Such was the case when Barack Obama won the US Presidency, only to have his plans for an upgrade to American society met by the competitive hostility of an opposition party seemingly more determined to display its dominance than serve the public. And always, it is voters who lose as their elected representatives spend more time playing alpha male war games than doing the work for which they were elected.

Racism was another factor that undermined the Obama Presidency in a nation still struggling to share its constitutional equality with all men, let alone women. In that regard, female leaders also encounter a similar wall of resistance from men conditioned to believe themselves superior to those born without a penis. In short, the attitude of such voters does not allow them to see women or those outside their own racial group as "real" leaders but only a temporary nuisance.

Moreover, little actually changed during that time of promised hope and change as wars and all the other problems that have long plagued human societies continued unabated. Then, things took a turn for the absurd as a backlash from angry white men had real estate mogul and reality tv icon, Donald Trump, promising to make America *great* again by putting dubious old white men back in charge.

Yet behind the chaotic swinging of the US political pendulum, what we saw was proof of how vulnerable our political systems can be when a single person or group is allowed to rule a nation. Moreover, given its high infant mortality rate, diminishing rights for women, and a people too divided to make meaningful progress, the US system is too broken to be considered a beacon of light for leading us to a better world.

Clearly, we must find a more realistic option for governing human societies if even the best will not allow all voices to be heard. Instead, they leave us to suffer the consequences of each new leader's misguided decisions on our behalf. And if the character of those leaders is tainted, it can leave the future of a nation tainted for generations to come.

On a more positive note, our world is transitioning toward a higher level of collective awareness. Yet as each new generation boldly steps forward to make its stand, others may attempt to draw them back into the past in a bid to regain control over their lives. This is evident in all regressive political, religious and business institutions that rally against the threat of higher education, human intelligence, or a recognition that our relationship with the natural world must be respectful. It is a social struggle best symbolized by the battle to save the last few rhinos from poachers with only self-interest in mind, regardless of the losses. In that regard, our nations are very much like those endangered rhinos in also being pushed to the brink of social, economic or environmental extinction by the ambitions of selfish men.

As to our social evolution, we cannot predict where it might lead, yet we can expect there there will be continued fighting among men in their quests for dominance and that our societies will also continue to suffer as a result of their destructive quests for glory. But while boxing matches and high stakes poker tournaments cannot put our species at risk, one area that must become off limits to the self-serving ambitions of men is the governing of our nations so that we do not suffer the ill affects of men's battles for alpha male glory. For this reason, we must find better options for organizing our nations and serving the needs of our future communities.

One such option is *Citizen Based Social Planning*, a truly democratic system of voting that protects us from the hazards of male competition by eliminating the threat of greed from politics while giving all citizens an equal voice in determining our collective future. As such, *CBSP* can lead us to create the kind of world wherein the promise of hope and change truly can exist as more than just an empty campaign slogan.

While history has provided us with a list of option for organizing human society, none offers what Citizen Based Social Planning does in that it overthrows thousands of years of men's natural born instinct to govern as a demonstration of one's power rather than than their accumulated wisdom.

The Next Step in the Evolution of Democracy

As a truly egalitarian system of governing by and for all people, Citizen Based Social Planning is the next step in the evolution of democracy. It is an essential milestone to reach in elevating our individual power and status to a level where we each have an equal voice in the planning of our collective future — rich, poor, or otherwise.

CBSP accomplishes this by having each citizen vote on ideas that can improve our society rather than having us vote for politicians who promise to make such improvements on our behalf. This immediately solves the problem of broken campaign promises by politicians who may be too busy defending their careers to make meaningful progress toward elevating our quality of life. Many of them think in two or four year terms, much of which is wasted on planning for the next election cycle. In short, little of substance ever gets done if campaigning is the primary focus of politicians rather than making actual progress.

CBSP puts an end to a long-standing game of political pretense and procrastination by giving decision-making power to the people who will directly benefit most making their own decisions, whether it be to improve local schools, the healthcare system, roads and infrastructure, or draft new laws to protect children from corporate greed and angry boys bringing their gun collection to school.

CBSP creates a direct way for people to impact the direction of their society by removing the "middleman" from political decision-making — along with the threat of his selfishness. This new voting system also makes obsolete the tradition of family dynasties and monarchies being entitled to special treatment. In short, it counters the threat of our societies being dominated by the privileged few.

In that regard, we currently have no way to know if a political leader is honest or qualified to deliver on his promises until it is too late to undo the damage. CBSP will eliminate that risk by getting rid of the need to elect political leaders. If the majority wants something done, its decision will stand and cannot be overruled to serve the interests of any one man or minority group. CBSP eliminates conflicts of interest by allowing us to determine via majority vote what we wish to achieve.

As to the real world benefits of a CBSP based system, it stands out in stark contrast to what our current modes of democracy can deliver. Here again, the USA's dysfunctional political system is a useful point of reference due to the imbalance of power evident between the people and their government leaders.

At present, a self-proclaimed "democracy" typically allows us a single vote every four years to choose one person to lead our nation with the end result making it indistinguishable from any other political system, be it communism or a theocracy. Our leader will also typically be male due to a lingering prejudice against women in "traditional" patriarchal systems. Elections are also not democratic given that ordinary citizens cannot compete for attention against wealthy businessmen, career politicians, or famous media personalities. In other words, the road to political life is also usually closed to all but a few. Moreover, in a world where money makes the loudest entrance into any room, it is difficult for those of lesser means to gain media attention if they do not exude the traits of material success as promoted by their society. This is why the "used car salesman" types excel in political theatre because being a good actor is necessary to market one's self to the masses. One example is disgraced former US congressman, George Santos, who faked his way to a political seat by pretending to be everything to everyone; he was Jewish when it was necessary, then a financial expert, and then a graduate of an ivy-league school — all of it a lie.

In addition, the halls of government can be like an exclusive country club wherein only those who can afford its prohibitive fees are allowed entry, including men of old money or political ties. Such gatekeeping was evident in the elections of Justin Trudeau and George W. Bush, whose fathers had both led their nations. This "boys club" aspect of social politics denies ordinary people entry, except as a groundskeeper. However, exclusionism of this type is typical of domination-based animal behavior, not democracy. What this also means is that a citizen of humble origins with credible ideas for improving society may not be heard in systems wherein media monopolies, economic privilege and family ties act as gatekeepers to those inner circles of power where decisions are being made. On the other hand, any wealthy industrialist can expect full access and even legislation to be tabled on his behalf to ensure the flow of his newest revenue into the awaiting hands of those wielding all the decision-making power.

This kind of incestuous deal-making was evident in the changes to the Canadian Fisheries Act in 2002. Here pro-business politicians gave mining companies the right to have lakes, streams or wetlands reclassified as "tailings impoundment areas" so they could be used as dump sites for industrial pollution. Yet if a CBSP voting system had been in place, those drinking that water would surely not have allowed such legislation to pass. But it was dirty business as usual and those alpha males in charge sided with the flow of money over protecting the health of their voters and the natural world.

...

A further problem arises when political parties choose candidates for us, thereby giving us no choice but to vote for whoever they prefer to be our next leader. One notable example was exposed by WikiLeaks wherein emails from campaign workers for Hilary Clinton detailed a coordinated effort to derail the presidential hopes of senator Bernie Sanders. Meanwhile, in Michael Moore's film, *Fahrenheit 11/9*, the Clinton team was shown claiming victory in regions where Sanders had won the most votes. In short, the democratic voting process was ambushed by insiders long before the election ever took place.

Such competitive hostility is inevitable in a top-down "alpha male" form of democracy wherein only one winner is declared to rule over all the rest. Yet if political power were shared equally among voters, then we would no longer be subject to betrayal by candidates trying to cheat their way to the top. Instead, we would be voting for intelligent ideas rather than scheming politicians.

Another weakness in modern political systems is that campaigns are often prone to meddling by the private interests of commercial media owners. For instance, televised debates may include only candidates who spent a lot of money on campaign ads; others may not be invited. Also, media companies may promote their own political biases or even mislead voters by broadcasting false information, as was the case when FOX News promoted Donald Trump's claim that the voting machines had been rigged for him to lose the 2020 election; a costly lie for which FOX was later sued by those companies it had falsely accused.

...

Although we are subjected to constant propaganda to influence our ways of thinking, our role as voting citizens in a democracy is actually quite limited. In fact, all we are asked to do is show up at a designated location, choose our favorite candidate, then hurry home to watch our future unfold from the comfort of the living room couch. And by then repeating this process ad infinitum, we call it "democracy." Yet all we have done is allow a stranger to make political decisions on our behalf for the next few years. And that is the limit of our legislative power as citizens in any modern democracy, with only slight variations.

Additionally, our voting systems are dangerously exposed not only to corruption by wealthy private interests, intelligence agencies and even dishonest campaign workers, but also to our own worst impulses. For instance, nihilistic voters may vote for candidates who promise to take down the government. Nor do we have safeguards to protect us from voting for liars. In effect, without a legitimate voice in the political process or the ability to oust corrupt leaders, we are little more than sitting ducks to wily political poachers.

Subsequently, the term "Democracy" itself is as misleading as is the word "freedom" in that it does not actually give us anything that our leaders do not agree to give us. Nor has it done away with the age-old patriarchal traditional of top-down dominance. And even if detractors say "It's a republic, not a democracy" the bottom line is that the system is not designed for sharing power except among politicians.

And yet, many believe democratic rule delivers miracles when even nations that appear peacefully mature are plagued by selfish alpha male behavior. In Ontario, Canada, for instance, voters cannot stop Doug Ford, a businessman turned politician, from offering prime watersheds to land developers. Yet a CBSP land referendum would end deals that only serve a privileged few. And that is why we don't have them.

How Will CBSP Work?

Citizen Based Social Planning is a voting system like any other. But as stated earlier, instead of voting for people, we will be given the chance to vote on practical ideas to improve our society. Rather than having to vote for someone unknown to us, we will be asked to vote on a social initiative that can impact our lives in a positive way, be it the building of a new bridge or refurbishing an old one. We may even be asked how many war planes our nation needs to keep families safe, or whether it may be more expedient to focus on affordable housing, higher pay for workers and better job security than attacking foreign nations.

There are many immediate advantages to governing ourselves in this manner because it will not only suppress greed and corruption, but also inspire greater public involvement in political issues now that citizens are determining the future direction of their societies.

Naturally, this will also fuel a need for greater social awareness and political discourse in schools, thereby elevating both the academic and intellectual standards of nations — a win-win situation for all but a few authoritarian dictators who need to keep their citizens in a state of fearful ignorance to more easily manipulate them. As such, CBSP represents an antidote to political monopolies and the competitive inclination of men to be the only one who speaks for everyone.

To gain a better understanding of the benefits of a CBSP system of governing, let's assess some of its anticipated benefits by category.

...

VOTING: Currently we are faced with the question of which wealthy businessman, career politician or media celebrity we wish to vote for. CBSP will present us instead with questions as to which ideas we favor over others using the same YES or NO checkbox format.

Questions will be based on projects that we value most as members of each society and nation, ranging from local concerns about water quality and housing to national concerns, such as whether to spend more taxes on social programs than weapons of war. Each project will be chosen based on its merits rather than its benefit to private political donors — which is a default consideration in many nations.

Clearly, this voting process will take longer than the few minutes we now invest to vote for a politician. Yet this greater commitment of time will also ensure that our nations do not fall prey to greedy opportunists as is the tradition in politics. As such, one day voting will be replaced by extended survey periods to gather public opinions on various social matters. This has the immediate benefit of giving the majority a voice in making political decisions now typically made by a small minority.

Surveying will involve a wide range of issues that politicians often grapple with alone, such as whether to ensure fair wages for workers or protect our ecology from the abuses of greedy industrialists.

Surveys will also include contentious topics including abortion and school prayer, or whether minority religious groups have the right to dictate their values and beliefs to the majority, as recently occurred by the USA's overturning the Roe vs Wade. As a truly democratic process, CBSP will allow all of us to decide what is acceptable, not just a few elected officials whose campaigns may be funded by lobbyists.

Furthermore, in modern democracies, no one asks us what we want once an election is over. In fact, it no longer matters what we want as such information was only used to win our vote. However, that will change under a CBSP system, which will year-round fill its databases with a precise analysis of what voters truly want, then prioritize those wants based on popularity. This avoids having to ask the permission of one politician if social progress can be made; a plight better suited for dictatorships, as stated before. Hence, CBSP is more proactive and productive than having to wait for uninspired leaders to act.

CBSP will also bring a greater level of maturity to governing by having us focus on critical issues rather than bicker about imaginary or hypothetical social conflicts.

INTEGRITY: Among its advantages, CBSP governing does not ask us to choose sides in a battle for political party dominance, nor does it seek to impose party values, beliefs or attitudes upon others by decree. Instead, it is a way of governing that promotes equality of power by the seeking of majority consensus on beneficial ideas. As such, CBSP will not force religious beliefs upon others, such as requirement to pray in school, as this is a matter of personal choice. In short, CBSP does not seek to govern our minds.

CBSP will be useful in dealing with real world concerns, such as the quality of drinking water, which is a public health issue that affects all people equally, regardless of their personal views. Yet in our currently divisive political climate, politicians may even use such issues to keep us divided. Subsequently, by making an issue about choosing sides, we may also make the worst choice on behalf of our health.

A similar division occurs when citizens vote for the worst candidates as an act of defiance against their government — which is the essence of the USA's MAGA movement — while others may not vote at all, thus giving fringe candidates a better chance to win elections.

Contrary to modern politics, CBSP does not promote such wasteful spending of our voting power. Nor does it promise unrealistic futures in return for our vote. What it can do, however, is protect the integrity of democracies by defending our freedom to choose and what actions are to be taken once a majority of voters has demanded them.

...

It's no secret that lies obstruct our ability to make informed decisions, whether in choosing a product or politician. Clearly, our future cannot stand on a foundation of fiction and empty promises. As such, CBSP will deliver only valid information to assist voters in making their own informed decisions about community or national level initiatives being considered. This will be done using already existing infrastructure, such as schools, community centers, and the internet. Government secrecy will also not be tolerated in a CBSP system as a relic of a past wherein leaders sought to take advantage of citizens or their enemies by way of holding back information. Honesty is a direct path to progress whereas lies inhibit our ability to move forward in confidence.

A further problem of modern governing systems is that only a few people are allowed to choose our social priorities for us, which can lead to disappointment if leaders fail to deliver on those agendas. CBSP lets us choose our own agendas and prioritize them by majority vote.

IMPLEMENTATION: Like any new program, CBSP will have to undergo an evolutionary process in becoming a viable solution to meet the challenges of governing. This will obviously be a learning process for all involved, from administrators to voters not used to having their opinions solicited or matter. Fortunately, most communities already have long-standing voting stations in place that can transition into year-round information collection centers for surveying the wants and needs of the people. Now, instead of casting a single vote, citizens will be asked to fill out a questionnaire that conveys their vision for a better future. And all votes will be tallied to choose the most popular ideas

In a CBSP style government, the public decides our social priorities based on a majority vote. While this may not protect voters from being swayed by outside opinions, it reduces the risk of meddling if the ideas presented are openly debated rather than discussed in secret behind closed doors among politicians, lawyers and leaders of industry.

Also, as history shows, having one person in charge is a gateway to misconduct. Our instinctual selfishness makes it too tempting to let one individual decide for all others. CBSP bypasses such self-serving impulses by functioning without need of political leaders. While it will still require bureaucrats to ensure the functioning of society, they will not be directed laterally by citizens rather than top down by a single alpha male leader or committee of alpha types.

Taking a "no man on top" approach will stabilize governing priorities by eliminating contests among ambitious men to control the direction of our societies. Currently, every incoming administration can change the priorities of the government, leading to essential social programs being eliminated on a whim, or to give a bigger tax cut to wealthy and business class voters. CBSP will stop our societies from falling victim to the short-sighted planning of politicians who treat governing like a drive-thru fast food restaurant and our futures like litter to be tossed out the window of their speeding careers. As such, it will also be a time of great reconciliation as we bring all sides together in the interest of bringing out the best in our local communities and nations.

...

Currently, most governments are legislatively lop-sided due to their being run by men fighting for dominance by way of social, economic and military warfare, whereas the interests of the people are largely attuned to living in peace and feeling safe.

A CBSP system will govern to maintain a peaceful environment for all citizens by preventing competitive male aggressors from turning us into refugees fighting for scraps against our neighbors. If those men truly want to compete for alpha male status as legitimate contenders based on natural law, then they can punch one another into oblivion in a boxing ring rather than use our incomes, families and future as a proving ground for their selfish glory-seeking games.

As human beings, we require food, shelter, access to education and clean air and water simply to exist in these artificial ecosystems of our modern era. As such, these basic necessities of life cannot be at the mercy of men fighting only to serve their selfish need for a bigger yacht.

Our societies are not meant to be toys in the hands of bigger boys, nor their governing a sport for men who are functionally illiterate in their ability to nurture and care. We must therefore stop allowing such men to turn our societies into battlegrounds that have us fighting for our lives as collateral damage in their selfish wars for status.

While religions have long filled us with advice about looking out for one another and treating others as we wish to be treated by them, in practice we see that nature continues to rule the minds of men. CBSP will help to put the spirit of human kindness into action by treating all of us as deserving of a voice in the destiny of our species.

Where Do We Go From Here?

As a system of governing, the role of *Citizen Based Social Planning* is to gather, organize and implement information related to proposed social initiatives. However, it does not offer a cure for willful ignorance or stupidity. As such, there will always be those kinds of people who believe that breast feeding is a form of communism or that kindness is a sign of weakness. Yet no matter a person's intellectual shortcomings, they also have a right to be heard in a CBSP-based democracy, where they may even be among the loudest demanding to be heard.

In this regard, CBSP plays the law of averages by putting faith in that the best of our humanity will prevail. It assumes that the majority of people are sufficiently kind-hearted to want what is best for all the people of society. CBSP further assumes that the self-serving demands of the socially challenged represents but a minority perspective that cannot prevail without need of armed mobs to overthrown the will of the people. CBSP also assumes that our judicial systems will have the integrity to act on behalf of the people rather than a privileged few.

Whether we implement CBSP or a similar system, we must work to expose the kind of men who seek to dominate us so that our world need never suffer the likes of an Adolf Hitler again, lest we want to continue finding our societies in ruins, again and again.

Nor must men be allowed to exclude women from power given that nature has made them ambassadors of the kindness and caring that are missing from our patriarchal systems. Their crucial feminine values of nurture and protection enhance life and will be a key ingredient in the rehabilitation of our governing systems toward becoming supportive, protective and sustainable human communities.

More importantly, as many will agree, we cannot solve a problem from the same state of mind that had created it. In that regard, many of our long-standing social problems are created by self-serving men who think only of themselves. Hence, we need more women to come forward and solve the problems of social inequity by treating nations more as a family than a for-profit business trading in human livestock.

For this reason, if pressed to elect only a single leader, then let it be a woman because men have proven for thousands of years that they are more likely to lead us toward destruction under the burden of their obsessive compulsion to compete for dominance.

Ultimately, CBSP can give an equal voice to all people and offer a system truly worth defending in that it is designed to empower us.

But before we can benefit from it, we must first create it — and that is where you come in.

Citizen Based Social Planning is in the early stages of conceptual development. To learn more, get involved, or share your ideas, visit the CBSP website address entered below.

Here you will find an insightful introduction and support material, as well as a mailing list to stay up to date with recent developments.

We can think of CBSP as a kind of tree wherein the seed of the idea germinated in the mind of one person, yet it must be exposed to all manner of conditions to assist in its growth. For CBSP, that requires conditions of nurture and protection to reach its full fruit-bearing potential. Democracy is all about participation, and CBSP can become a symbolic prototype of our willingness to work together for peace.

CBSP will allow us create the kind of ideal future wherein we all can thrive while showing respect for our planet and its many inhabitants.

Okay, are you ready? Then let's do this...

CITIZEN BASED SOCIAL PLANNING
The Official Website:
https://cbsp.rolandk.ca

Epilogue

Trying to understand one's self, let alone the rest of humanity, is surely a massive undertaking. And by the time we have some semblance of insight in that regard, it is often too late to make practical use of what we have learned. Subsequently, much of what I now know would have been very helpful in navigating my way through early adulthood. But I am nonetheless thankful that my curiosity has led me to take on this mission to share what I have learned with you.

As such, I hope that the insights within this book will energize your own life and give you some added courage to take on new challenges. Understanding can do that for us. That being said, I have come to the end of a book on a subject that could fill many more such books, and perhaps there will be more to say at some later date. But for now, I will dedicate myself to working on my music and writing at a leisurely pace to finish my next book, *Be Scene, Be Herd*, about group thinking.

In regard to this book, its first official draft began in April, 2023 and I was fully prepared to dedicate years to finishing it. But much to my surprise, the entire first draft — twenty chapters — was completed in roughly one month. I then began the editing process and was making great strides to have the book available by October, 2023. And then, a sudden turn of events forced a change in my plans.

My mother got very ill, and with my father largely unable to help himself, let alone her, I had to step up to ease her transition from this world. Five months later, in March 2024, she died of congestive heart failure, leaving me to look after my father, who is now also in a state of rapid decline. Ironically, as someone with dementia and suffering from various "personality disorders," he has allowed me to see how a man's urge to dominate can prevail even when his domination days are long over and he is utterly dependent. Life's little ironies. And that is what we also see from many aging leaders as the fear of losing grips them perhaps even more at the very end of life.

Understandably, caring for my parents has taken up a great deal of the time that I would otherwise have allotted to finishing this book. But as this unplanned episode in my life forced me to slow down, it also gave me some extra time to reflect on what I had written. As a result, I believe this has become a better book in that I was able to use various current events from that period of time as reference material.

In that regard, a fellow writer once advised me not to include events of the modern era in a book that is meant to be timeless. However, the frantic stirrings of our transitioning world and its more notable stage actors were too irresistible to ignore. I was also happy to witness the transformation of a near hopeless US presidential race to one that may well be historic in electing the first female president of that nation. I think the vaudeville act offered by the cult of Donald Trump has taken up enough of the public's time and attention and that we need to bring the adults back into the fold to take on the serious work of governing.

In that regard, I also hope that you explore the idea of *Citizen Based Social Planning* and give it some critical thought so that perhaps one day we can all live in a world where political grandstanding and empty promise-making are a relic of our misguided past.

CBSP can make that possible by giving voters legitimate power.

...

I'll leave you with that thought and the hope that you'll tell as many people as who will listen about this book (and my others) not only to support my efforts, but also to help more people to understand the world in which we live and thereby make it a little easier for them to navigate their way through it.

Oh, and let's give women a chance to rule our world — it certainly can't hurt. Finally, I wish each of you the best that life can offer.

Roland Kriewaldt, September, 2024.

Index

adolescent male 18
    prefrontal cortex and risk taking 40
alpha male status 49, 173, 207
    in serial killing 172
    the American Dream 203
Citizen Based Social Planning 275
Clearing a Path to Joy 27
    Physical States of Being 27
    Physics of Psychology 108
competition 16–17
    among wild animals 28
    as a social value 21, 34, 42, 46, 82, 108
    as gender prejudice (misogyny)
        the cult of masculinity. 159
    as natural instinct 40, 51
    as racism 141, 276
    as urge in women 15
    as urge to dominate 44, 181
    catch and kill 112
    copy cat killers 60
    fear of losing 28, 38, 43, 45, 66
        conspiracy theories 229
    in music 19–20, 164
        Bon Scott 18
        Edward Van Halen 49
        Milli Vanilli 186
        Randy Rhoads 49
        Rob Halford 164
    in police work 177, 181
    in politics and business 38, 112
    in serial killing 171, 174–175
    in sexuality 33, 39
        Gene Simmons 163
    playing by the rules 42
    risk taking behavior 40
    The Killer Instinct 46
conquest 183
domination 21, 23, 27
    by institutions 251
        terrorism 82
    economic 206
    in business 236–237, 246, 251
    of animals and nature 38, 184
    of women 115
    world dominance
        Hitler 57
Dunning-Kruger 54
extinction 38
fear 65–67, 72, 77, 82, 110
    among women 152
    as sales tool 229
    comfort-seekers 40
    homophobia 160–162
        Freddie Mercury 271
        Rob Halford 164
    of conflict 121
    of dying 26, 39, 41, 46
    of god 132, 183
    of oppression 226
    of ridicule 160, 165
    of smiling 167
feminine 130, 159–160, 162
    fear of the feminine 223
    feminine values 287
feminism 124, 133, 151
Gender Wall 129–132, 160, 243
glory-seekers 40, 42, 94, 194, 236
greed 15, 36, 75, 93, 274
guns
    gun manufacturers 61
    gun violence 58–59
    proxy killings 60
    school shootings 15, 60
leadership 21, 35, 51, 88, 117, 234
masculinity 92, 159, 164, 185, 223
    cult of masculinity 160–161, 163, 166, 224

society run like a business. 47
stereotypes 146, 163, 166, 263
patriarchy 129
   abortion 151
   feminism 119
   male entitlement 243
prejudice
   racial superiority 220
revenge
   proxy killings 15, 60
   terrorism 15, 162, 229
selfishness 243, 251
   as exploitation viii, 111, 129, 184
   as hoarding 37, 75, 93, 112
   as natural instinct vi, 22, 33, 221
   in politics and business 34, 48, 70, 73, 278
   in religion 120
   in sexuality 147
   versus sharing 33, 108, 246–247
slavery 37, 112
   slave traders 57
superstition 25, 38, 77
   mental terrorism 74
terror 46, 74
testosterone 25
the IPSFA Sequence 82
   mental conflicts 87
   Nazi propagandists 219
   removing mental obstacles 85
   social identity groups 83
trust 67, 70, 144, 186, 191, 215
   female chimpanzees 125
truth iv, 16, 45, 53, 87, 205, 242
   Edward Snowden 45, 70, 250
   Julian Assange 45, 250
   WikiLeaks 68
UFO
   propulsion systems 198

Steve Barone 197
United States of America 14
   the US political pendulum 276
   US politicians 187
   Wall Street and the US government 99
warfare ix, 126, 197
   male chimpanzees 216
   weapons sales 195
winning 40, 42, 94, 194, 236. See Also competition, domination
   as attention 208
   charlatans 187, 191
   cheating to win 42
   Donald Trump 37, 46, 55, 210
   fate of HMS Titanic as symptom of male competition 108
   lying 187, 194
   vs criminal justice 43

About the author:

Roland Kriewaldt is a German-born Canadian author and musician residing near Toronto, Canada. Aside from writing, he has spent years touring the US and Canada with live bands and also worked in graphic and web design. He also tries to make life easier for wild animals.

BOOKS:
Clearing a Path to Joy
(And finding contentment along the way)
website: www.ClearingAPathToJoy.com

The Worst Kind of People:
(How to identify and avoid energy vampires.)

Reality Checks for Everyday Life
(Loaded questions to enlighten and entertain the thinking class).

The IPSFA Sequence:
(Decoding the Greatest Cause of Human Suffering)

For upcoming books and projects by Roland Kriewaldt:
visit www.AuroraSkyPublishing.com
Roland's personal website:
visit www.RolandK.ca

MUSIC:
Too Big To Fail — A Music Video in support of CBSP
(Written and performed by Roland Kriewaldt).
(More info: www.music.Rolandk.ca)

Citizen-Based Social Planning (CBSP).
(The Next Step in the Evolution of Democracy)
(More info: www.cbsp.Rolandk.ca)

www.ingramcontent.com/pod-product-compliance
Lightning Source LLC
Chambersburg PA
CBHW030545080526
44585CB00012B/265